GUN CONTROL

LIBRARY IN A BOOK

GUN CONTROL

Harry Henderson

☑®
Facts On File, Inc.

To the victims of gun violence and to responsible gun owners

GUN CONTROL

Facts On File, Inc.
11 Penn Plaza
New York NY 10001

Library of Congress Cataloging-in-Publication Data

Henderson, Harry, 1951–
    Gun control/Harry Henderson.
        p. cm.—(Library in a book)
    Includes bibliographical references and index.
    ISBN 0-8160-4031-1
    1. Firearms—Law and legislation—United States. 2. Gun control—United States. I. Title. II. Series.
    KF3941 .H46 2000
    344.73'0533—dc21   3 3113 01930 2654   99-049843

Text design by Ron Monteleone

Printed in the United States of America.

MP Hermitage 10 9 8 7 6 5 4 3 2 1

This book is printed on acid-free paper.

CONTENTS

———————————

PART I

OVERVIEW OF THE TOPIC

CHAPTER 1

INTRODUCTION TO GUN-RELATED ISSUES

The issue of gun control includes a wide variety of approaches to the regulation of firearm ownership and use. Some of the details of gun control proposals can be arcane and subject to interpretation, such as what exactly constitutes an "assault weapon" or a "Saturday night special." But in general, the debate over gun control involves questions such as the following:

- Should ordinary citizens who are not involved with the military, law enforcement, or security be allowed to own a gun?
- If so, what should be the requirements for owning a gun? A minimum age? Background screening? Taking a safe gun-handling course?
- Should gun shows, pawnshops, and private gun sales be subject to the same restrictions as sales from licensed dealers? Should gun sales over the Internet be banned?
- Should all guns be registered in a permanent database that police can use to track guns used in crime? Might such a database be misused by an oppressive government?
- Should people be allowed to carry guns outside the home? Carry them concealed? If so, should a permit be required? How hard should it be to get the permit?
- Should some types of guns be banned, such as high capacity semiautomatic rifles and pistols, or cheap handguns, or all handguns?
- Should some types of ammunition be banned, such as armor-piercing or "cop-killer" bullets?
- Should gun purchasers be limited to buying one gun a month? Should there be limits on the purchase of ammunition?

- Should gun manufacturers have to meet safety standards like those applied to other consumer products? Should certain safety devices such as a trigger lock or a "loaded" indicator be required?
- Should parents be held responsible when children access guns?
- Should gun manufacturers be held liable if they market or distribute their products in a way that makes it easy for criminals to get them?

DIFFICULT QUESTIONS, CONFLICTING ANSWERS

It has been hard to find lasting agreement on any of these questions. Since the federal government first began to regulate firearms in 1927, there has been a national debate between gun control advocates and gun rights advocates[1] about a variety of proposals ranging from outright bans on certain kinds of firearms to minor changes in the way prospective gun purchasers are screened.

The intensity of the gun debate has varied and tends to peak in times of social turmoil. It was fueled by assassinations and racial violence in the 1960s, an upsurge in crime in the 1970s, and a new wave of drug-related violence in the 1980s. By the mid-1990s, however, it seemed that reductions in crime rates and the passage of new federal gun legislation (the Brady Bill and the Assault Weapons Ban) might have put the gun issue on the back burner.

However, in the mid- to late 1990s, a wave of high-profile mass shooting incidents in workplaces and schools occurred. It is true that the chance of a given individual becoming a victim of such a mass shooting is considerably less than that of being struck by lightning, but on April 20, 1999, when two teenagers opened fire in Columbine High School in Littleton, Colorado, killing 15 people (including themselves), statistics seemed to be beside the point. The intense media coverage and the shock of murder and mayhem in the supposedly secure environment of suburban America has led to a renewed search for the causes and possible cures for the persistent violence in American society. The apparent growth in violent hate crimes, such as the wounding of five people by gunfire in a Jewish community center in Los Angeles, has added further anguish and urgency to the debate.

One obvious place to look for the cause of mayhem is the widespread availability of firearms, including rapid-fire semiautomatic weapons. Immediately following the Littleton tragedy, President Clinton and many members of Congress promoted stricter gun controls, including raising the minimum age for firearms purchase to 21, requiring background checks for purchasers at gun shows, and requiring that all new guns be sold with trigger locks that could prevent unauthorized use.

The gun debate is especially difficult to analyze because it takes place on two levels. One level is pragmatic, concerned with the effectiveness and trade-offs involved in particular policies. In a typical statement in that debate, gun control advocate Naomi Paiss, director of communications of Handgun Control, Inc., sets out the pro-control agenda:

> *Guns kill 34,000 Americans a year, including almost 5,000 young people under the age of 20. At the current rate, guns will be the leading cause of injury-related fatalities in the U.S. by 2003. It's time to remove the gun from the untouchable position in which the gun lobby has placed it and regulate its manufacture, ownership and use. Let's treat guns like cars—through licensing, registration, and revoking the privilege of ownership from those too irresponsible to use them properly—and finally begin to curb the toll that gun violence has exacted from our society.[2]*

In an equally typical statement, the National Shooting Sports Foundation urges a very different approach: "Instead of passing a battery of new gun laws—that many lawmakers concede would not have and could not have prevented the tragedy in Littleton—political and opinion leaders should be focusing their energies on promoting strict gun law enforcement, government funding of proven firearms safety education programs, and an expansion of crime control programs that work."[3]

Gun control advocates generally want to exert a maximum effort to keep guns away from persons who are likely to use them irresponsibly. Gun rights advocates want to use a combination of education and law enforcement to deter gun abuse. However, people who don't have strong feelings one way or the other might well ask: Why not compromise and do a bit more of both?

One problem with finding a compromise is that the two sides often don't agree on even the basic facts or their significance. For example, Handgun Control, Inc., often cites a study that claims that a gun fired in the home is 43 times more likely to kill a family member or friend than to kill in self-defense. But criminologist and gun control critic Gary Kleck has suggested that the vast majority of successful uses of a gun to drive away a burglar or other criminal do not include the gun being fired, let alone result in the intruder being killed. Kleck believes that when the lives and property saved by such defensive gun uses are balanced against the risk of homicide or accident within the household, the balance strongly favors gun ownership.

But figures such as the number of defensive gun uses vary greatly with definitions and methodology. Kleck estimates about 2.5 million successful cases of armed self-defense per year. On the other hand, the Justice Department's National Crime Victimization Survey gives a figure of 108,000. Is Kleck's figure too high due to inadequate sampling (as some critics suggest), or does the Justice Department's low total reflect the likelihood that many people who drive away criminals don't feel a desire or need to inform the police? As Philip Cook of Duke University observes: "Many of the basic statistics about guns are in wide disagreement with each other depending on which source you go to."[4]

Other areas of contention in the analysis of gun violence include:

- Does making it easier for law-abiding citizens to carry concealed weapons deter criminals? Will it increase the number of traffic, barroom, or other confrontations that escalate to deadly force? If both, does the benefit of the first effect outweigh the cost of the latter?[5]

- A number of studies have found that having a handgun in the home increases the risk of a family member becoming a homicide or suicide victim. Is this presence of a gun a cause of or a response to crime or social pathology?

- Will requiring trigger locks and other safety devices on guns save lives? Or might it give people a false sense of security or cause more people to be victimized by crime because they can't get to their gun in time?

- Would banning the cheap handguns called Saturday night specials reduce crime by drying up a source of "starter guns" for beginning criminals? Or would it deprive poor people of the most effective means of self-defense they can afford?

- Do the semiautomatic rifles and handguns commonly called "assault weapons" play a significant part in crime? Do such weapons have any legitimate uses?

PRIVILEGE OR RIGHT?

As the questions framed above suggest, gun control and gun rights advocates find it very hard to resolve the trade-offs involved in proposed gun control measures, but the conflict between gun control advocates and gun rights advocates runs even deeper when it enters the area of political philosophy. As the statement from Handgun Control, Inc., cited earlier notes, to gun control advocates, gun ownership is a *privilege*, as is driving. From that point of view the question of whether or how to extend that privilege is a matter of social policy. Experts should analyze whether the social utility of gun ownership outweighs the social costs. Politicians and policy makers can make proposals based on expert findings, and voters can vote for or against them in true democratic fashion.

But to most gun advocates, gun ownership is not a mere privilege; it is a *right*, as are freedom of speech or of the press. For a privilege, the question is simply whether it is socially useful to extend or restrict it; for a right, much stricter standards come into play. According to the standards of the courts, the government must show a "compelling" interest before it can restrict a right, and the proposed restrictions must be "narrowly tailored" to accomplish their objective with as little interference to free exercise of the right as possible. Thus, with regard to the First Amendment rights of expression, there can generally be no "prior restraint" on speech or writing. Of course if the speaker, to use a famous example, shouts "fire" in a crowded theater when there is no fire, he or she can be held responsible for any resulting damages. People can also be held responsible for libel or slander. Finally, there can be some restrictions as to the "place and manner" in which the right is exercised.

Generally, gun rights advocates want gun ownership to be treated in a way similar to speech or writing. Every adult citizen who does not have a criminal or mental health record should be able to own and carry the gun of his or her choice with minimal restrictions (such as banning guns in some public places like schools). Any criminal who commits a crime with that firearm, however, should be prosecuted and punished.

The gulf between privilege and right thus makes it hard for the two sides in the gun debate to even speak the same language. The gun control advocate tends to see each proposed gun ban or restriction as an issue to be resolved politically on its own merits. The gun rights advocate, however, sees each proposal as being the latest attack on a fundamental right in furtherance of an agenda leading to a total ban on gun ownership. Emotionally, the gun control advocate tends to see the gun rights advocate as uncompromising, even fanatical in opposing even the most reasonable measures. In turn, the gun rights advocate tends to see the gun control advocates as untrustworthy and manipulative, proposing reasonable-sounding measures but unwilling to admit their ultimate goals.

Most people, of course, are not activists on either side of the gun issue. Polls (see Appendix A) record a high level of generalized support for gun control, though opinion on the most extreme measures (such as a total ban on handguns) is more evenly split between supporters and opponents. Our political system, however, gives the activists who can raise campaign contributions and mobilize voters a disproportionate influence on the outcome of legislative proposals. Traditionally the National Rifle Association (NRA) has had political influence out of proportion even to its considerable membership. In recent years, however, anti-gun groups have become more skillful in grassroots organizing and may also benefit from what opponents call a bias in the major national media in favor of gun control.

Neither the assertion of a right to bear arms nor the legislation of controls on their ownership or use is a recent development. Gun rights and gun control are simply the latest developments in the struggle of societies to determine how weapons should be used. We thus begin our review of gun issues with a look at their historical roots and development.

ARMS AND GOVERNANCE

Each society, past and present, has a particular balance of power among its influential classes such as religious leaders, intellectuals, and the wealthy, as well as the warriors or soldiers. Clearly the hunter-warrior in a hunter/gatherer culture, an armed and armored feudal noble, and a citizen-soldier in ancient Rome, modern Switzerland, or modern Israel are all arms bearers, but they have different forms of social status and responsibilities.

WARRIOR ELITE OR ARMED CITIZEN?

Societies since ancient times have adopted two general models with regard to weapons use. In some societies, such as medieval Europe and feudal Japan, an elite group of heavily armed and highly trained warriors formed the ruling class. In an economy barely beyond subsistence, a knight together with his weapons, armor, and horse represented a tremendous investment in resources. With that investment, the warrior elite offered protection and stability to the community, but it also used its weapons and skill to enforce its claim to the share of land, labor, or harvest that it needed to perpetuate itself. Medieval society was hierarchical, but also decentralized. Although the ideology of feudalism depicted a ladder of loyalty of responsibility that extended upward to the king, the feudal elite, holding land and equipped with the same weapons as the king and his retinue, could combine to restrict his power, as the English barons did to King John I with the Magna Carta in 1215.

But serfs, peasants, and even free tradespersons were no match for the heavily equipped noble who had been trained in arms since early childhood. Thus in 1381, when these classes revolted against the English ruling class, "some carried only sticks, some swords covered with rust, some merely axes and others bows more reddened with age and smoke than old ivory, many of their arrows had only one plume."[6] The leaders of the rebellion were tricked and the followers soon routed.

As the revival of the economy in Europe made independent landowners and tradesmen wealthier, they often sought the trappings of nobility, including fine swords and fancy clothes. The nobility resisted: After all, it was the nobility who were "armigerous"—entitled to bear a coat of arms whose symbology derived from the tools and uses of war. The weapons allowed to a person generally reflected social status: A noble could have a sword, and a yeoman (freeholder) farmer might be entitled to an axe or a bow (although the use of the latter for hunting was always a touchy issue).

A different model for arms bearing is found in varying degrees in the city-states of ancient Greece and the Roman Republic. In a republic, a person who was entitled to a voice in how the state was run was also responsible for helping to defend it. But just who should control the weapons was subject to dispute. Plato believed that because the state needed to train its citizens for defense, the state should have a monopoly on arms. Citizens could not own their own weapons but would be issued them for training and war as needed. Aristotle, on the other hand, believed in widespread arms ownership as a way to balance the power of the different social classes. In his *Politics* he noted that if weapons ownership were confined to a single elite group, "the farmers have no arms, the workers have neither land nor arms; this makes them virtually the servants of those who possess arms."7 In a republic where citizens had their own weapons, ambitious leaders could sometimes turn their popular following into a private army and engage in a coup or a civil war. On the other hand, the ability of a tyrant to rule in the face of significant popular opposition was reduced by the decentralization of weapons ownership.

GUNPOWDER AND THE NATION-STATE

The introduction of gunpowder weapons in Europe about 1300 had far-reaching effects on the social and political use of weaponry. In its first centuries, gunpowder was primarily used in siege guns that, while crude and unwieldy, could batter down the walls of castles of those who would not submit to the king. Even as artillery improved and developed into a form that could be used in field battles, it remained very expensive. The "iron argument of kings" could generally only be afforded by kings and tended to centralize power in a nation-state.

Small arms started out as cumbersome miniature "hand cannons," but with the development of improved firing mechanisms (matchlock in the 15th century; wheel lock and flintlock in the 16th century), handheld infantry guns became practicable. These weapons could not be fired rapidly because loading was an intricate, multistep process. Indeed, as late as the mid-19th century, a trained longbow user could shoot more often and to better effect than the user of a gunpowder weapon. But the gun had one big advantage: Training someone to be good with the bow took years, while a few weeks of training with a gun was sufficient. Of course early guns were also quite expensive—this was still a society of crafts, not industry.

Early guns had short range and poor accuracy. To use them effectively, soldiers had to be formed into lines and trained to fire in volleys. The individualized warfare of the knight was replaced by the machinelike precision of thousands of common soldiers drilled to act as one. By the 18th century, in Europe, the gun was the instrument of the standing army of an increasingly centralized state. Certainly, persons with the means and opportunity could have guns for hunting, and pistols were available as well. Nevertheless, the gun was not a commonplace tool of the ordinary citizen.

ARMS IN THE ANGLO-AMERICAN TRADITION

In most modern European nations, gun ownership is heavily regulated, and guns play little part in daily life. Gun control is embraced as a matter of course by the overwhelming majority of citizens. Europeans often express astonishment at widespread gun ownership in the United States and the contentiousness of the gun issue in the country's politics.

To understand how Americans acquired a distinctive attitude toward firearms, it is important to remember that the political culture of the United States grew out of the English rather than continental European experience.

THE MILITIA AND THE RIGHT TO BEAR ARMS

Once conquered by the Normans in 1066, Britain would not be invaded again successfully. By the 16th century, British rulers saw their first line of defense as being a navy that strove always to be able to defeat any combination of opponents. Compared to the emerging powers of the European mainland (Spain, France, and later, Germany) the English standing army would always be small; for one thing, the nation lacked the population and resources to create a large military establishment. But Britain had an additional military resource that it could call on in times of crisis: the armed, organized citizen.

Earlier, Anglo-Saxon Britain had the *fyrd*, in which all free men trained with basic weapons and which could be called out in times of emergency by the sheriff. In 1181, King Henry II revived this idea in his Assize of Arms, which specified the armor and weapons that could be used by each social class—full armor and the lance for the knight and lighter armor for the tradesman. Later, Henry III expanded the Assize to include serfs, as well as requiring the establishment of a group of men to guard cities at night (a primitive police force) and requiring that citizens respond to the "hue and cry" to help subdue criminals who resisted.

As lances gave way to pike and musket, the militia tradition continued to be important. At the outbreak of the English Civil War in 1642, the parliament declared that it, not the king, had the right to regulate the militia. "By God, not for an hour!" King Charles I exclaimed. He knew that without control of the militia, "Kingly power is but a shadow."[8] Even after the monarchists prevailed and Charles II came to the throne in 1660, the militia served as a partial check on the power of the king, though its importance faded after the Glorious Revolution of 1688–89 put England on the course to a limited, constitutional monarchy.

Several provisions in the Bill of Rights that arose from that revolution noted that abuses of Charles II and James II and showed the importance attached to the right to bear arms: "5. By raising and keeping a standing army within this kingdom in time of peace, without the consent of parliament, and quartering [housing] soldiers contrary to law. . . . 6. By causing several good subjects, being protestants, to be disarmed at the same time when papists [Catholics] were both armed and employed contrary to law." In its list of remedies for these abuses, the second part of the Bill of Rights specified "7. The subjects which are Protestants may have arms for their defence suitable to their conditions and allowed by law."[9]

Andrew Fletcher, who survived a death sentence from James II and went on to help establish the new government, discussed the role of the armed citizen in *A Discourse of Government with Relation to Militias* (1698), where he said the constitution should "put the sword into the hands of the subject . . . And I cannot see, why arms should be denied to any man who is not a slave, since they are the only true badges of liberty."[10]

EARLY ARMS CONTROL

Many of today's opponents of gun control look to the militia tradition and the English common law for their inspiration. But there is another side to this tradition: The same laws that established a right or duty to bear arms for the common defense often prescribed who could bear what kinds of arms. The Assize of Arms of Henry II in 1181 seized arms and armor from Jews to distribute to the "free men" it armed. The Glorious Revolution established a right to bear arms for Protestants, but not Catholics, and the arms to be borne were those "suitable to their conditions [social class] and allowed by law."

Crime on the streets and highways often provoked weapons regulations. The Statute of Northampton (1328) prohibited any person "great or small" from going armed in a public place, though in practice the law was generally used only against people who "terrified" others through their use of arms. Also, people of differing social status continued to be treated differently: Henry VIII, for example, barred anyone with an income of less than £300 annually from having a handgun or crossbow, in an attempt to keep such handy weapons out of the hands of common robbers.

COLONIAL AMERICA

At about the time the militia and the right to bear arms were becoming less important to many English people, they became essential for the colonists who were establishing settlements in America in the 1600s. As historian Daniel Boorstin notes, "Shooting small game with a bow or a gun and throwing a tomahawk became lifesaving skills when Indians attacked . . . civil and military uses of firearms dovetailed as they had not generally done in Europe."[11]

Native Americans quickly learned about the usefulness of firearms for hunting and war. They soon became subject to a gun control law: "Whereas the country by sad experience have found that the traders with Indians by their avarice have so armed the Indians with powder, shot, and guns . . . Be it enacted. . . that if any person . . . shall presume to trade, truck, barter, sell or utter, directly or indirectly, to or with any Indians any powder, shot, or arms . . . shall suffer death without benefit of clergy."[12]

The rival French colonists, too, posed a military threat to the British colonies until they were defeated by a combination of British and colonial volunteer forces in the French and Indian War of 1754–63. The British government did not want to undertake the expense of maintaining and supplying large numbers of professional soldiers on a frontier 3,000 miles away. The colonists would have to take primary responsibility for their own defense. They naturally adopted and refined the historical model of the militia to the needs of a very different society.

REVOLUTION AND CONSTITUTION

Following the end of the French and Indian War, disputes over the taxation and treatment of the colonists as well as their political rights eventually boiled over into revolution. In 1777, British colonial undersecretary William Knox proposed that to forestall rebellion, "The Militia Law should be repealed and none suffered to be reenacted and the Arms of all the People should be taken away & and every piece of Ordnance removed into the

King's Stores, nor should any Foundry or manufacturer of Arms, Gunpowder, or Warlike Stores, be ever suffered in America, nor should any Gunpowder, Lead, Arms, or Ordnance be imported into it without License; they will have but little need of such things for the future, as the King's Troops, Ships & Forts will be sufficient to protect them from danger."[13]

Colonial activists formed the militias known as Minutemen, creating a widespread network of resistance while leaders in the Second Continental Congress of 1775 debated whether to seek total American independence. But events overtook them when British officials, in the spirit of Knox's proposal, sent troops to Lexington and Concord to seize arms and ammunition. Although General Thomas Gage's forces won the first stand-up skirmish, the militias spontaneously unleashed guerrilla warfare on the returning Redcoats. In this effort, an accurate new weapon, the rifle, allowed snipers to pick off British troops from the distant cover of fences, rocks, and trees.

In the War of Independence, of the 231,771 men who served on the American side, 164,087 came from the militias. Militarily, the militias were a mixed bag, often poorly trained and ill prepared for major field battles, as well as being prone to desertion. But although it was the professional military efforts of George Washington, his colleagues, and French allies that ultimately won the war, the conflict could not have been started or sustained in its early years without the militia.

In creating its new charter of government, U.S. political leaders kept the importance of the militia and the traditional distrust of a standing army in mind. James Madison, for example, noted that liberty could be kept secure because "[To a U.S. army of about 25,000 or 30,000 men] would be opposed a militia amounting to near half a million citizens, with arms in their hands, officered by men chosen from among themselves, fighting for their common liberties, and united and conducted by governments possessing their affections and confidence."[14]

Although various wordings were proposed for the Second Amendment in the Constitution's Bill of Rights, the right to bear arms and the militia were always closely linked. The final version reads: "A well-regulated Militia, being necessary to the security of a Free State, the right of the people to keep and bear arms, shall not be infringed."

GUN CONTROL IN THE 19TH CENTURY

Although Americans in the early 19th century maintained a romantic view of the militia and the frontiersman, the militias themselves soon faded into disuse, many becoming little more than armed social clubs. But state constitutions retained explicit guarantees of the right to keep and bear arms. Kentucky's constitution for example stated "The right of the citizens to bear arms in defense of themselves and the state shall not be questioned."[15] And in some cases it was not questioned: In the Kentucky case of *Bliss v. Commonwealth* (1822), for example, the court overturned a prohibition against the carrying of concealed weapons.

But this absolutist position would not predominate. In the Tennessee case of *Aymette v. State* (1840), the court upheld a similar law in the case of a man wearing a concealed Bowie knife. The judges looked back into English history and noted that the conditions under which arms could be owned or carried had often been regulated. They also noted the intimate connection between arms bearing and service in the militia for the common defense. They thus concluded that "The legislature, therefore, have a right to prohibit the wearing or keeping weapons dangerous to the peace and safety of the citizens, and which are not usual in civilized warfare, or would not contribute to the common defense."

As cities grew, and with them concern about urban crime, many communities passed laws against the carrying of weapons often associated with criminals, such as knives, brass knuckles, and, in some cases, handguns. Often, as in *Nunn v. State* (1846), a distinction was made between banning some kinds of guns (small, concealable handguns in this case) and banning *all* firearms. The former was ruled to be a legitimate exercise of state or local police power, but the latter was presumed to violate the right to bear arms in the state constitution. [1]

Conditions on the frontier were obviously quite different than in cities, but contrary to Hollywood myth, the "Wild West" was not a totally lawless place where guns constantly blazed in the streets. With settlement came a need for law. Where the political organization or resources did not yet exist for regular law enforcement, members of the community often formed committees to apprehend criminal gangs. Such vigilantes were often surprisingly scrupulous in trying the suspects. Historian Richard Hofstader noted that vigilante organizations "often drew their leaders from the top levels of society . . . and their following came largely from the solid middle class."[16] And while gangs and gunfighters did exist, they killed each other, mainly, and not innocent civilians.

Post Civil-War America brought new challenges. During Reconstruction, African Americans gained citizenship and with it the right to keep and bear arms. Many militias became racially integrated, albeit often corrupt. But following Reconstruction, when white politicians or the Ku Klux Klan regained control of an area, "almost universally the first thing done was to disarm the negroes and leave them defenseless."[17] As another writer ironically notes, "The former states of the Confederacy, many of which had recognized the right to carry arms openly before the Civil War, developed a very sudden willingness to qualify that right."[18]

Federal legislation for the postwar South led the Supreme Court to its first major confrontation with the Second Amendment. The case of *United States v. Cruikshank* (1876) arose from the trial of a band of white farmers (and probable KKK members) who had attacked and burned a courthouse held by a group of armed blacks during an election dispute. The whites were tried under a Reconstruction civil rights statute and charged, among other things, with depriving the blacks of their right to bear arms. The lower court convicted them, but the Supreme Court overturned the conviction on appeal, ruling that the federal government could not enforce the right to bear arms in the Second Amendment against the states or private individuals.

In the late 19th century successive waves of immigrants flooded into U.S. cities from Italy, Ireland, Germany, and other countries. The neighborhoods in which they settled were often perceived to be crime ridden, and an increasing number of gun control measures were passed in response. Finally, in 1911, New York State enacted the Sullivan Law, which was the first state law that created a strict permit system for handgun ownership.

Thus by the early 20th century, guns remained in widespread use (particularly rifles and shotguns in rural areas). Gun control in some form existed on a state and local level in many areas. But as with many other laws, gun laws were often enforced against the poor and persons perceived to be criminally inclined, while "established citizens" could carry a concealed handgun with the blessing of the local sheriff or police chief.

GUN CONTROL IN MODERN AMERICA

As far as gun control is concerned, "modern America" can be said to have begun around 1919 when alcohol Prohibition created a raging thirst to be satisfied by the competing groups of gangsters who vied for control of the liquor business. They did so with the aid of a powerful new kind of gun, the Thompson submachine, or tommy, gun, a fully automatic weapon that would shoot as long as the trigger was held back. In the St. Valentine's Day Massacre (1929), horrified citizens were faced with the specter of seven dead mobsters; their bodies had been riddled with bullets by rival gangsters who had posed as the police. In 1933, after an assassination attempt against newly elected President Franklin D. Roosevelt, gun control for the first time became a topic for national debate. Wide press coverage and growing public pressure led to a demand for national firearms regulations.

Gun Control

THE 1930S: FEDERAL REGULATION BEGINS

In 1927 Congress passed the first federal gun law, making it illegal to mail concealable firearms. While still in effect, the law had little practical effect on the gun trade because guns could be shipped by a variety of other means. But the 1930s would see a more significant attempt to create national gun regulations.

The National Firearms Act of 1934 was rather modest by modern standards. It didn't actually outlaw machine guns or sawed-off shotguns, but it imposed a $200 tax on their manufacture, sale, and ownership—a rather high amount of money at that time. (Because they are short enough to conceal beneath a coat, sawed-off shotguns have long been considered a weapon of particular usefulness to criminals.) The law also required that purchasers of such weapons undergo an FBI background check.

In 1938 Congress extended the national firearm regulation system by passing the Federal Firearms Act. This law required that all manufacturers, importers, and dealers in firearms be licensed. It forbade delivery of a gun to a person who had been convicted of (or was under indictment for) a crime or who did not meet local licensing laws.

Thus by the end of the 1930s the federal government was significantly involved in firearms regulation. Control of automatic weapons became strict, though ironically very few crimes have been committed with fully automatic weapons. But the lack of systematic background checks and the existence of generally weak state laws meant that purchasers of handguns, by far the most common kind of gun used in crimes, were not tightly screened.

THE SECOND AMENDMENT DEBATE

Until the federal government began to regulate firearms in the 1930s, the Second Amendment was not a major factor in gun-related litigation. The Supreme Court as well as state courts had made it clear that whatever rights it guaranteed, the Second Amendment applied only to the actions of Congress or the federal government, not to state or local legislatures. (Under their own constitutions, state courts generally found that there was an individual right to keep and bear arms but decided to varying the extents that state or local governments could regulate how arms were used, such as by banning concealed handguns.)

However once the National Firearms Act was passed, the question of the Second Amendment's applicability to federal firearms control could no longer be escaped. The key case arose when two bootleggers, Jack Miller and Frank Layton, were accused of "unlawfully, knowingly, willingly, and feloniously transport[ing] in interstate commerce . . . a double-barrel 12-gauge Stevens shotgun having a barrel less than 18 inches in length."

A lower court ordered Miller and Layton freed, ruling that the Second Amendment prevented Congress from regulating commerce in weapons. The two bootleggers promptly disappeared into the countryside. But meanwhile, the government lawyers appealed the conviction. Because there was no longer anyone to pay for the defense, the Court heard only the government's side.

The Second Amendment begins with the phrase "A well-regulated militia, being necessary to the security of a free state" and then goes on to say "the right of the people to keep and bear arms, shall not be infringed." This rather curious phrasing leads to two major questions: (1) Does the reference to the militia simply state the framer's *purpose* in guaranteeing the right to bear arms, or does it *limit* that right to arms that can be used in the militia? (2) Does "the people" refer to a *collective* right to maintain a militia or to an *individual* right to keep and bear arms?

The Court's ruling suggests an answer to the first question that sees the militia clause as limiting or qualifying the right to bear arms. The key part of the decision said that the Court "can not take judicial notice that a shotgun having a barrel less than 18 inches long has today any reasonable relation to the preservation or efficiency of a well regulated militia; and therefore can not say that the Second Amendment guarantees to the citizen the right to keep and bear such a weapon." In other words, the Court based its decision on whether the weapon in question had military application and thus could further the development of the militia.

Ever since then, gun control advocates have argued that the Second Amendment thus applies only to bearing arms as part of an organized militia, which today is the National Guard: "The contemporary meaning of the Second Amendment is the same as it was at the time of its adoption. The federal government may regulate the National Guard, but cannot disarm it against the will of state legislatures. Nothing in the Second Amendment, however, precludes Congress or the states from requiring licensing and restrictions of firearms; in fact, there is nothing to stop an outright congressional ban on private ownership of all handguns and all rifles."[19]

Gun rights advocates, however, bring up a number of objections to this view. In his influential article "The Embarrassing Second Amendment," Sanford Levinson, while a supporter of some forms of gun control, argues that if Congress had wanted only to protect the right of the states to have militias, it would have said so. Further, he notes, *militia* has a much broader historical meaning that cannot be restricted to today's National Guard. Thus George Mason, who refused to sign the Constitution because it initially lacked a Bill of Rights, declared "Who are the militia? They consist now of the whole people?"[20] Indeed, federal statutes define the militia as consisting of all able-bodied male citizens (today women would have to be included as well.) As for the question of whether the right to bear arms is intended to be individual or collective, Levinson and others have noted that in the rest of the Bill of Rights, *the people* always means *individuals*, even if they choose to act collectively—as in "the right of the people to peacefully assemble" in the First Amendment.

Levinson points out that the Second Amendment debate reveals a curious reversal of conservatives and liberals from their usual positions on civil rights. Liberals interpret the rest of the Bill of Rights broadly without worrying too much about the social cost of freeing criminals. However, they want to interpret the Second Amendment narrowly because of what they consider to be the social costs of gun ownership. Conservatives, on the other hand, often complain about the courts finding "new rights" in broad interpretations of the Bill of Rights but favor a broader interpretation where the Second Amendment is concerned.

Levinson urged that the scholarly community begin to take the Second Amendment seriously. To some extent, academic opinion has indeed shifted from a collectivist to an individualist interpretation of the Second Amendment.

But gun control advocates have a powerful bottom-line argument. Since *Miller*, the Supreme Court has not significantly revisited the Second Amendment and has not turned down any gun laws based on it. This is true even of cases involving weapons of definite military usefulness, despite the implication in *Miller* that such weapons might, unlike the sawed-off shotgun, find constitutional protection. In practice, therefore, unless and until the courts confront it again, the Second Amendment will remain primarily a philosophical rather than a legal issue.

GUNS AND SOCIAL CONFLICT

The 1940s and 1950s saw little new firearm legislation. But the 1960s brought rapid change and upheaval to U.S. society. In the five years from 1963 to 1968, three national leaders were assassinated: President John F. Kennedy, civil rights leader Martin Luther King, Jr., and Senator (and Democratic presidential favorite) Robert F. Kennedy. Black militants and anti-Vietnam war protesters took to the streets and challenged the legitimacy of government and other institutions.

As the turmoil grew, many groups began to arm themselves, ranging from the Ku Klux Klan and other racist organizations to the Black Panthers, who proclaimed their rights under the Second Amendment and marched with their rifles to the California statehouse. Destructive riots flared in the ghetto districts of Los Angeles and other large cities.

Reaction to the worst social turmoil since the 1930s led to a second great wave of federal gun legislation. Gun control advocates pointed out that Lee Harvey Oswald had obtained the rifle he had used to kill John F. Kennedy through the mail. (Such sales were already illegal under the 1927 act, but there was little practical enforcement.)

President Lyndon B. Johnson put his formidable political skills on the side of gun control. In his 1968 State of the Union Address, he urged Congress to pass a law to prevent "mail-order murder." He also came out for universal gun registration and licensing. A few months later, the King and Kennedy assassinations gave a tremendous impetus to the gun control advocates, and their supporters in Congress were able to overcome the objections of the powerful National Rifle Association, which had begun to take a larger role in fighting gun control legislation.

Congress passed the Gun Control Act of 1968. It restricted nearly all interstate sales of firearms and tightened penalties for selling guns to minors or persons with criminal records. Every sale of a gun or ammunition had to be recorded in detail.

Gun rights advocates questioned whether these tight new laws would actually have any effect on crime. Gun control advocates endorsed a 1969 report by the National Commission on the Causes and Prevention of Violence, which had undertaken a massive study of the conditions that had led to urban riots and other violence during the past decade. The commission's report recommended national regulation of handguns and, echoing President Johnson's speeches, urged the requirement of registration of all guns and licensing of all purchasers.

GUNS, CRIME, AND SELF-DEFENSE

The 1960s had also marked the beginning of an overall increase in crime rates that would generally continue until the mid-1990s. Although large-scale social conflict had subsided by 1970, crime—and what to do about it—became a major political issue. An important part of that issue was the role played by guns. Did the widespread availability of guns—particularly, handguns—contribute to the crime rate by making it easy for criminals to terrorize their victims, or did it actually reduce crime by giving law-abiding citizens the means of self-defense?

Starting in the 1970s, gun control advocates began to focus on a type of inexpensive, often poorly made handgun commonly known as a Saturday night special. They have argued that these cheap guns provided criminals with a ready supply of weapons. Gun rights advocates, however, have argued that banning cheap guns would deprive poor people—who live in the most crime-ridden neighborhoods with the least reliable police protection—of the means to defend themselves from criminals.

But the whole idea that guns were an effective means for defense against criminals would be called into question. A 1986 paper by Arthur Kellermann and Donald T. Reay in the *New England Journal of Medicine* concluded that a gun kept in the home was 43 times more likely to be used to kill a family member or friend than to kill a criminal intruder.[21] As noted earlier, however, such studies are filled with assumptions that are difficult to evaluate and have led to a war of numbers.

Criminologist Gary Kleck soon replied with a study estimating that people use their guns to drive away criminals as many as 2.2 million times a year, usually without firing a shot. If this is true, guns are used many times to defend people or property for each time they kill an innocent person. If so (and Kleck's estimates have in turn been challenged), does that mean guns do more good than harm?

Although dueling numbers play a part in the gun debate, the debate itself is often reduced in the media to a war of anecdotes in which tragic personal experience is cited by both sides. Gun control advocates see the armed citizen not as a deterrent to criminals, but as part of the problem. In 1993, Colin Ferguson used his semiautomatic handgun to shoot a number of people in a car on the Long Island Railway. One injury victim, a former law enforcement officer, testified at a congressional hearing that "There is no question in my mind that I would have done more damage if I had possessed such a weapon than the six deaths and the nineteen injuries that occurred on the train . . . And with people running and knocking one another down, if someone behind me had started firing, I dare say I would then think I was in a crossfire."[22]

On the other hand, when George Henard opened fire in Luby's Cafeteria in Killeen, Texas, Suzanna Gratia, an experienced shooter, had left her gun in the car before entering the restaurant, complying with a recently passed law. She testified before Congress that she had to watch helplessly as Henard killed her parents and other customers. "I had a clear shot at him,"[23] she insisted.

Generally, the war of anecdotes favors the gun control advocates. When guns are used to massacre people in a restaurant or schoolyard, the media shows the carnage in full detail. But generally speaking, someone who simply brandishes a gun to drive away a criminal is not news, nor is what *might have* happened if someone like Suzanna Gratia had had a gun.

With action in Washington, D.C., blocked by the continued political power of the NRA, the gun control battle shifted to local government, with gun control activists trying to come in under the radar. In 1981, Morton Grove, Illinois, passed the first total handgun ban in modern times. The law withstood all challenges, with the court ruling that whatever rights people might have to keep and bear arms in general, there was nothing wrong with banning *some* types of guns.

Gun rights advocates generally react to the initiatives of the gun control advocates, but they have sometimes taken the offensive. The National Rifle Association has persistently and loudly pushed proposals for tough sentencing for all persons convicted of using a gun in a crime and for enforcement of existing gun laws rather than the passing of new ones that they see as having dubious value.

The biggest pro-gun crusade in recent years, however, is found in the debate over concealed carry laws. States differ widely in whether they allow people to carry guns concealed in a holster within their coat or waistband or in a container such as a fanny pack. In his overall work, which includes his latest book *More Guns, Less Crime*, pro-gun criminologist John Lott has conducted large-scale studies that he says show that states that make it easy for law-abiding citizens to have concealed handguns have lower crime rates than comparable states that do not. On the other hand, the Center to Prevent Handgun Violence issued its own study that claimed Lott was wrong and that crime rates in states with liberal concealed-carry laws either did not decrease as rapidly as in those with stricter laws or actually increased. The debate moves quickly into complicated issues of sampling and statistical methodology.

During the early 1990s gun rights activists have had considerable success in promoting liberalization of state concealed-carry laws, though the impact of the Littleton massacre has at least stalled such efforts.

THE DRUG WAR, ASSAULT WEAPONS, AND THE NEW MILITIA

Just as bootleg liquor helped make the 1920s roar, the growing use of illegal drugs (particularly crack, a type of cocaine) brought a new wave of gangsterism in the 1980s. The focus of attention in the gun control debate became the so-called assault weapons, which had become the badge of the new gangster.

The term *assault weapon* can be confusing. Originally, it was a military term for a fully automatic rifle (such as the M-16) that could also be fired in short bursts. The purpose of these weapons (first introduced by the Germans in World War II and quickly adopted by the Soviets in the form of the AK-47), is primarily to give an infantry soldier enough firepower to cover an assault on an enemy position.

Some gun enthusiasts began to use the term to refer to civilian, semiautomatic versions of military weapons, but gun control advocates are also accused of taking advantage of the confusion in which the popular media often seem to blur the distinction between a true assault weapon or machine gun and a semiautomatic rifle or handgun. The latter shoots only one time for each pull of the trigger; it doesn't "spray" bullets. Gun rights advocates point out that there is no fundamental difference in operation between an Uzi or Tec-9 and the kind of semiautomatic pistols and rifles that have been in use since the 19th century. They accuse their opponents of using the scary, militarylike appearance of modern guns to create more support for gun control. Further, they point out that semiauto rifles are used in only a tiny fraction of crimes. Gun control advocates, however, point out that the ability to shoot rapid single shots and the use of a large (10 round or more) magazine (bullet holder) certainly allows a shooter to kill many more people in a short time. They point to the use of such weapons by gang members and the way in which they facilitate mass shooting incidents.

Gun control advocates (including President Clinton) frequently argue that assault weapons have no "sporting use" or place in hunting and are not needed for defense against crime. Irritated gun rights advocates reply that "the Second Amendment isn't about hunting ducks" and that such weapons can be needed for community defense, citing the Korean merchants in Los Angeles who used them to drive off a mob of looters during the L.A. riots in 1992.

Assault weapons also became associated with the gun-toting antigovernment activists in Montana, Michigan, and other states who had begun to organize private militia groups in response to what they saw as an out-of-control federal government that, among other things, was trying to disarm the people of the United States. Even though their ideological roots ranged from racist to libertarian beliefs, the members of the new militias generally said that they simply wanted to be left alone and that they were asserting the historical rights that had motivated the Minutemen of the American Revolution.

Some militia activists reacted strongly to the killing of white separatist Randy Weaver's wife, son, and friend by FBI agents during a siege of his Ruby Ridge, Idaho, cabin. They accused the government of first entrapping and then targeting a man whose only crime had been selling a shotgun whose barrel was too short. They were also outraged by the federal assault and siege of the church of the Branch Davidians religious sect, leading eventually to the fiery death of its leader, David Koresh, and dozens of followers, including many children. The revelation in the summer of 1999 that FBI agents had used pyrotechnic devices (capable of starting fires) during the final attack on the compound and the possible concealment of evidence of government wrongdoing has led to renewed investigations and has served to keep Waco alive in the public mind.

Some gun rights activists pointed to these incidents to show why citizens must have the right to bear arms to deter abuses by government. Although gun control advocates, on the other hand, admitted to errors by law enforcement agencies, they considered the tragedies to be largely the fault of the gun-toting victims themselves. Since the Oklahoma City Bombing of 1994, however, these militias seem to have faded from public view.

THE 1990S: BRADY AND BEYOND

Growing popular support for gun control and the efforts of the Clinton Administration and many Democrats in Congress have led to two substantial federal gun control laws. In 1981, James S. Brady, press secretary to President Ronald Reagan, was wounded along with President Reagan in an assassination attempt by John Hinckley. Brady was badly wounded, faced a long recovery, and still has to use a wheelchair. His wife, Sarah Brady, became a crusader for gun control, joining Handgun Control, Inc. (HCI) and later becoming the organization's formidable chairperson. While lacking the resources of the NRA, HCI became adept at grassroots organizing and legal action.

While gun control advocates were increasing their organization and public visibility, the NRA was becoming increasingly militant and absolutist in its opposition to gun control. In 1986, they lobbied Congress to pass the Firearms Owners' Protection Act, which permitted rifles and shotguns (but not handguns) to be sold by mail, eased dealer record-keeping requirements, and increased penalties for criminal misuse of guns. The NRA, however, also seemed to stumble in public opinion in the 1990s, such as when a widely publicized comment in a fund-raising letter about federal "jack-booted thugs" led President George W. Bush to cancel his membership. (Later, veteran actor Charlton Heston was appointed president of the NRA, and recent polls suggest that he remains well regarded, though other celebrities such as Spike Lee take the other side of the gun issue.)

By the end of the 1980s, Brady and other gun control activists had mobilized considerable public support (including President Reagan, who had changed his mind) for a proposal to require a waiting period before a person could buy a gun. They believed that a waiting period was necessary for doing a proper background check of gun purchasers so that criminals and the mentally ill could be weeded out. They also believed that a mandatory waiting period could reduce impulsive gun purchases by people who were angry with someone and bent on violence. Gun rights advocates have suggested, however, that a person being stalked or harassed might be killed while waiting for a gun that is urgently needed for self-defense.

Although the Brady Bill failed in its first attempt at passage in 1991, Congress passed the Brady Handgun Violence Prevention Act in November

1993. The law established a five-day waiting period, after which the gun could be sold if the purchaser met an expanded list of requirements. (In addition to barring convicted felons and the mentally ill, the law also barred from gun purchase anyone who was currently under a court order for stalking or harassment.)

The Brady Act was challenged in court, but only the part requiring state officials to carry out the background checks was overturned by the Supreme Court in *Printz v. U.S.*, on the grounds that Congress lacked the power to commandeer the services of local officials. This decision would have little impact because the Brady Act already had a provision that after five years (in 1998) the waiting period would be replaced by a computerized national instant check system that would verify a gun purchaser in much the same way that stores validate credit cards.

Another big victory for gun control advocates came in 1994 with the passage of the Violent Crime Control Act, which banned the manufacture, sale, and import of a large variety of semiautomatic weapons such as the Uzi and Tec-9 and similar "copycat" weapons. The list of banned weapons was later expanded, but weapons manufactured or imported before the ban took effect can still be owned.

NEW APPROACHES TO GUN CONTROL

Given the difficulty of passing gun control legislation against the opposition of the NRA and other pro-gun rights groups, gun control advocates have explored and implemented a variety of other approaches to gun control. In general, they involve the attempt to create scientific or legal models to change the behavior of gun manufacturers, dealers, and owners.

THE MEDICAL MODEL AND GUN VIOLENCE

There is little disagreement that a significant number of deaths and injuries are caused by firearms, although gun deaths peaked at about 40,000 in 1995 and then started to decline. According to the Centers for Disease Control and Prevention (CDC), firearms are the second-leading cause of injury death in the United States and may surpass motor vehicles for the number one spot shortly after the year 2000.

Starting in the 1980s, a number of medical professionals including some involved with the CDC and with the *Journal of the Medical Association* (*JAMA*) began to write about what they called "an epidemic of gun violence" that they said was causing up to $4 billion in medical expenses every year. They suggested that the same approach taken toward traditional public health problems should also be taken toward gun violence. For example, in responding to the growing number of deaths from AIDS, doctors had to isolate the cause of the disease, identify practices that promoted infection, and devise educational and public policy strategies to contain it; similarly, these medical researchers and activists suggest that guns are the "pathogens" that promoted a growing epidemic of violence. They hope to use their authority as medical professionals to publicize the dangers of guns in the home—in particular, the danger of accidental gun deaths, especially those involving children. They have compiled studies that claimed that gun ownership increased the risk of homicide, suicide, and accidental death.[24]

Gun rights advocates (including a small group of doctors such as Edgar A. Suter) have attacked the "medicalization" of the gun issue. Philosophically, they argue that a gun is not an active organism like HIV, the virus that causes AIDS. It can't do anything by itself. Also, unlike HIV, a gun is a tool that has legitimate uses such as self-defense. Treating the misuse of tools as an "epidemic" promotes the viewpoint that people are helpless, passive victims of their impulses, and not responsible for their actions. Gun advocates also argue that the proponents of the "gun epidemic" theory use poor statistical techniques and make many unwarranted assumptions; for example, with regard to suicide, they disagree with the conclusion that reducing the number of guns would necessarily reduce the number of suicides, noting that Japan, which has very tight gun control, has a high suicide rate. Would banning guns simply lead to people finding other means, such as jumping, gas asphyxiation, or sleeping pills? Gun control advocates point out, however, that a gun is an "impulse weapon"—it takes only the pull of a trigger to commit a potentially irrevocable act. Gun injuries are also much more likely to be fatal, while people who try other means of suicide often survive.

Medical and sociological gun control advocates have also pointed out that such countries as Britain and Japan, with strict firearm controls, have far lower homicide rates than the United States. Gun rights activists question whether such cross-cultural comparisons are valid, noting that European and Japanese societies are more conformist and that it is social control, not gun control, that is responsible for their low rate of violence.

"FOR THE CHILDREN"

Politics in the late 1990s seemed to be characterized by the framing of many issues in terms of how they affect children. Because people care deeply about their (and others') children, this may be good politics, though critics argue that it promotes an emotionally distorted approach to making public policy.

Gun Control

With regard to guns, the debate focuses on the easy access of guns to children, the potential for accidental or intentional shootings in the home, and the mass shooting incidents in schools and playgrounds (such as the 5 children killed and 30 wounded by Patrick Purdy in 1989 in Stockton, California, or the 15 killed in Columbine High School in Littleton, Colorado).

Although the federal Gun-Free School Zones Act (which bans gun possession in and near schools) was overturned by the Supreme Court, there are plenty of laws and policies that forbid students or others from bringing guns onto school property. John Lott suggests that the characterization of gun violence in schools is rather misleading.

> *Thirteen "children" are said to die every day from guns in the United States. Indeed, in 1996, 4,643 people under age 20 died from homicides, suicides, accidents, or other gun related events. What is not explained is that 53 percent involved homicides for 15- to 19-year-olds, and that almost all of these involved gangs fighting over drug turf. As long as these gangs have something valuable to fight over, banning guns is unlikely to stop gangs from obtaining weapons. For children under age 15, a total of 693 died from guns, about 1.9 per day. Despite the horrific shootings at Littleton and a few other schools, gun violence and crime in schools has been declining steadily.[25]*

The debate over violence in the schools involves not only gun access, but the influence of violent movies, TV shows, and computer games, as well as parental neglect. Although a strong majority favor stronger gun control, there is also considerable support for regulations involving the media and their marketing practices. In the 1999 crime bill debates, opponents of stricter gun controls tried to add amendments dealing with the media, while gun bill advocates accused them of delay and diversionary tactics. (Conservative gun rights advocates tend to support restrictions on the media, while libertarians support both gun rights and freedom of speech.)

By late 1999, efforts to pass new federal gun legislation had bogged down, but gun control advocates promised to make gun control a major issue in the 2000 presidential campaign. Most Democrats saw gun control as a winning issue, while many Republicans found themselves caught between growing public pressure for gun control and a vocal, well-organized minority of gun rights advocates who see the gun issue as being, like abortion, a litmus test for political support.

Although the extent of the problem and the efficacy of the cure are in dispute, gun control advocates make a powerful appeal, however, when they suggest that only comprehensive gun control can stop the killings in the schools. They hope that this appeal, combined with already strong support for gun control, will enable them to overcome the political power of the NRA and other gun rights advocates.

GUNS AND PRODUCT SAFETY

Faced with a protracted struggle in the political arena, some gun control activists have launched a new offensive by filing liability suits against gun manufacturers. Suing the shooter is a possibility, of course, but most criminals have little in the way of recoverable assets.

Another possibility is to sue the gun dealer who sells a firearm to a person who is obviously intoxicated or otherwise incompetent. In 1997, for example, Deborah Kitchen was shot by her ex-boyfriend, leaving her paralyzed. The boyfriend had obtained a .22 caliber rifle from a local K-Mart store, despite his having, according to his testimony, consumed a fifth of whiskey and a whole case of beer during the day. The appeals court ruled that under such circumstances the store could be guilty of "negligent entrustment" of the gun.

A basic ground for suing a manufacturer is that the product has a defect or design flaw that makes it unreasonably hazardous. In the 1998 case of *Dix v. Beretta*, one teenager shot and killed another with a Beretta handgun. He had carefully replaced the loaded magazine with an empty one, not knowing that the gun held an additional round in the firing chamber. The plaintiff argued that this characteristic of the gun was a design flaw and that the gun did not have any indicator to warn that it was not empty. Beretta, however, noted that its guns did have a standard safety device that had to be disengaged before the gun could be fired. The jury refused to find Beretta liable for an industry-standard design. (Gun control advocates frequently note, however, that guns are subject to few of the safety regulations or standards that are applied to other products.)

Another legal approach is to argue that a product is inherently hazardous, despite not having a defective design. In *Addison v. Williams* the plaintiff claimed that manufacturing assault weapons was an "ultrahazardous activity" that was inherently and unreasonably dangerous and imposed an unacceptable cost on the community. But in this case and others courts have ruled that the ultrahazardous activity doctrine applies only to activities involving the use of land, such as having a leaky gas tank. The plaintiff had also charged that by being much more dangerous than ordinary handguns, assault weapons posed "an unreasonable risk of harm to the public." Pointing out that all guns are dangerous in various ways, the court in *Addison* declined that claim as well.

Kelley v. R.G. Industries dealt with a victim injured by a robber using a Saturday night special rather than an assault weapon. At first, the court started out in fashion similar to that in the *Addison* case. It dismissed the ultrahazardous activity complaint on the same grounds of it not being land related. It also dismissed the possibility that the gun was inherently defective in design. The court refused to extend strict liability to all handguns, despite agreeing that they contributed to a significant social problem. But the court then looked at the Maryland legislation concerning Saturday night specials and its characterization of the cheap, inaccurate, and poorly made guns as being of use only to criminals. The court also looked at evidence that the manufacturer was targeting poor, high-crime neighborhoods and held the company liable for the shooting injury.

Gun control advocates hail such legal efforts as an attempt to at long last hold an irresponsible industry accountable for the consequences of its marketing of dangerous products. They claim that the result will be safer guns and fewer crimes and accidents.

Gun rights advocates, however, see such efforts as an attempt to stretch reasonable concepts of liability into a form of "backdoor gun control," in effect obtaining through the courts what they could not obtain through political means. They argue that if such suits are widely successful, gun manufacturers may be forced out of business, or at least forced to market only expensive handguns, affordable only by the well-off and by criminals.

Thus, in a law journal article, Philip D. Oliver warns that "courts tempted to impose gun control through tort law should recognize that they are ill-suited to carry out carefully calibrated regulatory schemes, and that manifest injustice would result from imposing liability on suppliers who have done nothing that is not fully sanctioned by society . . .".[26]

The legislatures, however, may be catching up with the courts in promoting gun safety. In the fall of 1999, the California legislature enacted a bill that requires that all guns sold in California pass strict safety tests. However, critics (including some gun control supporters) suggest that the legislation is flawed and that it will create a large black market in used guns that can no longer be sold legally because private owners will have no way to have them tested. Meanwhile, large gun manufacturers who can afford to set up testing labs continued to sell all the guns they wanted, and police departments benefited from a loophole introduced at the last minute that exempted the Glock pistol, a very popular police weapon.

THE NEXT TOBACCO?

Gun makers are now facing an even more potent legal threat: the class-action suit. Starting in late 1998, 20 cities have begun the process of suing gun manufacturers. They argue that the guns are unsafe (lacking such safety devices as trigger locks), are negligently distributed (with no effective control to prevent guns from going into the criminal black market), and are being deceptively marketed as well. If they succeed, the suits could cost the gun industry billions of dollars in claims for the medical, police, and other expenses caused by firearms injuries.

The precedent for the effort is, of course, the successful legal campaign against the tobacco industry that began in 1994. The result was a $250 billion settlement to be shared by 46 states. Gun control advocates and litigators point to similarities between the tobacco and gun industries. They argue that both industries market a product that is inherently unsafe, is advertised and marketed in a way that is deceptive, and targets vulnerable groups such as young people.

The gun industry and gun rights advocates believe the gun–tobacco analogy is flawed, however. They point out that the gun industry, unlike the tobacco industry, did not try to conceal the fact that its products could be dangerous. As noted earlier, they also argue that guns save many lives by stopping crime and that any accounting of the social costs of guns would have to be balanced against the benefits of security and successful defense. However, there is another difference between the tobacco and gun industries: The tobacco industry has much more money for fighting legal battles.

Although the large class action suits have not yet gone to court, the verdict in *Hamilton v. Accu-Tek* may give gun makers some cause for concern. In this case, a Brooklyn jury found that 15 of the 25 gun makers sued by gun victims had some degree of negligence or liability, although only 3 had to pay actual damages. The jury reached their conclusion after reviewing evidence that the companies should have known that their marketing practices would lead to a disproportionate number of guns ending up in criminal hands in New York.

THE FUTURE: CONFLICT OR COMPROMISE?

As the century drew to a close, the gun control arena was more turbulent and confused than ever. Although general support for gun control reached to 70–80 percent of the public, the gun rights side still had the edge in numbers of passionately committed activists. In 1999, Congress debated relatively minor changes in gun laws, such as requiring all purchasers at gun shows to undergo background checks; the two sides divided not over whether to have the checks, but rather, whether to require that they be completed in 24 or 72 hours.

It is possible that gun rights, rather than being abolished by sweeping legislation, may be gradually restricted and removed from the public sphere in much the way smoking has been. For example, local jurisdictions, such as Los Angeles and Alameda counties in California, are beginning to ban gun possession (and thus gun shows) on public property. High costs, whether imposed by regulation or legal liability, and community pressures may reduce the number of gun shops as well.

It is also possible that the Littleton shootings have ignited a far-reaching examination not only of the role of guns in our society, but also the role of the entertainment and media companies and the responsibilities of parents. But as this survey has shown, the gun control debate has repeatedly flared up and died down, usually with gun control advocates making only gradual and limited progress toward their goals. Meanwhile, gun rights advocates continue to speak for what they consider to be a position in keeping with the original U.S. balance of liberty and responsibility. The possibility and shape of a compromise that would be acceptable to the majority of both sides remains unclear.

---

[1] In the interest of even-handedness, I have adopted the term *gun control advocates* to refer to those seeking to maintain or to increase restrictions on firearms or their use, and *gun rights advocates* to refer to those seeking to preserve or increase rights involving firearms or their use.

[2] Naomi Paiss, quoted in David Phinney et. al. "Gun Fight: Seeking a Cease-Fire." ABC News online. URL: http://abcnews.go.com/sections/us/DailyNews/guns_essays.html. Posted on June 8, 1999·

[3] Statement by National Shooting Sports Foundation, quoted in David Phinney et. al. "Gun Fight: Seeking a Cease-Fire."

[4] Philip Cook, quoted in David Phinney, et. al. "Gun Fight: Seeking a Cease-Fire."

[5] Appendix A summarizes studies and arguments relating to many of these questions.

[6] W. Marina, "Weapons, Technology and Legitimacy," in D. B. Kates, *Firearms and Violence*. Pacific Institute for Public Policy Research, San Francisco, 1984, p. 429.

[7] Aristotle, quoted in Kruschke, p. 60.

[8] King Charles I of England, quoted in David Hardy, *Origins and Development of the Second Amendment*. Chino Valley, Ariz.: Blacksmith, 1986, p. 25.

[9] Bill of Rights of 1689, William III and Mary, sess. 2, chapter 2.

[10] Andrew Fletcher, quoted in Stephen P. Halbrook, *That Every Man Be Armed: The Evolution of a Constitutional Right*. San Francisco, Calif.: Liberty Tree Press, 1984, p. 47.

[11] Daniel Boorstin, *The Americans: The Colonial Experience*. New York: Random House, 1965, p. 365.

[12] Virginia statute, quoted in Stephen P. Halbrook, *That Every Man Be Armed*, p. 56.

[13] William Knox, quoted in Benedict D. LaRosa. "Gun Control: A Historical Perspective," in Jacob Hornberger and Richard M. Ebeling, *The Tyranny of Gun Control*. Fairfax, Va.: Future of Freedom Foundation, 1997, p. 49.

[14] James Madison, *Federalist*, No. 46, quoted in Marjolijn Bijlefeld. *The Gun Control Debate*. Westport, Conn.: Greenwood Press, 1997, p. 5.

[15] See Chapter 2 for several cases involving the interpretation of state constitutions.

[16] Richard Hofstadter, "Reflections on American Violence in the United States," in Hofstadter and Wallace, *American Violence*, p. 22.

[17] Albion Tourgeé, quoted in David Kopel, *The Samurai, the Mountie, and the Cowboy*. Buffalo, N.Y.: Prometheus Books, 1992, p. 333.

[18] Clayton E. Cramer. "The Racist Roots of Gun Control." Available online. URL: http://www.magi.com/~freddo/racist.html. Posted in 1993.

[19] Roy G. Weatherup. "Standing Armies and Armed Citizens: An Historical Analysis of the Second Amendment." *Hastings Constitutional Law Quarterly 2* (Fall 1975), p. 1000–1001.

[20] Sanford Levinson. "The Embarrassing Second Amendment." *Yale Law Journal* 99 (1989), p. 637–659.

[21] See Appendix A for summaries of these and other significant gun-related studies.

[22] Tamara L. Roleff, editor. *Gun Control: Opposing Viewpoints*. San Diego, Calif.: Greenhaven Press, 1997, p. 13.

[23] Suzanna Gratia, quoted in Tamara L. Roleff, editor. *Gun Control: Opposing Viewpoints*, p. 13.

[24] See Appendix A for representative studies and critiques.

[25] John Lott, quoted in ABC News Online, URL: http://more.abcnews.go.com/sections/us/DailyNews/guns_essays.html. Updated on June 28, 1999.

[26] Philip D. Oliver, "Rejecting the 'Whipping-Boy' Approach to Tort Law," *University of Arkansas at Little Rock Law Journal* 14 (1991), n.p.

CHAPTER 2

THE LAW OF GUN CONTROL

Firearms are primarily regulated by the states, along with several important federal laws. The recent upsurge of interest in gun control, particularly following the Littleton, Colorado, high school shootings, is likely to lead to changes in both state and federal legislation. In general, the existence of a law at a higher jurisdiction (state or federal) is not a bar to more restrictive legislation at a lower level (city or state). Therefore determining the firearms laws in force in a given locale requires study of federal, state, and county or municipal laws.

The following discussion groups firearms laws by topic. Under each topic, any relevant federal laws are given first, followed by a list of states that have legislated in that area.

For a summary of features of state gun laws as of the time of this writing, see Appendix B. For the latest information about new or pending state or federal legislation, see the web sites described in Chapter 7. "How to Research Gun Control Issues."

BANS ON SPECIFIC WEAPONS AND OTHER ITEMS

AUTOMATIC WEAPONS/MACHINE GUNS

The National Firearms Act of 1934 (Pub. L. No. 73–474) placed high taxes on the manufacturers, sellers, and purchasers of automatic weapons (machine guns). Fully automatic weapons made after May 19, 1986, are now banned; earlier ones can be sold by federally licensed Class III firearm dealers on payment of tax and after passing a background check.

SEMIAUTOMATIC WEAPONS/ASSAULT WEAPONS

The Assault Weapons Ban in the 1994 Omnibus Crime Bill prohibited the following specific weapons: Norinco, Mitchell and Poly Technologies

Automat Kalashnikovs (i.e., AK-47 type guns; all models) Action Arms Israeli Military Industries UZI and Galil, Beretta Ar70 (SC-70), Colt AR-15, Fabrique National FN/FAL, FN/LAR, and FNC, SWD M-10, M-11, M-11/9, and M-12, Steyr AUG INTRATEC TEC-9, TEC-DC9 and TEC-22, revolving cylinder shotguns, such as (or similar to) the Street Sweeper and Striker 12.

In addition, the law banned all semiautomatic weapons that are equipped with a detachable magazine and two or more of the following: bayonet lug, flash suppressor, protruding pistol grip, folding stock, or threaded muzzle. Magazines that hold more than 10 rounds are also prohibited. Weapons and magazines manufactured before September 13, 1994, however, are exempt.

The following states ban all or some types of assault weapons: California, Connecticut, New Jersey, and New York (in some jurisdictions). A number of cities have their own assault weapons bans. These include: Albany, New York; Atlanta, Georgia; Berkeley, California; Cleveland, Ohio; Columbus, Ohio; Denver, Colorado (ban on sale); Los Angeles, California; and New York City.

SHORT-BARRELED ("SAWED-OFF") WEAPONS

The National Firearms Act of 1934 placed high taxes on the manufacturers, sellers, and purchasers of short-barreled guns such as sawed-off shotguns and carbines.

SATURDAY NIGHT SPECIALS

The federal Gun Control Act of 1968 banned the import of guns "generally recognized as particularly suitable for, or readily adaptable to sporting purposes." This has been interpreted as a ban on inexpensive handguns known as Saturday night specials, as well as certain types of semiautomatic shotguns (Street Sweepers) and some assault weapons. A number of cities such as Los Angeles, San Francisco, and Denver have also banned Saturday night specials.

HARD-TO-DETECT GUNS

The federal Undetectable Firearms Act of 1988 (Public Law 100–649) bans the manufacture, import, or sale of guns that cannot be detected by metal detectors or airport screening equipment (such as guns made mostly of plastic).

HANDGUNS (GENERAL)

Court decisions (such as *Quilici v. Morton Grove*) have generally held that cities or other jurisdictions are free to ban all handguns if they wish, though few have done so. In 1981, Morton Grove, Illinois, became the first town to do so in modern times. Washington, D.C., Chicago, and a number of towns in Illinois also ban handguns.

BANNED ACCESSORIES AND AMMUNITION

Under federal law, silencers are banned. Armor-piercing ammunition (popularly called cop-killer bullets) were banned in 1986, with an expanded definition of banned bullets in the Violent Crime Control and Law Enforcement Act of 1994 that includes bullets made of tungsten, beryllium, depleted uranium, and other exotic materials. Other accessories can also cause a weapon to be banned (see Assault Weapons above).

RESTRICTIONS ON GUN OWNERSHIP

BASIC REQUIREMENTS

Age

Under federal law (18 U.S.C. §922(b)(1)), federally licensed firearm dealers cannot sell a handgun to a person under 21 years of age or a long gun (rifle or shotgun) to anyone under 18 years of age. The following states prohibit all sales (including private sales) of guns to persons under 21: Connecticut, Georgia, Hawaii, Iowa, Maryland, Missouri, Nebraska, Ohio, Rhode Island, and South Carolina.

Residence

An individual cannot "transfer, sell, deliver or transport" a gun to a resident of another state. Mail-order gun sales between states are prohibited. (There are some exceptions, such as for guns that have been inherited and antique firearms.)

Background

Under the Brady Act, all purchasers of guns must first pass a background check before buying. (For more details on this check, see Buying and Selling Firearms below.) Guns cannot be sold to any person who

- has been convicted of a crime with a sentence of a year or more (except for state misdemeanors with a sentence of two years or less).
- has a court restraining order based on violent activity (such as for harassment, spousal abuse, or stalking).

- has been convicted of domestic abuse.
- has been arrested for selling or using drugs.
- is a fugitive from justice.
- has been certified as mentally unstable or is in a mental institution.
- is an illegal alien or has renounced his or her U.S. citizenship.

LICENSES AND PERMITS

The following states require licenses or permits for buying a handgun: Hawaii, Illinois, Iowa, Kansas (in some areas), Massachusetts, Michigan, Minnesota, Missouri, Nebraska, New Jersey, New York, North Carolina, and Ohio (in some areas). Hawaii, Illinois, Massachusetts, and New Jersey also require a permit for buying a long gun (the term used for long-barreled guns such as a rifle or a shotgun). The District of Columbia does not allow ownership of handguns.

REGISTRATION

Registration involves completing a form for the gun itself, in addition to holding the necessary license or permit. Hawaii, Kansas (in some areas), Michigan, Nevada (in some areas), New Jersey, New York, and Ohio (in some areas) require registration.

BUYING AND SELLING FIREARMS

BACKGROUND CHECK AND WAITING PERIOD

Two closely related firearms provisions are for a background check (to confirm that a prospective gun purchaser does not have a criminal, mental health, or other record that would make him or her ineligible to buy a gun) and for a waiting period, or the minimum time before a gun can be handed over to the purchaser.

Starting February 28, 1994, the Brady Handgun Violence Prevention Law (the Brady Act) required a five-day waiting period for all handguns purchased from dealers (but not private sales). This resulted in waiting periods being enforced in 32 states that did not previously have them. The federal waiting period requirement expired in November 30, 1998, and as of late 1999 was still in the process of being replaced by the National Instant Check System (NICS), which gives dealers the ability to confirm instantly a purchaser's eligibility to buy a firearm.

Although the federal waiting period has expired, states are still free to impose their own waiting periods. The following states have waiting periods, ranging from a few days to several months: Alabama, California, Connecticut, Florida, Illinois, Indiana, Kansas (in some areas), Maryland, Massachusetts, Minnesota, Missouri, New Jersey, New York, North Carolina, Ohio (in some areas), Rhode Island, South Dakota, Washington, and Wisconsin.

LICENSING OF MANUFACTURERS

The Gun Control Act of 1968 requires that firearms and ammunition manufacturers obtain a federal license and pay a fee of $50 per year for firearms manufacturers and $10 per year for ammunition makers unless the manufacturer makes "destructive devices" or "armor-piercing ammunition," in which case the fee is $1,000 per year.

LICENSING OF DEALERS

The Federal Firearms Act of 1938 (Pub. Law No. 75–785) required that all dealers who buy or sell weapons across state lines hold a Federal Firearms License (FFL). The Gun Control Act of 1968 (Pub. Law No. 90–618) superseded the 1938 law. It increased license fees and prohibited most sales of firearms or ammunition across state lines. All gun dealers now had to be licensed and had to record all sales of firearms or ammunition so that they could be traced by police. Maximum penalties were raised to $5,000 and imprisonment for five years.

The Firearms Owners Protection Act of 1986 liberalized some of these requirements. Long guns (rifles and shotguns), but not handguns, could be sold across state lines. Guns and ammunition could be purchased through the mail subject to various restrictions. Gun dealers could sell firearms in a place other than a store (such as a flea market or a gun show). Record-keeping requirements were reduced.

The Violent Crime Control and Law Enforcement Act of 1994 made further changes to the system. License holders are now photographed and fingerprinted and are required to comply with applicable state and local laws. Dealers must report any thefts of weapons within 48 hours and must immediately respond to the federal Bureau of Alcohol, Tobacco, and Firearms requests for firearm traces.

FIREARMS IMPORTS

A number of laws regulate the importing of firearms. The Mutual Security Act of 1954 (Pub. Law No. 83–665) led to the establishment of import controls under the Office of Munitions Control of the Department of State. The Omnibus Crime Control and Safe Streets Act of 1968 (Pub. Law No. 90–351) together with the Gun Control Act of 1968 banned the import of Saturday night specials and restricted imports of automatic weapons. Further restrictions on semiautomatic assault weapons were added by the Omnibus Violent Crime Control and Prevention Act of 1994 (Pub. Law No. 103–322).

GUN SHOWS, PAWN SHOPS, AND PRIVATE SALES

As noted in the above sections, some federal laws apply also to private sales, but sales other than those by licensed dealers have generally been regulated (if at all) by state or local jurisdictions. However, proposals that were pending in Congress in mid-1999 (and likely to eventually pass in some form) would require that all purchasers at gun shows (or persons seeking to redeem firearms left at pawn shops) undergo instant background checks. Other proposals would require that all private gun sales be conducted through a licensed dealer and would ban sales of guns or ammunition via the Internet.

"ONE GUN A MONTH"

Maryland, South Carolina, and Virginia have passed laws limiting purchases to one gun per month. The city of Los Angeles also has such a law.

STORAGE AND CARRYING OF FIREARMS

CONCEALED CARRY

The following states prohibit the carrying of concealed weapons: Illinois, Kansas, Missouri, Nebraska, New Mexico, Ohio, and Wisconsin.

The following states "may issue" a concealed weapons permit (this is usually at the discretion of police officials; permits are often hard to obtain): Alabama, California, Delaware, Georgia, Hawaii, Iowa, Maryland, Massachusetts, Michigan, Minnesota, New Jersey, New York, Rhode Island, and South Carolina.

The following states "shall issue" a concealed weapons permit to anyone who meets basic objective requirements (such as lack of a felony or mental health record): Alaska, Arizona, Arkansas, Colorado, Connecticut, Florida, Idaho, Indiana, Kentucky, Louisiana, Maine, Mississippi, Montana, Nevada, New Hampshire, North Carolina, North Dakota, Oklahoma, Oregon,

Pennsylvania, South Carolina, South Dakota, Tennessee, Texas, Utah, Virginia, Washington, West Virginia, and Wyoming. (Handgun Control, Inc., notes that Colorado, while having a "shall issue" law, in practice exercises discretion by law enforcement and issues very few permits.)

One state, Vermont, requires no permit at all for carrying a concealed weapon.

The following states require some training or experience with firearms use to receive a concealed carry permit: Alaska, Arizona, Arkansas, Connecticut, Florida, Kentucky, Montana, North Carolina, Oklahoma, Oregon, South Carolina, Texas, West Virginia, and Wyoming. In practice, this can range from completing a fairly rigorous approved course to performing a vaguely defined "demonstration of competence" to a local sheriff.

SAFE STORAGE AND CHILD ACCESS

Proposals pending in Congress in mid-1999 would require that trigger locks be offered with all new handguns sold.

A number of states have recently enacted laws that include some or all of the following features:

- penalties for allowing a child access to a gun (in some cases, penalties do not apply if the gun is in locked storage or is obtained through a break-in),
- a requirement that dealers offer a trigger lock for sale with each handgun, and/or
- a requirement that guns be kept in locked storage or are fitted with a locking device that prevents unauthorized operation.

States with such laws are Connecticut, Delaware, Florida, Hawaii, Maryland, Massachusetts, Minnesota, Nevada, New Jersey, North Carolina, Rhode Island, Texas, Virginia, and Wisconsin. A pending bill in Wisconsin would require that all handguns be sold with trigger locks.

GUNS IN PUBLIC BUILDINGS (SCHOOLS, ETC.)

The Gun-Free Schools Zones Act (part of the Crime Control Act of 1990) made it illegal for anyone (other than a police officer or security guard) to have a firearm in a school zone, or to carry unloaded firearms (unless in a locked container) within 1,000 feet of school grounds. The Supreme Court overturned this law in 1995 in *U.S. v. Lopez* (see Representative Court Cases).

Texas, Oklahoma, and Utah ban the carrying of guns into schools or other public buildings, bars, sporting events, or private businesses that post "No Guns Allowed" signs. Most, if not all, school districts have rules banning guns and other weapons.

REPRESENTATIVE COURT CASES

There have been a wider variety of cases at all levels dealing with the regulation of firearms and, more recently, with civil liability of firearm manufacturers or dealers. However, because there are so many constitutional and civil issues involved in gun control litigation, the following list breaks down the decisions by topic. (Note that some cases involve more than one topic.) Cases under each topic are listed in chronological order.

TOPICAL GUIDE TO COURT CASES

Assault weapons and machine guns: *Sonzinsky v. United States; Addison v. Williams; Arnold v. Cleveland; Cincinnati v. Langan; Benjamin v. Bailey; Springfield Armory v. City of Columbus*

Attainder argument: *Springfield Armory v. City of Columbus; Benjamin v. Bailey*

Commerce Clause in the U.S. Constitution: *Cases v. U.S.; U.S. v. Lopez*

Concealed weapons: *Bliss v. Commonwealth; Aymette v. State; Nunn v. State; In re Brickey*

Equal protection of the laws: *Cases v. U.S.; Cincinnati v. Langan; Benjamin v. Bailey*

Ex post facto laws: *Cases v. U.S.*

Federal Gun Control Legislation: (divided in subsections per law)
Brady Bill: *Printz v. U.S.*
Federal Firearm Act of 1938: *Cases v. U.S.*
National Firearms Act of 1934: *Sonzinsky v. United States; United States v. Miller*
Gun Control Act of 1968: *U.S. v. Warin*
Gun Free School Zones Act: *U.S. v. Lopez*
Omnibus Violent Crime Control and Prevention Act of 1994: *U.S. v. Emerson*

Federalism: *Printz v. U.S.*

Gun Control

"Grandfather" provision in laws: *Cincinnati v. Langan*

Handgun ban: *Nunn v. State; Andrews v. State; In re Brickey; State v. Rosenthal; Quilici v. Morton Grove; California Rifle and Pistol Association v. City of West Hollywood*

Handgun permit: *Application of Atkinson; Schubert v. DeBard*

Intoxication and weapons use: *City of Salina v. Blaksley; Kitchen v. K-Mart*

Liability (civil): (divided into subsections)

> Gun manufacturer: *Kelley v. R.G. Industries, Inc.; Perkins v. F.I.E. Corp.; Dix v. Beretta; Hamilton v. Accu-Tek*

> Negligent entrustment: *Kitchen v. K-Mart*

> Retailer: *Kitchen v. K-Mart*

> "Unreasonably dangerous" or "ultrahazardous" products doctrine: *Kelley v. R.G. Industries, Inc.; Perkins v. F.I.E. Corp.; Addison v. Williams*

Militia and military weapons: *Andrews v. State; Presser v. Illinois; City of Salina v. Blaksley; United States v. Miller; Cases v. U.S; U.S. v. Warin*

Ninth Amendment: *Quilici v. Morton Grove*

"Right to Bear Arms" in state constitutions: *Bliss v. Commonwealth; Aymette v. State; Nunn v. State; Andrews v. State; In re Brickey; City of Salina v. Blaksley; Arnold v. Cleveland; Benjamin v. Bailey; Schubert v. DeBard; Quilici v. Morton Grove*

Saturday Night Specials: *Kelley v. R.G. Industries, Inc.; California Rifle and Pistol Association v. City of West Hollywood*

Second Amendment

> Applied to states: *Andrews v. State; United States v. Cruikshank; Presser v. Illinois; In re Brickey; Quilici v. Morton Grove*

> Applied to federal government: *United States v. Miller; Cases v. U.S.; U.S. v. Warin*

Supremacy and Preemption:

> State over local: *State v. Rosenthal; Quilici v. Morton Grove; California Rifle and Pistol Association v. City of West Hollywood*

> Federal over state/local: *Presser v. Illinois; Arnold v. Cleveland; Quilici v. Morton Grove; Printz v. U.S.*

Taxation on firearms: *Sonzinsky v. United States*

Tenth Amendment: *Printz v. U.S.*

Travel and weapons use: *Application of Atkinson*

Vagueness argument: *Cincinnati v. Langan; Springfield Armory v. City of Columbus; Benjamin v. Bailey*

Welfare Clause in the U.S. Constitution: *Sonzinsky v. United States*

The Law of Gun Control

BLISS V. COMMONWEALTH, 2 LITTELL 90 (KENTUCKY, 1822)

Background

The defendant (Bliss) was convicted of violating a Kentucky law that stated "any person in this commonwealth, who shall hereafter wear a pocket pistol, dirk, large knife, or sword in a cane, concealed as a weapon, unless when traveling on a journey, shall be fined in any sum not less than $100 . . ."

Legal Issues

The defendant argued that by forbidding his sword-cane, the statute violated the state constitution, which provided "that the right of the citizens to bear arms in defense of themselves and the state, shall not be questioned." The State argued that it agreed that there was a constitutionally protected right to bear arms, but that the means of doing so could be regulated, including by regulating the carrying of concealed weapons.

Decision

The court suggests that the constitutional provision is "as well calculated to secure to the citizens the right to bear arms in defense of themselves and the state, as any that could have been adopted by the makers of the constitution." The court noted that later in the constitution "it is expressly declared, 'that every thing in that article is excepted out of the general powers of government, and shall forever remain inviolate; and that all laws contrary thereto, or contrary to the constitution, shall be void.'"

The court declared, ". . . to be in conflict with the constitution, it is not essential that the act should contain a prohibition against bearing arms in every possible form; it is the right to bear arms in defense of the citizens and the state, that is secured by the constitution, and whatever restraint [of] the full and complete exercise of that right, though not an entire destruction of it, is forbidden by the explicit language of the constitution." The statute was therefore declared unconstitutional.

Impact

Although not involving a firearm, this is one of the earliest state decisions relating to weapon laws and the most absolute in its insistence on a totally unfettered right to bear arms. Its precedent is not followed in most subsequent decisions, which find at least some arms regulations (such as the prohibition of concealed weapons) to be compatible with the constitutional right to bear arms.

Gun Control

AYMETTE V. STATE, 2 HUMPHREYS 154 (TENNESSEE, 1840)

Background

William Aymette was convicted of carrying a concealed bowie knife, in violation of a state law providing that "if any person shall wear any bowie knife, or Arkansas tooth-pick [a type of bowie knife], or other knife or weapon, that shall in form, shape, or size resemble a bowie knife or Arkansas tooth-pick, under his clothes, or keep the same concealed about his person, such person shall be guilty of a misdemeanor." He appealed the conviction.

Legal Issues

Aymette argued that a ban on such weapons is a violation of the provision of the Tennessee constitution "that the free white men of this state have a right to keep and bear arms for their common defense." He claimed that the decision of what weapons to carry and how to carry them is an individual one, beyond the power of the legislature to regulate.

Decision

The appeals court pointedly rejected the absolute right declared in *Bliss v. Commonwealth* above. It examined the history of the right to bear arms in English law because the framers of the state legislation had used that tradition. It noted, for example, that an act passed by Parliament during the reign of Charles II had declared that the people may have arms "suitable to their condition and as allowed by law," which implied a regulatory power. Further, the right to bear arms in English law was tied to a *common* defense of the people (against tyranny or disorder). The court concluded, "The legislature, therefore, have a right to prohibit the wearing or keeping weapons dangerous to the peace and safety of the citizens, and which are not usual in civilized warfare, or would not contribute to the common defense." Aymette's conviction was thus upheld.

Impact

Although it involves a knife rather than a gun, this case illustrates two continuing themes that will be applied to firearm regulation: (1) the question of whether the right to bear arms is collective or individual, and (2) the application of the "police power" of the state to the types of weapons people may have and the manner in which they may be carried. This case cast an early vote for the "collective" position and upheld the state's police power.

The Law of Gun Control

NUNN V. STATE, 1 KELLY 243 (GEORGIA, 1846)

Background

Hawkins H. Nunn was indicted and convicted "for having and keeping about his person, and elsewhere, a pistol, the same not being such a pistol as is known and used as a horseman's pistol, under an act of the General Assembly of the State of Georgia, entitled 'An Act to guard and protect the citizens of this State against the unwarrantable and too prevalent use of deadly weapons.'" (The law, an early example of strict gun control, also banned the sale of a variety of weapons, including bowie knives and concealable pistols. The "horseman's pistol" is a larger, hard to conceal weapon, usually kept in a saddle holster.) Nunn's appeal reached the Georgia Supreme Court.

Legal Issues

Nunn challenged his conviction on several grounds, some of which related to the indictment process and are not relevant here. He asserted that the law under which he was convicted violated both the United States Constitution and the Constitution of the State of Georgia by infringing the right to keep and bear arms for self-defense.

Decision

The court first observed that the statute in question was badly written and vague. As for the plaintiff, "It is not pretended that he carried his weapon secretly, but it is charged as a crime, that he had and kept it about his person, and elsewhere. And this presents for our decision the broad question, is it competent for the legislature to deny to one of its citizens this privilege? We think not."

After reviewing similar cases in other states, the court ruled that "so far as the act of 1837 seeks to suppress the practice of carrying certain weapons secretly, that it is valid, inasmuch as it does not deprive the citizen of his natural right of self-defence, or of his constitutional right to keep and bear arms. But that so much of it, as contains a prohibition against bearing arms openly is in conflict with the Constitution, and void . . ."

Impact

This decision suggests that the state and federal constitutions convey an individual, not merely a collective, right to keep and bear arms for their defense. The state or a local jurisdiction can use its police power to ban the carrying of concealed arms as dangerous to the community or can make other regulations, so long as they don't destroy the efficacy of the right to self defense and they still permit the effective exercise of constitutional rights.

ANDREWS V. STATE, 50 TENN. 165 (TENNESSEE, 1871)

Background

The case of James Andrews was combined with several other cases for appeal purposes. Altogether, the cases involved the violation of a Tennessee law prohibiting "any person to publicly or privately carry a dirk, sword-cane, Spanish stiletto, belt or pocket pistol or revolver."

Legal Issues

The appellants argued that the weapons laws violated both the Second Amendment to the U.S. Constitution and the Tennessee Constitution. They noted that in the *Aymette* case the court ruled that the knife could be banned because it was not a weapon of war that would be protected by the constitution's interest in promoting the common defense. A pistol, they argued, was a weapon that could be used in war, and the state could not make a regulation that amounted to a prohibition of such a weapon.

The State argued that the Second Amendment did not apply to the states. Further, even "if [the State] can not prohibit carrying arms, they may, by regulation, determine what arms may be carried, what shall be proscribed; may declare where they may be carried, and when they may be carried, as well as declare the mode. If weapons of warfare are protected by the Constitution, still they are subject, by the exception, to regulation in respect to times, places and modes."

Thus according to the State, even if a pistol were considered a military weapon, the allowable conditions for carrying it could be specified by regulation.

Decision

The court reiterated the collective nature of the right to bear arms for defense as found in English law, asserting "It was this great political right that our fathers aimed to protect; not the claims of the assassin and the cut-throat to carry the implements of his trade. They would as soon have protected the burglar's jimmy and skeleton key." They also noted that English precedent did not object to specifying allowable weapons according to the class or condition of the person.

The Second Amendment argument was disposed of quickly by declaring that the amendment restrained only Congress and had no application to the states. (This, indeed, was the generally accepted view about all provisions of the Bill of Rights until the 20th century when the process of incorporating some rights into the Fourteenth Amendment and applying them against the states gradually took hold.)

The court noted that the Tennessee Constitution specified that "That the citizens of this State have a right to keep and bear arms for their common defense. But the Legislature shall have power by law, to regulate the wearing of arms, with a view to prevent crime." In interpreting this, the court focused on the language about "common defense" and the importance of the militia expressed elsewhere in the state constitution. In this context the constitution protects "the usual arms of the citizens of the country, and the use of which will properly train and render him efficient in defense of his own liberties, as well as of the State. Under this head, with a knowledge of the habits of our people, and of the arms in the use of which a soldier should be trained, we would hold, that the rifle of all descriptions, the shot gun, the musket, and repeater, are such arms; and that under the Constitution the right to keep such arms, can not be infringed or forbidden by the Legislature."

However, the court noted that constitutional reference to the prevention of crime meant that "a man may well be prohibited from carrying his arms to church, or other public assemblage, as the carrying them to such places is not an appropriate use of them, nor necessary in order to his familiarity with them, and his training and efficiency in their use. As to arms worn, or which are carried about the person, not being such arms as we have indicated as arms that may be kept and used, the wearing of such arms may be prohibited if the Legislature deems proper, absolutely, at all times, and under all circumstances."

The court left it to a factual examination to determine whether a revolver might be considered a military weapon whose carrying was protected by the constitution (although the manner of carrying could still be regulated in any case).

Impact

This decision continues in the tradition of the keeping of arms being an individual right, but one exercised in the context of promoting a collective defense (the well-trained militia). The state's police power can prohibit weapons that are not suitable or customary for this purpose. The keeping of military weapons cannot be banned, but the manner of bearing them can be regulated.

Gun Control

UNITED STATES V. CRUIKSHANK, 92 U.S. 542 (1876)

Background

The background in this case is somewhat unclear, but it seems to have arisen from the killing of two African Americans by a group of Ku Klux Klan members in Louisiana. They were charged with banding together "unlawfully and feloniously . . . to injure, oppress, threaten, and intimidate," which was in violation of a federal civil rights statute called the Enforcement Act. The act was part of the apparatus set up during the Reconstruction period in an attempt to protect the rights of blacks in the South.

The indictment goes on to charge the defendants with trying to "hinder and prevent in their respective free exercise and enjoyment of their lawful right and privilege to peaceably assemble with each other and with other citizens of the said United States for a peaceable and lawful purpose." The second count charges them with hindering the black citizens in their exercise of their "right to keep and bear arms for a lawful purpose." (To note in passing, laws that prevented blacks from carrying weapons, either directly or indirectly—such as by banning the cheaper weapons that they could afford—were a common part of the strategy for regaining white control in the South in the latter part of the 19th century.) Other counts involved interference with other rights, such as the right to vote. The defendants (including one William Cruikshank) were convicted and appealed. The Supreme Court agreed to hear their appeal directly.

Legal Issues

The relevant and underlying issue is whether the federal government has the right to prohibit citizens in the states from violating basic constitutional rights such as the freedom of assembly (First Amendment) or the right to keep and bear arms (Second Amendment). In other words, does the specification of rights in the U.S. Constitution restrain only the federal government and its agents, or does it also restrain state and local governments or the actions of private citizens?

Decision

The Court declared that as with the right of assembly in the First Amendment, the right to bear arms for a peaceful purpose as specified in the Second Amendment "is not a right granted by the Constitution. Neither is it in any manner dependent upon that instrument for its existence. The Second Amendment declares that it shall not be infringed; but this, as has been seen, means no more than that it shall not be infringed by Congress." The Second Amendment therefore cannot be used as the basis for a law enforced against the states or individual citizens. The Court overturned the other counts of the indictment on various grounds (including vagueness), and the defendants were ordered released.

Impact

This decision is rather confusing. Some gun control advocates say that it means that the right to bear arms is not protected at all by the Second Amendment. Gun rights advocates, however, say that it is simply a statement of the basic doctrine that the Constitution does not create rights but declares or affirms rights arising out of the common or natural law.

What is undisputed is that the Supreme Court decided that the Second Amendment, whatever sort of right it declared, was a restraint only on Congress, not on the states, localities, or citizens. As noted earlier, many parts of the Bill of Rights would later be "incorporated" into the Fourteenth Amendment and enforced against the states (notably, to protect the civil rights of African Americans and other minorities), but to date the Second Amendment has not been included in this process.

PRESSER V. ILLINOIS, 116 U.S. 252 (1886)

Background

The military code of the state of Illinois specifies: "It shall not be lawful for any body of men whatever, other than the regular organized volunteer militia of this State, and the troops of the United States, to associate themselves together as a military company or organization, or to drill or parade with arms in any city, or town, of this State, without the license of the Governor thereof . . ."

Herman Presser was indicted for violating this statute as part of a German-American social and military society called the Lehr und Wehr Verein ("Education and Defense Society"). The group was incorporated under Illinois law with the stated purpose "of improving the mental and bodily condition of its members so as to qualify them for the duties of citizens of a republic." In December 1879, the group, lead by Presser, engaged in a march and drill, armed with rifles, without the required license from the governor.

Legal Issues

Presser argued that the Second Amendment gave him and his group the right to bear arms in keeping with its goal of maintaining a well-trained militia. He said that the state cannot restrict that right to the official, organized militia (the Illinois National Guard) because under Article I, Section 8 of the U.S. Constitution, only Congress has the power "To provide for organizing, arming, and disciplining the militia, and for governing such part of them as may be employed in the service of the United States, reserving to the States, respectively, the appointment of the officers, and the authority of training the militia, according to the discipline prescribed by Congress . . ."

The State made the usual argument that the Second Amendment was not applicable to the states. It also argued that the prohibition of private militias was not in conflict with the power of Congress to oversee the organization of state militias.

Decision

The Court sided with the State's argument. There is no constitutionally protected right to march as part of a private armed militia. The Second Amendment does not apply to the states.

Impact

This decision gained some recent relevance with the formation of many private militias in the 1980s. Gun control advocates see *Presser* as denying any constitutional protection to such organizations, as well as reaffirming that the Second Amendment is not a bar to state or local gun regulations.

Gun rights advocates, however, point to the following part of the decision as affirming that the right to bear arms usable in connection with the official militia is an individual right that cannot be infringed: "It is undoubtedly true that all citizens capable of bearing arms constitute the reserved military force or reserve militia of the United States as well as of the States, and in view of this prerogative of the general government, as well as of its general powers, the States cannot, even laying the constitutional provision in question out of view, prohibit the people from keeping and bearing arms, so as to deprive the United States of their rightful resource for maintaining the public security, and disable the people from performing their duty to the general government."

IN RE *BRICKEY*, 8 IDAHO 597 (1902)

Background

The Territory (not yet a state) of Idaho had a law against carrying a deadly weapon within the limits of a city. The defendant was convicted and imprisoned in county jail for having carried a loaded revolver in violation of the law. (The gun had been carried openly; it was not concealed.) He filed a writ of habeas corpus with the Idaho Supreme Court, arguing that the law was unconstitutional.

Legal Issues

The basic issue was whether the weapons law violated either the Second Amendment or the Idaho constitution. The latter states that "The people have the right to bear arms for their security and defense, but the legislature shall regulate the exercise of this right by law."

Decision

The court sided with the petitioner, ruling: "Under these constitutional provisions [federal and state], the legislature has no power to prohibit a citizen from bearing arms in any portion of the state of Idaho, whether within or without the corporate limits of cities, towns, and villages. The legislature may, as expressly provided in our state constitution, regulate the exercise of this right, but may not prohibit it. A statute prohibiting the carrying of concealed deadly weapons would be a proper exercise of the police power of the state. But the statute in question does not prohibit the carrying of weapons concealed, which is of itself a pernicious practice, but prohibits the carrying of them in any manner in cities, towns, and villages. We are compelled to hold this statute void."

Impact

The decision suggests that the state's police power can be used to regulate how weapons can be carried but not completely prohibit it. It is also one of the relatively few decisions that seems to also apply the federal Second Amendment to the state, though it can be viewed as superfluous to the state constitution.

STATE [OF VERMONT] V. ROSENTHAL, 75 VERMONT 295 (1903)

Background

The defendant was convicted of carrying a loaded pistol within the limits of the city of Rutland, Vermont, in violation of an ordinance that "provides that no person shall carry within the city any steel or brass knuckles, pistol, sling shot, stiletto, or weapon of similar character, nor carry any weapon concealed on his person, without permission of the mayor or chief of police, in writing." He appealed to the Supreme Court of Vermont.

Legal Issues

The defendant argued that the city ordinance conflicted with state law, which did not prohibit the carrying of an unconcealed firearm, except at a school. State law should take precedence.

Decision

The court agreed with the defendant that the local law conflicted with that of the state because "unless a special permission is granted by the mayor or chief of police for that purpose, a person is prohibited from carrying such weapons in circumstances where the same is lawful by the Constitution and the general laws of the state," and conversely, "there is nothing in the ordinance to prevent the granting of such permission, notwithstanding it be in circumstances to constitute a crime under the general laws" (e.g., such as by allowing a gun to be carried in a school).

Impact

In recent years many cities have passed firearms laws more restrictive than those of the state. This frequently leads to the issue of "state preemption"—whether any aspect of firearms law specified by the state precludes a city or county from making its own legislation in that area. This issue is fought out on a state-by-state basis and depends on the relationship between the language of the conflicting laws and the intentions expressed by the legislature.

CITY OF SALINA V. BLAKSLEY, 72 KANSAS 230 (1905)

Background

James Blaksley was convicted by the police court of Salina, Kansas, for "carrying a revolving pistol within the city while under the influence of intoxicating liquor." His conviction was upheld by the district court and was then appealed to the Supreme Court of Kansas.

Legal Issues

The defendant argued that his conviction violated his right to keep and bear arms under the Kansas Constitution, which states "The people have the right to bear arms for their defense and security; but standing armies, in time of peace, are dangerous to liberty, and shall not be tolerated, and the military shall be in strict subordination to the civil power."

Decision

The court noted: "The power of the Legislature to prohibit or regulate the carrying of deadly weapons has been the subject of much dispute in the courts. The views expressed in the decisions are not uniform, and the reasonings of the different courts vary. It has, however, been generally held that the Legislatures can regulate the mode of carrying deadly weapons, provided they are not such as are ordinarily used in civilized warfare."

Further, "The provision in section 4 of the Bill of Rights 'that the people have the right to bear arms for their defense and security' refers to the people as a collective body. It was the safety and security of society that was being considered when this provision was put into our Constitution." The court went on to point out that the provisions for the maintenance of the state militia implied that the state could regulate the way in which weapons were to be carried.

The constitutional provision is thus ". . . a limitation on legislative power to enact laws prohibiting the bearing of arms in the militia, or any other military organization provided for by law, but is not a limitation on legislative power to enact laws prohibiting and punishing the promiscuous carrying of arms or other deadly weapons."

Impact

This view of the state constitutional provision is close to the viewpoint of most modern gun control advocates with regard to the Second Amendment: Only the right of the state to form and operate a militia is protected; the legislature is free to regulate or even prohibit the individual carrying of weapons. Certainly few people would assert that anyone has the right to carry a weapon while drunk.

SONZINSKY V. UNITED STATES, 300 U.S. 506 (1937)

Background

The previously discussed cases all dealt with state or local laws regulating firearms. In 1934, however, the federal government entered the arena when Congress passed the National Firearms Act in response to public concern about the machine-gun–toting gangsters of the Prohibition era. This law banned certainly highly destructive devices (such as bombs and grenades) outright, but it did not ban the machine guns. Instead, it placed a tax of $200 on every sale of a machine gun, sawed-off shotgun, or rifle with either a barrel shorter than 18 inches or a silencer. (This was a rather large amount of money at that time, both in absolute terms and in relationship to the market value of the weapon.) In addition, all firearm dealers would have to be registered and pay a $200 annual "special occupational tax." The case arose when a dealer was convicted for not paying the tax. The appeal came to the Supreme Court.

Legal Issues

The appellant raised several arguments. He argued: "The Constitution made no grant of authority to Congress to legislate substantively for the general welfare, and no such authority exists, save as the general welfare may be promoted by the exercise of the powers which are granted. . . . The power of taxation which is expressly granted may be adopted as a means to carry into operation another power also expressly granted, but resort to the taxing power to effectuate an end which is not legitimate, not within the scope of the Constitution, is obviously inadmissible." In other words, Congress could only tax to raise revenue to pay for some activity for which it has a power enumerated (listed) in the Constitution.

Furthermore, the petitioner argued that the National Firearms Act was constructed and written in a way that made it clear that it was not intended to raise revenue but rather to discourage dealing in the specified weapons. He also argued that if the purpose of the tax was really to exercise a form of police power, that power belonged not to Congress but to the states. "Congress is not empowered to tax for those purposes which are within the exclusive province of the States."

The government replied that the taxes in the National Firearms Act were authorized by Congress's broad power in Article 1, Section 8, clause 1 of the Constitution "To lay and collect taxes, duties, imposts and excises to pay the debts and provide for the common defense and general welfare of the United States." Further, "It is no objection that the size of the tax tends to burden and discourage the conduct of the occupation of petitioner. . . . Nor is it material that Congress may have anticipated and even intended such an effect. Where a tax is laid on a proper subject and discloses a revenue purpose, it is of no consequence that social, or moral, or economic factors may have been considered by Congress in enacting the measure."

Decision

The Court rejected the petitioner's argument, agreeing with the government's contention that the tax was legitimate and the motives of Congress irrelevant. The conviction was affirmed subject to factual review by the lower court.

Impact

This case is interesting in that the petitioner's argument relied not on the Second Amendment or some similar clause in a state constitution but ultimately on a theory that the powers of Congress are limited to those spelled out in the Constitution and that the power to tax is thus similarly limited. Although this was largely the intention of the framers of the Constitution, the power of Congress had been allowed to expand greatly by the 1930s and indeed was the subject of a number of cases challenging Franklin Roosevelt's New Deal legislation. Although of considerable philosophical interest, this line of argument has not prevailed in modern times.

United States v. Miller, 307 U.S. 174 (1939)

Background

This case began with an indictment that charged that two suspected bootleggers, Jack Miller and Frank Layton, "did unlawfully, knowingly, wilfully, and feloniously transport in interstate commerce from the town of Claremore in the State of Oklahoma to the town of Siloam Springs in the State of Arkansas a certain firearm, to-wit, a double barrel 12-gauge Stevens shotgun having a barrel less than 18 inches in length" without paying the $200 tax required under the National Firearms Act of 1934.

The lower court judge threw out the case on the grounds that the law violated the Second Amendment. The government appealed. Meanwhile, the bootleggers disappeared. When the case was finally heard in the Supreme Court, only the government was represented.

Legal Issues

There are two legal issues: Does the federal firearms tax encroach on powers reserved to the states, and does it infringe on the right to keep and bear arms specified in the Second Amendment?

Decision

The court quickly disposed of the issue of the taxation power, citing its previous decision of *Sonzinsky v. U.S.* As for the Second Amendment, the court simply noted that it "can not take judicial notice that a shotgun having a barrel less than 18 inches long has today any reasonable relation to the preservation or efficiency of a well regulated militia; and therefore can not say that the Second Amendment guarantees to the citizen the right to keep and bear such a weapon."

Impact

This short, rather cryptic decision has been interpreted in two different ways in the continuing debate over the meaning of the Second Amendment. Gun control advocates cite it as clearly stating that the Second Amendment must be interpreted in terms of the militia clause and does not give individuals the right to keep and bear any sort of firearm they want.

Gun rights advocates suggest that the same reference to the militia might imply that an individual would have the right to carry a weapon that *is* of a military nature (such as a fully automatic AK-47 or M-16 rifle). They also note that the defendant was not represented and that, therefore, the judges heard only one side of the case. (They also note in passing that short-barreled shotguns and carbines were in fact military weapons used by some cavalry units.)

Gun control advocates observe, however, that the Court has not directly revisited the issue of the scope and applicability of the Second Amendment in the more than 60 years since *Miller* was decided. Unless and until they do, a direct attack on gun laws based on the Second Amendment seems unlikely to succeed.

CASES V. U.S., 131 F.2D 916 (1ST CIR. 1942)

Background

In 1938 Congress passed another Federal Firearms Act. Among its provisions, it prohibited a convicted felon from purchasing or otherwise receiving a gun or ammunition. Jose Cases Velazquez of the U.S. territory of Puerto Rico was convicted of violating the Federal Firearms Act "by transporting and receiving a firearm and ammunition" while being a convicted felon. Cases's appeal was heard by the U.S. District Court of Appeals.

Legal Issues

As the court noted in its opinion, the defendant contends that the Federal Firearms Act is unconstitutional because (a) it is an ex post facto law; (b) it violates the Second Amendment by infringing the right of the people to keep and bear arms; (c) it is an undue extension of the commerce clause; (d) it creates an unreasonable presumption of guilt; and (e) it denies equal protection of the laws.

Decision

The court rejected all five of the defendant's arguments. It declared that the Federal Firearms Act of 1938 was not an ex post facto ("after the fact") law—that is, it didn't punish someone for an act committed before the law took effect—rather, "it is abundantly plain that in enacting it Congress was in no way interested in imposing an additional penalty upon those who at some time in the past had been convicted of a crime of violence. In the act Congress sought to protect the public by preventing the transportation and possession of firearms and ammunition by those who, by their past conduct, had demonstrated their unfitness to be entrusted with such dangerous instrumentalities . . ."

With regard to the Second Amendment, the court cited the recent Supreme Court case of *U.S. v. Miller* to indicate that the amendment did not convey an absolute or unqualified right to keep and bear arms. The court noted the reference in *Miller* to a sawed-off shotgun not being a military weapon but did not conclude that Cases's pistol might be such a weapon and be protected by the Constitution: "Apparently, then, under the Second Amendment, the federal government can limit the keeping and bearing of arms by a single individual as well as by a group of individuals, but it cannot prohibit the possession or use of any weapon which has any reasonable relationship to the preservation or efficiency of a well regulated militia. However, we do not feel that the Supreme Court in this case was attempting to formulate a general rule applicable to all cases. The rule which it laid down was adequate to dispose of the case before it and that we think was as far as the Supreme Court intended to go."

The court went on to note: "While the weapon [the pistol] may be capable of military use, or while at least familiarity with it might be regarded as of value in training a person to use a comparable weapon of military type and caliber, still there is no evidence that the appellant was or ever had been a member of any military organization or that his use of the weapon under the circumstances disclosed was in preparation for a military career."

The court declared that the commerce clause of the Constitution (allowing Congress to regulate interstate commerce) did apply to Puerto Rico as a U.S. territory. It also disposed of the due process and equal protection arguments, citing the rational and practical need for lawmakers to make assumptions based on a person's prior conviction for a crime.

Impact

This case illustrates a possible path that the Supreme Court might take if it ever revisits its view of the Second Amendment in *Miller v. U.S.* The decision here implies that the Supreme Court's rejecting constitutional protection for a nonmilitary weapon doesn't necessarily mean that possession by an individual of a military weapon outside an organized military context would be protected. Gun rights advocates view such an approach as contradictory and as a failure to honor the intent of the Constitution's framers.

U.S. V. WARIN, 530 F.2D 130 (6TH CIR. 1976)

Background

The defendant, a firearms designer, was convicted of possessing a "9-millimeter prototype machine gun" in violation of the National Firearms Act as amended by the Gun Control Act of 1968. The two sides stipulated that "9-millimeter submachine guns have been used by at least one Special Forces Unit of the Army in the Vietnam War, although they are not in general use. 9-millimeter submachine guns have been used by the military forces of the United States on at least one occasion during the Vietnam war. . . . [T]hat submachine guns are part of the military equipment of the United States military and that firearms of this general type, that is, submachine guns, do bear some relationship, some reasonable relationship to the preservation or efficiency of the military forces."

Legal Issues

The defendant argued that because the weapon was a military weapon and he was a member of the "sedentary" (or reserve) state militia, he was entitled under the Second Amendment to have it, as implied by the Supreme Court rejecting the shotgun in *U.S. v. Miller* as not being a military weapon.

Decision

The court disagreed:

> *In Miller the Supreme Court did not reach the question of the extent to which a weapon which is "part of the ordinary military equipment" or whose "use could contribute to the common defense" may be regulated. In holding that the absence of evidence placing the weapon involved in the charges against Miller in one of these categories precluded the trial court from quashing the indictment on Second Amendment grounds, the Court did not hold the converse—that the Second Amendment is an absolute prohibition against all regulation of the manufacture, transfer and possession of any instrument capable of being used in military action.*

The court went on to reiterate the common themes of the Second Amendment being a collective, not an individual, guarantee and that the common law has long recognized the right of the state to regulate the details of weapon ownership and use.

Impact

By dealing with what was clearly a military weapon, the circuit court in *Warin* seemed to be making an even stronger statement that courts are unwilling to draw the conclusion that the Second Amendment gives individuals an unqualified right to carry at least military weapons.

APPLICATION OF ATKINSON, 291 N.W2D 396 (MINNESOTA, 1980)

Background

The plaintiff, Berton Atkinson, had been carrying a pistol in the glove compartment of his car "while traveling appreciable distances away from [his] home on public roads and highways." In 1975, the city of Bloomington, Minnesota, passed an ordinance requiring that persons wishing to carry or possess a pistol in a public place to obtain a permit from a police chief or county sheriff. Further, the applicant had to demonstrate that he or she had "an occupation or personal safety hazard requiring a permit to carry." Atkinson's permit was denied on the grounds that he had not satisfied that requirement. He appealed that decision to the court.

Legal Issues

The court saw two issues being raised by this case: Does the constitution or common law give individuals an absolute right to carry a loaded gun on a public highway? And failing that, does travel on a public highway automatically constitute the "personal safety hazard" required by the statute?

Decision

The court concluded that neither the common law nor the constitution conveyed an "absolute" right to carry weapons for individual self-defense. Therefore, there was scope for the state to exercise its police power in regulating the carrying of weapons. Further, the court [found] "it difficult to believe that such travel [on highways] was intended by the legislature to be a personal safety hazard. . . . The hazard plaintiff has identified is vague, general, and speculative. He has not made the showing of real and immediate danger, which the statute requires in order to justify issuance of a handgun permit. The permit was properly denied."

Impact

This decision is an example of a court upholding what is called a discretionary gun permit. Gun rights advocates often argue that such laws amount to gun control for everyone except well-connected and favored persons who have an inside track with the police chief or sheriff. Accordingly, they have sometimes organized successful campaigns to remove the element of "discretion" from gun permit laws.

SCHUBERT V. DEBARD, 398 N.E.2D 1339 (INDIANA, APP. 1980)

Background

In June 1975, Joseph L. Schubert applied for a license to carry a handgun. He had previously held a handgun permit and had held commissions from two police agencies. All had expired. When his new application was denied, he made an administrative appeal.

The Indiana licensing statute provided:

> *The officer to whom the application is made shall conduct an investigation into the applicant's official records and verify thereby the applicant's character and reputation, and shall in addition verify for accuracy the information contained in the application, and shall forward this information together with his recommendation for approval or disapproval . . . to the superintendent who may make whatever further investigation he deems necessary. In addition, whenever disapproval is recommended, the officer to whom the application is made shall provide the superintendent and the applicant with his complete and specific reasons, in writing, for the recommendation of disapproval. If it appears to the superintendent that the applicant has a proper reason for carrying a handgun and is of good character and reputation and a proper person to be so licensed, he shall issue to the applicant either a qualified or an unlimited license to carry any handgun or handguns lawfully possessed by the applicant.*

Schubert had claimed that he needed the gun to protect himself from threats and presented as evidence "a copy of a picture of a pig with appellant's name written above it." The other was a letter, signed "The Assassinater's," demanding $1,250 or "Pig, you are dead." However, he apparently had not contacted police about these threats. The court record also notes: "A report summarizing a background investigation made of appellant when he applied for a private detective's license in 1971 was admitted without objection. That report concluded that appellant was a 'chronic liar' suffering from a 'gigantic police complex.'"

The superintendent of the Indiana state police upheld the permit denial, saying that Schubert "did not have a proper reason."

Legal Issues

The Indiana Constitution says "The people shall have a right to bear arms, for the defense of themselves and the State." According to the court record, "Schubert contends . . . that the Indiana Constitution affords him the right to bear arms for his own defense. Thus, he urges that where self-defense is properly asserted as the reason for desiring a firearms license, and the applicant is otherwise qualified, the license cannot be withheld upon an administrative official's subjective determination of whether the applicant needs defending."

Decision

The court concluded that "the [police] superintendent [had] decided the application on the basis that the statutory reference to 'a proper reason' vested in him the power and duty to subjectively evaluate an assignment of 'self-defense' as a reason for desiring a license and the ability to grant or deny the license upon the basis of whether the applicant 'needed' to defend himself." The majority of the court found that "Such an approach contravenes the essential nature of the constitutional guarantee. It would supplant a right with a mere administrative privilege which might be withheld simply on the basis that such matters as the use of firearms are better left to the organized military and police forces even where defense of the individual citizen is involved."

Acknowledging that there had been legitimate concerns about Schubert's suitability to receive a permit, the court ordered a new administrative hearing.

Impact

Some "discretionary" gun laws have been overturned, and others upheld. There are a number of factors that may come into play in such decisions: whether the state constitution has an unequivocal guarantee of the right to carry arms for self-defense, the specificity and apparent rationality of the permit statute, and the extent to which a court might defer to its own beliefs about the carrying of firearms as a matter of social policy.

Gun Control

QUILICI V. VILLAGE OF MORTON GROVE, 695 F.2D 261 (7TH CIR. 1982)

Background

Depending on one's point of view, the village of Morton Grove, Illinois, became either famous or notorious when it enacted an ordinance that banned, among other weapons, "Any handgun, unless the same has been rendered permanently inoperative." This total ban on handguns was challenged in a civil action by Victor D. Quilici in state court. The village of Morton Grove had the case transferred to federal court, where it was joined to two other cases.

The district court rejected Quilici's suit (*Quilici v. Village of Morton Grove*, 532 F. Supp. 1169 [N.D. Ill. 1981]). The plaintiffs then appealed to the circuit court.

Legal Issues

The original district court proceeding and the review of that decision by the circuit court had the following main issues:

1. Did the Morton Grove ordinance conflict with the clause in the Illinois Constitution that states "Subject only to the police power, the right of the individual citizen to keep and bear arms shall not be infringed"? The appellants conceded that "laws which require the licensing of guns or which restrict the carrying of concealed weapons or the possession of firearms by minors, convicted felons, and incompetents are valid." They argued, however, that a total ban on handguns was not reasonable and that it might well lead to a situation where some towns banned handguns, others permitted them with certain restrictions, and still others had no laws. This would create a chaotic situation and make it too easy for travelers to fall afoul of the law. Morton Grove contended that the constitution, in referring to "arms" in general, could be satisfied as long as *some* arms were permitted, and the town ordinance did allow the keeping of some types of rifles and shotguns.

2. Did the Second Amendment to the U.S. Constitution apply to this local law? The appellants argued that the Supreme Court case *U.S. v. Presser* implied that firearms ownership, through its connection to "national citizenship" and the ability of the national government to ensure public security through the militia, could not be interfered with so radically by local governments. Morton Grove, however, pointed to the straightforward statement in *Presser*: "The Second

Amendment declares that it shall not be infringed, but this . . . means no more than that it shall not be infringed by Congress. This is one of the amendments that has no other effect than to restrict the powers of the National government . . ." For the circuit appeal, the appellant added an argument that the statement in *Presser* was no longer valid because many provisions of the Bill of Rights had later been incorporated into the Fourteenth Amendment's guarantees of the rights of citizens that could be enforced against the states.

3. Finally, the appellant raised the issue of whether the Morton Grove ordinance conflict with a fundamental right to self-defense implied in the Ninth Amendment to the U.S. Constitution. The amendment says that "the enumeration in the Constitution, of certain rights shall not be construed to deny or disparage others retained by the people."

Decision

In looking at the Illinois Constitution, the circuit court disagreed with Morton Grove's contention that handguns were not contemplated in the constitutional protection of the right to keep and bear arms. However, the court said: "We agree with the district court that the right to keep and bear arms in Illinois is so limited by the police power that a ban on handguns does not violate that right." In coming to that conclusion they were guided partly by statements by delegates at the state constitutional convention, such as one named Foster who said that the constitutional provision "would prevent a complete ban on all guns, but there could be a ban on certain categories." Finally, the court noted that under the doctrine of "Home Rule," municipalities could enact whatever legislation they wished so long as it was not in conflict with a "positive constitutional guarantee." Any problems that might be caused by conflicting local laws were not legally relevant.

The court found no evidence that the Second Amendment had been applied to the states by the Supreme Court and that "The Supreme Court has specifically rejected the proposition that the entire Bill of Rights applies to the states through the Fourteenth Amendment." Further, the court agreed that "As the Village [of Morton Grove] correctly notes, appellants are essentially arguing that *Miller* was wrongly decided and should be overruled. Such arguments have no place before this court. Under the controlling authority of *Miller* we conclude that the right to keep and bear handguns is not guaranteed by the Second Amendment."

The Ninth Amendment argument was quickly dismissed as lacking any convincing precedents. "Appellants may believe the Ninth Amendment should be read to recognize an unwritten, fundamental, individual right to own or possess firearms; the fact remains that the Supreme Court has never embraced this theory."

The circuit court thus upheld the Morton Grove statute as being constitutional.

Impact

The Morton Grove decision shows the general tendency to construe constitutional guarantees of the right to keep and bear arms narrowly, although it gives wide scope to a legislature's exercise of police power, extending even to banning whole classes of firearms. So far, however, a total ban on *all* firearms and all circumstances of possession has not been tested in the courts.

KELLEY V. R.G. INDUSTRIES, INC., 497 A.2D 1143, 304 MD. 124 (MARYLAND, 1985)

Background

Olen J. Kelley was shot and injured during an armed robbery at the store where he worked. The gun used was assembled and sold by R.G. Industries, a subsidiary of the West German firm Rohm. Kelley sued both firms. Rohm and R.G. Industries had the case transferred to the U.S. District Court in Maryland and asked that it be dismissed. (Rohm argued that "the [p]laintiffs' contentions [must] fail because the handgun performed as it was supposed to perform and because Rohm Gesellschaft is not responsible for the criminal and tortious acts of Mr. Kelley's assailant." Not finding a "controlling precedent on the strict liability issue" the district court "certified" it and transferred it to the Maryland State Court of Appeals.

Legal Issues

The Maryland court addressed the following issues:

1. *Is the manufacturer or marketer of a handgun, in general, liable under any strict liability theory to a person injured as a result of the criminal use of its product?*
2. *Is the manufacturer or marketer of a particular category of small, cheap handguns, sometimes referred to as Saturday night specials and regularly used in criminal activity, strictly liable to a person injured by such handgun during the course of a crime?*
3. *Does the Rohm Revolver Handgun Model RG38S, serial number 0152662, fall within the category referred to in question 2?*

The Law of Gun Control

Decision

The court said that under Maryland law, gun manufacturers could not be held liable under the first theory because this kind of liability applied only to the misuse of land (for example, having buried fuel tanks that leak and cause injury or damage to neighbors). The activity of making or shooting a gun has nothing to do with land. "Therefore, the abnormally dangerous activity doctrine does not apply to the manufacture or marketing of handguns."

But could the gun itself be defective and "unreasonably dangerous" even if the manufacturer took all reasonable care in selling it and even if the person who uses it had not bought it directly from the manufacturer? Noting that the product had to be defective in design (not just dangerous), the court ruled that "A handgun manufacturer or marketer could not be held liable under this theory. Contrary to Kelley's argument, a handgun is not defective merely because it is capable of being used during criminal activity to inflict harm. . . . For the handgun to be defective, there would have to be a problem in its manufacture or design, such as a weak or improperly placed part, that would cause it to fire unexpectedly or otherwise malfunction."

Moving from the gun itself to its use, the court said: "The fact that a handgun manufacturer or marketer generally would not be liable for gunshot injuries resulting from a criminal's use of the product, under previously recognized principles of strict liability, is not necessarily dispositive. This Court has repeatedly said that 'the common law is not static; its life and heart is its dynamism—its ability to keep pace with the world while constantly searching for just and fair solutions to pressing societal problems.'" Looking at Maryland's handgun regulations, the court concluded, however, that because some kinds of handgun use were permitted, it would not be appropriate to assign liability to use of all types of handguns.

However, the court recognized that Congress and state legislators had identified a particular category of handguns popularly known as Saturday night specials, characterized by "by short barrels, light weight, easy concealability, low cost, use of cheap quality materials, poor manufacture, inaccuracy and unreliability." The court said such guns were of use only to criminals and not for legitimate purposes of sport or self-protection.

Turning to Rohm's product, the court observed: "Moreover, the manufacturer or marketer of a Saturday night special knows or ought to know that he is making or selling a product principally to be used in criminal activity. For example, a salesman for R.G. Industries, describing what he termed to be a 'special attribute' of a Rohm handgun, was said to have told a putative handgun marketer, 'If your store is anywhere near a ghetto area, these ought to sell real well. This is most assuredly a ghetto gun.' The R.G. salesman allegedly went on to say about another R.G. handgun, 'This sells real well, but, between you and me, it's such a piece of crap I'd be afraid to fire the thing.'"

Because ". . . the manufacturer or marketer of a Saturday night special knows or ought to know that the chief use of the product is for criminal activity. Such criminal use and the virtual absence of legitimate uses for the product are clearly foreseeable by the manufacturers and sellers of Saturday night specials. . . . it is entirely consistent with public policy to hold the manufacturers and marketers of Saturday night special handguns strictly liable to innocent persons who suffer gunshot injuries from the criminal use of their products."

The court returned the case to the district court for determination of whether the gun used met the definition for a Saturday night special and, if so, for trial.

Impact

This decision begins by concluding that handguns in general are not inherently defective or unreasonably dangerous, but then the decision uses findings from legislators to conclude that a particular kind of handgun, the Saturday night special, is so and that a manufacturer can be held liable for use of such guns in criminal activity. This illustrates the fact that courts can create new criteria for liability and that gun control advocates may be able to further their goals by filing civil suits that end up making more categories of guns subject to liability. Gun rights advocates would argue, however, that the court is going beyond its proper role and is, in effect, legislating.

PERKINS V. F.I.E. CORP., 762 F.2D 1250 (5TH CIR. 1985)

Background

On September 18, 1981, Claude Nichols fought with someone in a bar parking lot. He went into the bar, shooting wildly at his opponent with a .25 caliber revolver. Three bystanders were wounded including Joseph Perkins, who, as a result of the gunfire, became permanently paralyzed from the waist down. Nichols was convicted of aggravated battery and sentenced to five years at hard labor. Perkins sued F.I.E. Corporation, the manufacturer of the handgun used by Nichols. The suit was transferred to federal court.

Legal Issues

The district court noted: "The plaintiff admitted in answers to interrogatories—that there was no defect in the design of the gun, no defect in the manufacture or assembly of the component parts of the gun, no statutory prohibition to the manufacture or distribution of the gun, and that Claude Nichols was not at the time of the shooting an agent, employee, or servant of F.I.E. Corp." The plaintiff (Perkins) thus did not claim any of these traditional causes of possible liability for the manufacturer.

However, Perkins claimed that the pistol "is defective in that it is unreasonably dangerous in normal use, that the hazard of injury to human beings exceeds the utility of the pistol and this defect constitutes a proximate cause [of the injury]."

According to the court: "The plaintiffs present two theories of recovery. First, they argue that the marketing of a dangerous weapon to the general public is an ultrahazardous activity giving rise to absolute liability under Louisiana law. Second, they argue that the handgun used in the two crimes is an unreasonably dangerous product giving rise to strict products liability . . . because of its small size, enabling it to be easily concealed, coupled with marketing of it to the general public."

Decision

The district court rejected both the strict product liability and the ultrahazardous activity theory in Perkins's suit and granted summary judgment in favor of the gun manufacturer. In a similar case, *Richman v. Charter Arms Corp.* (involving a robbery, rape, and murder committed using a .38 caliber handgun), the court granted summary judgment to the defendant on product liability but not on ultrahazardous activity. The two cases were then combined in an appeal to the U.S. Circuit Court of Appeals, Fifth District.

The circuit court observed that the doctrine of "ultrahazardous activity" had only been applied to activities involving the use of land or property in a way that was inherently dangerous: for example, building a dangerous high-pressure gas line, blasting, using hazardous chemicals, and so on. The court, however, noted a general standard that had emerged from the case of *Langlois v. Allied Chemical* where the Louisiana Supreme Court had advised that: "The activities of man for which he may be liable without acting negligently are to be determined after a study of the law and customs, a balancing of claims and interests, a weighing of the risk and the gravity of harm, and a consideration of individual and societal rights and obligations." This would seem to allow for an argument that small handguns were "ultrahazardous." However, the circuit court decided that this statement of suggested methodology did not determine what sorts of cases it should be applied to. The court concluded that to be ultrahazardous, "1. The Activity Must Be An Activity Relating to Land or to Other

Immovables. . . . 2. The Activity Itself Must Cause the Injury and the Defendant Must Have Been Engaged Directly in the Injury-Producing Activity. . . . 3. The Activity Must Not Require the Substandard Conduct of a Third Party to Cause Injury."

Clearly, manufacturing a handgun has nothing to do with the use of land. The manufacturing of a handgun doesn't directly cause injury, and indeed, it requires that a third party (the shooter) be involved. The court thus declared that manufacturing a handgun is not an ultrahazardous activity, granting summary judgment in favor of the manufacturer.

Impact

Although decided under Louisiana's unique French-inspired laws, the decision here reflects a widespread rejection of the theory that simply manufacturing a gun is an "ultrahazardous activity" comparable to setting off explosives on one's land. (However, note that *Kelley v. R.G. Industries* concluded that certain types of handguns—Saturday night specials—could be considered unreasonably hazardous.) Some later firearms liability has also focused on the possibility that the way some handguns are *marketed* constitutes an unreasonable risk or danger to the community.

ADDISON V. WILLIAMS, 546 SO.2D 220 (LOUISIANA APP. 1989)

Background

According to the court record, "on New Year's Eve 1986, shortly before midnight, Cody Wayne Williams caused a disturbance at the Hub Lounge in Bossier City. Employees of the lounge took a handgun from him, and he was ordered to leave the premises. To protect themselves, customers and employees closed and locked the two steel doors to the lounge. Williams returned to the lounge with a Colt AR-15 model SP1 semiautomatic rifle and opened fire on the lounge, firing 56 rounds of .223 caliber ammunition into the building through the steel doors. Bullets and bullet fragments struck six of the occupants of the lounge, fatally injuring one person and injuring five others. Williams later pled guilty to first degree murder and is serving a life sentence in the state penitentiary."

Several lawsuits were filed on behalf of the victims against Colt Industries (manufacturer of the gun) and Olin Corporation (maker of the ammunition), and other gun manufacturers. Colt and Olin filed to have the suit dismissed for lack of a valid cause of action, and the district court agreed. The plaintiffs appealed.

The Law of Gun Control

Legal Issues

The appeals court reviewed the following theories of liability:

1. *the manufacturing and marketing of the AR-15 assault rifle and its ammunition to the civilian public is an ultrahazardous activity rendering defendants absolutely liable;*
2. *the weapon and its ammunition are unreasonably dangerous and defective per se rendering defendants liable under strict products liability;*
3. *the manufacturing and distribution of the products presented an unreasonable risk of harm, amounting to negligence and rendering defendants liable under LSA-C.C. Art. 2316; and*
4. *assuming defendants had a legal right to distribute the products to the public, defendants are liable because they abused that right.*

Decision

The court rejected the "ultrahazardous" and "unreasonably dangerous" theories, citing the earlier decisions of *Strickland v. Fowler* and *Perkins v. F.I.E. Corp.*, which concluded that the manufacturing or marketing of handguns was not ultrahazardous (because it did not apply to activities involved with use of land) nor unreasonably dangerous. Also, "Strickland and Perkins likewise correctly dealt with and disposed of the contention that the manufacturer was liable under a theory of strict products liability. In general, to recover in a products liability case the plaintiff must prove that the product was defective, that is, unreasonably dangerous to normal use, and that the plaintiff's injuries were caused by reason of the defect."

The court then dealt with another possibility, that

> *there is a distinction with legal effect to be drawn between the manufacture and sale of handguns and the manufacture and sale of assault rifles. Plaintiffs argue that comparing a handgun to an assault rifle is like comparing a firecracker to dynamite. It is argued that handguns are primarily defensive weapons and assault rifles are primarily offensive weapons, and that while there may be some social utility for handguns there is none for assault rifles. Plaintiffs emphasize the greater power, penetrating capabilities, and rapid fire of the assault rifle. It is argued that the manufacture of assault rifles and the manner in which they are marketed create an atmosphere of violence and an increased risk beyond that presented by other guns, thereby rendering this product unreasonably dangerous and defective and presenting an unreasonable risk of harm to the public.*

However, the court (unlike *Kelley v. R.G. Industries* with regard to Saturday night specials) declined to characterize a particular kind of gun as creating inherent liability. "We recognize the difference in physical characteristics and capabilities of assault rifles as compared to handguns or other guns. However, all guns are dangerous and have the capacity to kill. Each type of gun has characteristics that make it more dangerous than another type, depending on the circumstances of its use. A handgun can be concealed and in that sense is more susceptible to criminal misuse than larger guns. . . . Thus, attempting to characterize one type of gun as presenting a greater risk of harm or as being more susceptible of criminal misuse than another type becomes extremely tenuous." Therefore, "The manufacturers of the weapon and the ammunition used in it are not liable for injuries resulting from the intentional criminal misuse of the gun."

Impact

This is a case where the court chose not to "legislate" beyond traditional product liability law. There has been a great increase in gun liability litigation in recent years, and it is far from clear whether most courts will eventually follow the approach in *Kelley* or the one here.

ARNOLD V. CLEVELAND, 67 OHIO ST.3D 35 (OHIO 1993)

Background

In 1989 the City Council of Cleveland, Ohio, passed an ordinance banning "assault weapons"—basically, semiautomatic rifles or shotguns with high-capacity magazines. Harry W. Arnold and others appealed to the courts to overturn this law as being unconstitutional.

Legal Issues

The appellants argued that the Cleveland law placed too great a restriction on rights specified in Section 4, Article 1 of the Ohio Constitution, which states: "The people have the right to bear arms for their defense and security; but standing armies, in time of peace, are dangerous to liberty, and shall not be kept up; and the military shall be in strict subordination to the civil power." They argued that this section referred to a fundamental individual right to bear arms.

They also argued that the law interfered with a federal civilian marksmanship program created by the U.S. code by banning certain rifles used by that program. Under the doctrine of supremacy, a local or state law that conflicts with constitutionally valid federal law is void.

Decision

The lower appeals court rejected the argument based on the Ohio Constitution, saying that the ordinance "was a valid exercise of the police power." It did agree that part of the law did conflict with the U.S. code. The appellants then appealed to the Ohio Supreme Court.

That court began by noting: "The question as to whether individuals have a fundamental right to bear arms has, seemingly, been decided in the negative under the Second Amendment to the United States Constitution," citing *Cruikshank, Presser, Miller, Quilici v. Morton Grove* and other cases. "These decisions signify, and history supports the position, that the amendment was drafted not with the primary purpose of guaranteeing the rights of individuals to keep and bear arms but, rather, to allow Americans to possess arms to ensure the preservation of a militia."

The court did note, however, that state courts were free to interpret their state constitutions in ways that offered greater liberties or rights than those founded by the U.S. Supreme Court in the federal Bill of Rights. The Ohio Constitution refers to a specific right of the people to "to bear arms for their defense and security." The court asserted that "The right of defense of self, property and family is a fundamental part of our concept of ordered liberty. To deprive our citizens of the right to possess any firearm would thwart the right that was so thoughtfully granted by our forefathers and the drafters of our Constitution."

Thus, the court said that the individual citizens of Ohio have a right to possess firearms for their self-defense and security. The court then quoted the great British legal scholar Blackstone: "And we have seen that these rights consist, primarily, in the free enjoyment of personal security, of personal liberty, and of private property. So long as these remain inviolate, the subject is perfectly free; for every species of compulsive tyranny and oppression must act in opposition to one or other of these rights, having no other object upon which it can possibly be employed. To preserve these from violation, it is necessary that the constitution be supported in its full vigor."

However, the court then stated that "the people of our nation, and this state, cannot have unfettered discretion to do as we please at all times. Neither the federal Bill of Rights nor this state's Bill of Rights, implicitly or explicitly, guarantees unlimited rights." The court gave the famous example that freedom of speech does not allow one to shout "fire!" in a crowded theater. Each right may be restrained in certain ways to secure the safety of society. Therefore, "we find that Section 4, Article I of the Ohio Constitution confers upon the people of Ohio the fundamental right to bear arms. However, this right is not absolute."

The court then discussed the "police power" as embodied in a community's right to "exercise all powers of local self-government and to adopt and enforce within their limits such local police, sanitary and other similar regulations, as are not in conflict with general laws." The court stated that "Laws or ordinances passed by virtue of the police power which limit or abrogate constitutionally guaranteed rights must not be arbitrary, discriminatory, capricious or unreasonable and must bear a real and substantial relation to the object sought to be obtained, namely, the health, safety, morals or general welfare of the public."

Finally, the court applied this test to the assault weapons law. It quoted the part of the law that expresses the city council's reasons for enacting it: "The Council finds and declares that the proliferation and use of assault weapons [are] resulting in an ever-increasing wave of violence in the form of uncontrolled shootings in the City, especially because of an increase in drug trafficking and drug-related crimes, and pos[e] a serious threat to the health, safety, welfare and security of the citizens of Cleveland. The Council finds that the primary purpose of assault weapons is antipersonnel and any civilian application or use of such weapons is merely incidental to such primary antipersonnel purpose. The Council further finds that the function of this type of weapon is such that any use as a recreational weapon is far outweighed by the threat that the weapon will cause injury and death to human beings. Therefore, it is necessary to establish regulations to restrict the possession or sale of these weapons. It is not the intent of the Council to place restrictions on the use of weapons which are primarily designed and intended for hunting, target practice, or other legitimate sports or recreational activities."

The court concluded that the Cleveland City Council's purposes in banning assault weapons were reasonable and bore a reasonable relationship to the goal of promoting public safety. It suggested that a ban on all firearms might, though, be unacceptable. Finally, the decision stated that city ordinance did not interfere with the federal Civilian Marksmanship program because residents can practice marksmanship without using types of rifles banned by the city. The city ordinance was thus upheld.

Impact

This decision is interesting in that it begins with a sweeping declaration of fundamental rights and even classifies the bearing of arms for personal protection as a fundamental individual right. It then, however, interprets the police power to allow the banning of a whole class of firearms. Gun rights advocates have argued that this is contradictory: If gun ownership is a fundamental right as is free speech, then the "strict scrutiny" test should have been applied, requiring a "compelling" state interest and a "narrowly tailored" means to accomplishing it rather than the broader "rational basis" test applied here.

CINCINNATI V. LANGAN, 94 OHIO APP.3D 22, REVIEW DENIED, 70 OHIO ST.3D 1425 (1994)

Background

In another Ohio case, Peter Langan was convicted of violating an assault weapons ban similar to that in Cleveland. He appealed the conviction on various grounds, and the case went to the Ohio Court of Appeals.

Legal Issues

The defendant's arguments relevant to gun control were that the Cincinnati ordinance infringed the right to bear arms in the Ohio Constitution, that the ordinance was "unconstitutionally vague" in its description of the banned weapons, and that by "grandfathering" (allowing residents who had such guns prior to the law's taking effect to keep them) it denied later residents the equal protection of the laws.

Decision

The court quickly disposed of the first constitutional argument by citing its earlier decision of *Arnold v. Cleveland*, where it had held that an assault weapons ban was a reasonable exercise of the city's police power. It ruled that the law was not vague because it clearly described specific weapons as well as general features of weapons that would be banned. Finally, the court concluded that because the law did not violate a fundamental right, its grandfathering feature need only be judged as being reasonable: "The fact that persons who did not possess semiautomatic firearms on a certain date are not allowed to possess them thereafter, while persons who did possess semiautomatic weapons prior to that date do not have to surrender those weapons they legally owned prior to the enactment of the statute, does not violate the equal protection rights of one who did not previously possess a semiautomatic weapon. The fixing of a date by which to prohibit the influx of semiautomatic weapons into the city is rationally related to the city council's goal to protect its citizenry from violent crimes and the use of semiautomatic weapons and, thus, the resulting classification contained within the ordinance is neither arbitrary nor unreasonable." Langan's conviction was upheld.

Impact

Because arguments based on the Second Amendment or a state constitution seem to have little chance of succeeding in modern litigation, gun rights advocates have relied more on arguments such as unconstitutional vagueness. However, a law that is both narrow and specific in describing banned weapons is unlikely to be judged vague. The idea of arguing that a group of people can be discriminated against "chronologically" by grandfathering also seems to be ineffective.

SPRINGFIELD ARMORY V. CITY OF COLUMBUS, 29 F.3D 250 (6TH CIR. 1994)

Background

A firearms dealer and two prospective purchasers joined together to challenge the constitutionality of a ban on assault weapons enacted by the city of Columbus, Ohio.

Legal Issues

According to the court: "The ordinance defines 'assault weapon' as any one of thirty-four specific rifles, three specific shotguns and nine specific pistols, or '[o]ther models by the same manufacturer with the same action design that have slight modifications or enhancements. . . .'" The plaintiffs claimed that because the law referred only to specific models by specific manufacturers (or possible future models by the same manufacturers), it was an unconstitutional "bill of attainder." (A bill of attainder is a law that punishes specific individuals without trial.) The plaintiffs also argued that the law was unconstitutionally vague.

Decision

The U.S. District Court of Appeals rejected the attainder argument but said that parts of the law were vague with regard to its descriptions of two of the weapons it listed. The plaintiffs appealed to the U.S. Court of Appeals, Sixth Circuit.

This court agreed that the Columbus law was "fundamentally irrational and impossible to apply consistently by the buying public, the sportsman, the law enforcement officer, the prosecutor or the judge. [It] outlaws assault weapons only by outlawing certain brand names without including within the prohibition similar assault weapons of the same type, function or capability. The ordinance does not achieve the stated goal of the local legislature—to get assault weapons off the street. The ordinance purports to ban 'assault weapons' but in fact it bans only an arbitrary and ill-defined subset of these weapons without providing any explanation for its selections."

The court also agreed with gun manufacturers who complained that the law gave no idea of what "slight modifications" of the named weapons would cause them to also be banned, such as a faster trigger pull, different ammunition capacity, or different caliber of ammunition. The court declared the Columbus law to be "invalid on its face."

Impact

As the court itself noted, communities can draft assault weapons bans that specify general characteristics of banned weapons rather than naming specific models and using vague language about "modifications." Laws drafted in that way are much less likely to be overturned as being unconstitutionally vague. (Note that because the court rejected the law on vagueness grounds, it did not decide the question of whether or not the law was a bill of attainder.)

U.S. V. LOPEZ, 115 S.CT. 1624 (1995)

Background

In 1990 Congress passed the Gun-Free School Zones Act, which "forbids any individual knowingly to possess a firearm at a place that [he] knows . . . is a school zone." The defendant, a 12th grade student, was convicted of violating this law by carrying a concealed handgun into his school.

The defendant appealed his conviction, arguing that the Gun-Free School Zones Act was an unwarranted intrusion on an area traditionally regulated by the states. The district court denied his appeal, ruling that the law "is a constitutional exercise of Congress' power to regulate activities in and affecting commerce." However, the defendant then appealed to the U.S. Circuit Court, which overturned the conviction on the grounds that the law had not been established as a proper exercise of Congress's power to regulate interstate commerce. The government appealed, and the case went to the U.S. Supreme Court.

Legal Issues

Article I, Section 8, Clause 3 of the U.S. Constitution gives Congress the power to "[t]o regulate Commerce with foreign Nations, and among the several States, and with the Indian Tribes." The original intention for giving this power to Congress was primarily to allow Congress to create uniform regulations to prevent clashes between conflicting state laws and to prevent states from passing laws that discriminated against imports from other states.

However, starting during the New Deal era of the 1930s, the Supreme Court began to take an increasingly broader view of the Commerce Clause. In the 1935 case *A. L. A. Schecter Poultry Corp. v. United States*, the Court said that Congress could regulate commercial activities directly involved in interstate commerce but not activities that had only an indirect effect on the economy. However, as political pressure on the Court increased, the Court seemed to change its criteria and uphold New Deal legislation. Finally, in the case of *Wickard v. Filburn*, the Court declared. "[E]ven if appellee's activity be local and though it may not be regarded as commerce, it may still, whatever its nature, be reached by Congress if it exerts a substantial economic effect on interstate commerce, and this irrespective of whether such effect is what might at some earlier time have been defined as 'direct' or 'indirect.'" Thus, in *Wickard*, the Court upheld a wheat quota even in a case where the farmer consumed all the wheat he grew rather than selling it. By not having to buy any wheat, they ruled, the farmer was reducing the demand for wheat and thus affecting commerce.

Such a broad standard would seem to give Congress almost unlimited power to regulate just about any sort of activity that had any economic effect. But did possession of a gun in a school meet even that very liberal standard?

Decision

The Court noted "Even *Wickard*, which is perhaps the most far reaching example of Commerce Clause authority over intrastate activity, involved economic activity in a way that the possession of a gun in a school zone does not." The Court also concluded that the law was not a necessary part of a legitimate scheme to regulate commerce. Further, Congress had not established a reasonable relationship between this legislation and commerce, and the law had no mechanism for determining whether a particular case of gun possession had the necessary "nexus" or connection with interstate commerce. For all of these reasons the Supreme Court overturned the Gun-Free School Zones Act as not being a proper exercise of congressional power.

Impact

This case has a number of important features. From the point of view of challenging gun control, it should be noted that the Second Amendment played no part in the challenge. Unless the Supreme Court revisits its view of the Second Amendment, challenges to federal gun control laws are likely to be based on the Commerce Clause or federalism (the division of powers between the federal government and the states, as in *Printz et al. v. U.S.*).

Beyond gun control, this decision may signal the willingness of the Supreme Court to rein in its interpretation of the Commerce Clause. In a concurring opinion Justice Thomas indeed urges the Court to consider doing so. In dissent, Justices Stevens and Breyer, however, believe the majority was wrong in not seeing the vital link between education and the future success of commerce as being a reason for a federal ban on guns in schools.

Finally, it should be noted that Congress has a way to get around such limitations on its power. Congress can appropriate money for a purpose such as helping to fund educational programs and then require that states adopt certain policies (such as a ban on guns in schools) to receive the funds.

BENJAMIN V. BAILEY, 662 A.2D 1226, 234 CONN. 455 (CONNECTICUT, 1995)

Background

This case is a challenge to a Connecticut assault weapons ban brought by DeForest H. Benjamin and a variety of other plaintiffs, including a gun manufacturer called Navegar, which was doing business as Intratec. The ban involved both a list of specific weapons (such as the AK–47) as well as specifying similar weapons such as AK–47-type guns. The trial and appeal courts rejected the suit, which was then appealed to the Connecticut Supreme Court.

Legal Issues

There were three major issues: (1) Did the assault weapons ban violate the state constitution's guarantee of the right of a person "to bears arms in defense of himself and the state"? (2) Did the ban violate "equal protection" principles by treating gun owners differently based on hard-to-distinguish characteristics of their weapons? (3) Was the law an unconstitutional "bill of attainder" because it punished the owners of specific weapons but not owners of others that were functionally equivalent?

Decision

The Connecticut Supreme Court upheld the lower courts in rejecting all three challenges. The court ruled that the state could not ban *all* guns because this would make the right of defense in the constitution ineffective, but it could ban *some* types of guns—such as assault weapons, as a reasonable exercise of its police power. The court rejected the equal protection argument because the gun ban did not violate a fundamental right (as previously noted), nor did it deal with a "suspect class" of persons (such as a racial or religious group). Therefore, the law need only be "be rationally related to some legitimate government purpose in order to withstand an equal protection challenge. . . ." Finally, the law was not a bill of attainder because it does not directly "punish" anyone, nor did it apply only to a specified individual or class of individuals. Rather, it prohibited *anyone* from selling the banned weapons.

The court also threw out a "vagueness" challenge accepted by a lower court, ruling that it was not too vague to refer to something like AK–47-type weapons because a person of normal intelligence would understand what was meant.

Impact

If the approach shown by the Connecticut court continues to predominate, a carefully written state assault weapons ban is likely to withstand all legal challenges.

Kitchen v. K-Mart Corp., 697 So.2d 1200 (Florida, 1997)

Background

As stated in court records, "On the night of December 14, 1987, petitioner Deborah Kitchen was shot by her ex-boyfriend, Thomas Knapp, and rendered a permanent quadriplegic, shortly after Knapp purchased a .22 caliber bolt-action rifle from a local K-Mart retail store. Knapp testified that he had consumed a fifth of whiskey and a case of beer beginning that morning and up until he left a local bar around 8:30 P.M. Knapp drove from the bar to a local K-Mart store where he purchased a rifle and a box of bullets. He returned to the bar and, after observing Kitchen leave in an automobile with friends, followed in his truck. He subsequently rammed their car, forcing it off the road, and shot Kitchen at the base of her neck."

Kitchen sued K-Mart for damages, and the jury agreed that K-Mart had been negligent in selling a firearm to an intoxicated person. K-Mart appealed, and the appeals court overturned the verdict, ruling that as in cases involving incompetent or drunk driving, existing statutes covering the offense precluded the claim of negligence.

Legal Issues

The case came for review before the Florida Supreme Court, which was asked to answer the following question: "Can a seller of a firearm to a purchaser known to the seller to be intoxicated be held liable to a third person injured by the purchaser?"

Decision

The court noted that the existence of a law governing an activity doesn't automatically mean that there can't also be civil liability for that act. "Where a defendant's conduct creates a foreseeable zone of risk, the law generally will recognize a duty placed upon defendant either to lessen the risk or see that sufficient precautions are taken to protect others from the harm that the risk poses." Further, "as the risk grows greater, so does the duty, because the risk to be perceived defines the duty that must be undertaken." Because firearms are so dangerous, the duty of the seller is quite substantial.

The generally accepted doctrine of "negligent entrustment" says that part of that duty involves not giving a dangerous object (or *chattel*) to someone known to be incompetent to use it safely. "One who supplies directly or through a third person a chattel for the use of another whom the supplier knows or has reason to know to be likely because of his youth, inexperience, or otherwise, to use it in a manner involving unreasonable risk of physical harm to himself and others whom the supplier should expect to share in or be endangered by its use, is subject to liability for physical harm resulting to them."

Therefore, the court ruled that Kitchen could pursue her claim for "negligent entrustment" against K-Mart.

Impact

Few people would argue that a person selling or giving a firearm to a person known to be intoxicated or otherwise incompetent should not be subject to criminal and civil penalties. From a gun control perspective, the decision suggests that legislatures enacting gun regulations should not fear that doing so would preclude civil liability. Gun rights advocates, however, have responded to increased litigation by promoting state legislation that would limit the liability of gun dealers in other circumstances, such as a shooting by a legally qualified purchaser.

PRINTZ V. U.S., 521 U.S. 98 (1997)

Background

The federal Brady Handgun Violence Prevention Act ("Brady Bill") of 1994 required the "chief law enforcement officer" of each local jurisdiction to conduct background checks of all persons wishing to buy a firearm, but no federal money was appropriated for the purpose. Two sheriffs, Jay Printz of Ravalli County, Montana, and Richard Mack of Graham County, Arizona, filed separate suits that challenged this provision of the Brady Act, claiming that forcing sheriffs to perform the checks at their own expense went beyond the powers of Congress as restricted by the Tenth Amendment to the U.S. Constitution.

In both cases, the district courts of appeals ruled that the background check provision was unconstitutional, though other parts of the law (such as the waiting period) could remain in force. However, federal attorneys appealed to the Circuit Court of Appeals, Ninth Circuit, which ruled that the background checks were constitutional. The sheriffs' appeals, now combined, came to the U.S. Supreme Court.

Legal Issues

The key issue was whether the Constitution allows Congress to enact legislation that forces local law enforcement officials to carry out a federal mandate (in this case, running background checks on firearms purchasers.)

The federal government argued that "the earliest Congresses enacted statutes that required the participation of state officials in the implementation of federal laws." They also pointed to the Constitution's Supremacy Clause, which states that "the Laws of the United States. . . shall be the supreme Law of the Land; and the Judges in every State shall be bound thereby." Finally, they argued that portions of *The Federalist* (writings considered to reveal the intentions of the Constitution's framers) implied that in the structure of the new government, the federal government would be able to require the assistance of state officials for the carrying out of constitutionally valid federal legislation.

Decision

The Court did not agree that the Supremacy Clause and historical experience could be applied to local sheriffs. The justices pointed out that any precedent applied only to state judges, not law enforcement officers. They found no evidence, at least until recent times, that Congress had asserted a power to "commandeer" local officials. Further, "None of [the statements in *The Federalist*] necessarily implies—what is the critical point here—that Congress could impose these responsibilities without the States' consent."

Instead, the Court pointed to the concept of dual sovereignty, implied by the Tenth Amendment to the Constitution, which states: "The powers not delegated to the United States by the Constitution, nor prohibited by it to the States, are reserved to the States respectively, or to the people."

In view of this, the Court noted: "The Framers rejected the concept of a central government that would act upon and through the States, and instead designed a system in which the State and Federal Governments would exercise concurrent authority over the people. The Federal Government's power would be augmented immeasurably and impermissibly if it were able to impress into its service—and at no cost to itself—the police officers of the 50 States."

Thus, by a narrow 5–4 majority, the Supreme Court voided the requirement that state officials perform the background checks.

Impact

The immediate impact of the decision is limited. First, all other provisions of the Brady Act remain intact. Second, the background check provision was set to expire in November 1998, to be replaced by a federal system to be used directly by gun dealers.

In the long term, however, the decision may limit the ability of Congress to create "unfunded mandates" (requirements that are imposed by a higher legislature but paid for by local jurisdictions). It is also relevant to the growing interest in the Tenth Amendment by activists who are attempting to restrain the exercise of federal power in favor of local control. Of course Congress can always require that certain procedures be carried out if a state wishes to receive federal money for law enforcement or other purposes.

DIX V. BERETTA, USA CORP., (ALAMEDA COUNTY, CALIFORNIA, 1998)

Background

Young Kenzo Dix was at the home of Michael S., a 14-year-old friend. Michael took his father's 9-millimeter Beretta pistol from a camera bag. He removed the loaded magazine and replaced it with an empty one. He then pointed the gun at Kenzo and pulled the trigger. Unfortunately, he did not know that in addition to the magazine, the gun can hold one round in the firing chamber. The gun fired, killing Kenzo.

With the assistance of Handgun Control, Inc., Kenzo's parents, Griffin and Lynn Dix, filed suit against Beretta, charging that the gun was defectively designed. They also sued the shooter's parents, charging that they had stored the gun unsafely. The latter case was settled out of court for $100,000, but the case against Beretta went to trial in Alameda County, California.

Legal Issues

The plaintiff argued that the Beretta pistol was defective in design because it did not have an indicator that would show when there was a round in the firing chamber. They also said the gun should have a lock to prevent an unauthorized person from using it. Beretta, they argued, should have foreseen that their product was liable to be misused in a way that could lead to tragic accidents.

Beretta replied that the gun already had a safety device that the young shooter had to disengage before firing. They also argued that trigger locks and locked gun cases were readily available, but Michael's parents had not chosen to use such devices. Finally, Beretta pointed out that the manual that came with the gun mentioned safety practices such as storing the weapon unloaded, separate from ammunition, and inaccessible to children.

Decision

The jury determined that Beretta's product was not defective and that the company was not responsible for Kenzo's death. (The jury foreman was later quoted as saying: "It's really the consumer buying the gun, I feel, who has ultimate responsibility for storage and safety.")

The judge required the Kenzos to pay Beretta's court costs. Kenzo appealed the verdict after learning that one juror may have carried a gun herself during the trial and screamed at other jurors during deliberations. However the appeal was denied.

Impact

So far, juries have usually not found that guns as normally designed are defective. However, this may change as cities and other jurisdictions file more suits and as there are more demands for safer guns.

CALIFORNIA RIFLE AND PISTOL ASSOCIATION V. CITY OF WEST HOLLYWOOD, 66 CAL. APP. 4TH 1302 (CALIFORNIA, 1998)

Background

The City of West Hollywood, California, passed a law banning handguns on a list of inexpensive guns often referred to as Saturday night specials. Two local storeowners, aided by the California Rifle and Pistol Association and joined by the NRA and California attorney general Dan Lungren, sued to overturn the local ordinance on the grounds that it was "preempted" by state law. A variety of pro-gun and anti-gun organizations lined up on either side of the case.

Legal Issues

According to the appeals court, "The primary legal issue is whether the Legislature has completely preempted the field of regulation of handgun sales. In the absence of state preemption, every municipality is authorized by the California Constitution to exercise its police power to deal with local situations." The idea of preemption is that a lower jurisdiction (such as a city) cannot make a law that deals with a matter that a higher jurisdiction (such as the state) has already definitively covered. The lower court found that the local ordinance was not preempted.

Decision

The appeals court agreed with the lower court: "Although it is clear that the Legislature could preempt all local ordinances regarding handgun sales, it is equally clear that the Legislature has not done so. Instead, the Legislature has studiously avoided comprehensive preemption of such local laws despite several legislative opportunities to enact a complete preemption. Since the Legislature has avoided preemption of all local regulation of handgun sales, the City continues to enjoy at least some of its constitutional right to regulate handgun sales. The ordinance in question here does not directly conflict with any state statute, and the question of whether to have such an ordinance is a decision within the authority of local elected legislators."

Impact

In general, courts find that a local law is preempted by the state only when at least one of the following is true: (1) the state and local laws contradict each other; or (2) the state law says it intends to preempt or effectively does so by exhaustively covering the subject matter. Gun rights advocates have sometimes tried (with only modest success) to enact state laws with more moderate gun controls, hoping to prevent municipalities from passing stricter controls.

HAMILTON V. ACCU-TEK, 13 F.SUPP.2D 366 (E.D. NEW YORK 1998)

Background

The success of massive class action suits against tobacco companies has encouraged litigators to try a similar approach against firearms manufacturers.

In this case, a shooting victim (and the surviving family members of six other victims) in Brooklyn, New York, joined together to sue Accu-Tek and 24 other gun manufacturers for negligent marketing that they said contributed to the victimization of their loved ones by criminals. (Although the case was originally filed in 1995, it went through a number of preliminary appeals before going to trial in 1998.)

Legal Issues

The plaintiffs argued that the gun manufacturers deliberately marketed their products in a way that they should have known increased the danger that the guns would be misused, leading to injuries or deaths. For example, they charged, an effort was made to sell more guns in areas in the southern states that had weak gun control laws; they said that the manufactures should have known that such guns were more likely to get into the black market and thus into the hands of criminals in urban areas such as New York City.

The defendants urged the judge to dismiss the case because someone should not be liable for selling a nondefective product in a legal manner. The judge refused this request and sent the case to the jury.

Decision

After evaluating contracts and sales policies from the manufacturers, the jury decided that three of the manufacturers were both negligent and liable and ordered them to pay $560,000. Six companies were found to be negligent and liable but did not have to pay damages. Six other companies were found to be negligent, but their negligence was not determined to be the cause of the plaintiffs' injuries. Finally, 10 companies were found to be neither negligent nor liable. The defendants said that they would appeal.

Impact

The jury deliberations were intense and frequently deadlocked, but the judge refused to accept a hung jury, probably leading to a compromise verdict. It is too early to tell whether the argument of negligent marketing will prevail in upcoming class action suits.

U.S. V. TIMOTHY EMERSON, CRIMINAL ACTION NO. 6:98-CR-103-C (U.S. DISTRICT COURT FOR THE NORTHERN DISTRICT OF TEXAS, SAN ANGELO DIVISION, 1999)

Background

When defendant Timothy Emerson's wife filed for divorce, she applied for a restraining order against him, seeking financial restrictions and a prohibition against his making threats or doing violence against his wife or family. In the hearing for the order, she claimed that Emerson had threatened a man with whom she had been carrying on an affair. Although no actual evidence of a threat was presented, the order was granted as a routine precaution.

One consequence of the order of which Emerson was apparently unaware was that under a 1994 federal law (18 U.S.C. § 922(g)(8)) he was now prohibited from possessing a firearm. He did not dispose of his gun, and he was indicted for violating this law.

Legal Issues

Emerson argued that the federal law violated the Constitution's Commerce Clause as well as the Second, Fifth, and Tenth amendments. He said the law was not a proper exercise of the power of Congress to regulate interstate commerce because possession of a gun had nothing to do with commerce and that it also violated the Tenth Amendment by intruding on the power of the states. Emerson also argued that the law violated his rights under the Second Amendment, which he said gave him a personal right to bear arms that could not be removed by the simple act of issuing a restraining order in a proceeding that lacked due process and in which no evidence was presented. Similarly, he argued that the lack of due process in taking away an important right violated the Fifth Amendment.

Decision

Judge Sam R. Cummings rejected the Commerce Clause challenge, noting that a superior court had already ruled that the law did not violate that part of the Constitution. By implication if the law had been passed under a valid power of Congress, it could not violate the Tenth Amendment, which assigns all powers not specified to Congress to the states or the people, nor had Congress violated the proper sovereignty of the states.

However, in a ruling that was quickly hailed by gun rights advocates, Judge Cummings ruled that the law did violate the Second Amendment. In a decision that reads like a minitutorial on the original intent and historical background of the amendment, he agreed with legal scholars such as Sanford Levenson who insist that the Second Amendment guarantees an individual right to keep and bear arms. Citing a parenthetical part of the Supreme Court decision *United States v. Verdugo-Urquidez*, (494 U.S. 259, 265, 1990) he noted that the Court held that the phrase *the people* throughout the Bill of Rights was intended to refer to individuals, not merely a collective group.

Cummings also decided that the Supreme Court's ruling in *U.S. v. Miller*, with its reference to a sawed-off shotgun not having been shown to have military use, was a very narrow decision that did not resolve the question of whether the Second Amendment guaranteed an individual right to keep and bear arms. In his view, this gave him room to make such a determination. He therefore ruled that the law violated Emerson's Second Amendment rights, declaring that:

> *It is absurd that a boilerplate state court divorce order can collaterally and automatically extinguish a law-abiding citizen's Second Amendment rights, particularly when neither the judge issuing the order, nor the parties nor their attorneys are aware of the federal criminal penalties arising from firearm possession after entry of the restraining order. That such a routine civil order has such extensive consequences totally attenuated from divorce proceedings makes the statute unconstitutional. There must be a limit to government regulation on lawful firearm possession. This statute exceeds that limit, and therefore it is unconstitutional.*

Cummings suggested that what this law attempted to do was different from depriving a felon, who had been convicted in a full proceeding under rules of evidence, of the right to own a gun. Further, he agreed that the defendant's Fifth Amendment rights had also been violated by the lack of due process and noted that at the time the restraining order was issued no one had informed him about this rather obscure law.

Impact

As of mid-1999, the government was in the process of appealing the decision. If a higher court reinstates the indictment, the case has the potential of eventually reaching the Supreme Court, challenging that body to make a broader decision about just what rights the Second Amendment guarantees. If the Court decided that the Second Amendment conferred an individual right to bear arms, federal (though perhaps not state) gun legislation might have to meet a much stricter test of constitutionality.

CHAPTER 3

CHRONOLOGY

This chapter provides a chronology of important events relating to gun issues. Some historical events are included because they are often cited by gun control or gun rights advocates in support of their positions.

871

- King Alfred of Saxon England's laws give every man the right to keep and bear arms but prohibit murder and other crimes.

1020

- England's King Cnut's laws recognize the right to keep and bear arms, the right to self-defense, and the right to hunt on one's own land.

1181

- In his Assize of Arms, King Henry II gives "every knight and freeman" the right to have weapons and armor. Arms holders had to swear to obey the king and defend the kingdom. The result is a kind of protomilitia.

1215

- King John tries to disarm both nobles and commoners, but the barons force him to recognize the right to bear arms as part of the Magna Carta, which later becomes a model for the American colonists in their struggle against the English monarchy. The militia is restored.

1252

- Under Henry II, the arming of citizens is extended to serfs. An "arming of the whole people" rather than a large standing army gradually becomes the basis for England's defense.

1300s

- Gunpowder, already in use in China, is introduced into Europe. At first it is used primarily in crude siege cannons that can blow holes in castle walls, enforcing the power of the monarch over the nobles.

1328

- In response to rowdiness by knights and others, Edward III issues the Statute of Northampton. It prohibits "persons great or small" from carrying weapons in public, though it allows for defense of the home. The law is widely disobeyed, and, in practice, courts applied it only to those who used arms to "terrify the good people of the land."

1485

- King Henry VII forbids hunting in an attempt to reduce the number of people with weapons who could start a rebellion against the crown.

1500s

- Portable firearms such as the arquebus become more common on the battlefield. At first the unwieldy guns are fired from tripodlike supports, but versions that can be fired from the shoulder soon appear.
- King Henry VII implements "crossbow control," decreeing that no one may shoot a crossbow in hunting or otherwise, except to protect his property and land

1511

- King Henry VIII places tighter controls on crossbows but ordered that all fathers should teach their sons to shoot the longbow, which had been a devastating weapon against French knights in earlier wars.

1541

- King Henry VIII restricts the lengths of guns that citizens may possess. People are allowed to keep other guns in their homes but not carry them in their travels on the king's highways.

1557

- Under Queen Mary I, a statute details exactly which weapons people can and must possess for the defense of the state. The kind and amount of weapons a person may have depends on the kind and amount of property they own.

1600s

- Permanent British settlement in America begins. The colonists use firearms daily for hunting as well as in ongoing conflicts with Native Americans and French colonists.

1642

- The English Civil War between the king and parliament breaks out. One of the issues of contention is control of the militia, the trained bands of armed citizens who make up an important part of the nation's military power.

1659

- With Cromwell dead and the English Civil War coming to an end, a London ordinance requires that every householder give the government a list of all arms and ammunition owned. Weapons owned by Catholics or others who had fought against the Parliament or by other "dangerous" persons could be seized. Later, King Charles II continued the seizing of weapons from such persons.

1670

- King Charles II restricts guns and bows to large landowners (who make up the nobility), thus disarming the emerging middle class and the poor. At its time, this was the most restrictive English weapons control law ever passed.

1686

- Sir John Knight is accused of walking to and entering a church while armed. The judge acquits him because the law in question specified persons who went armed "to terrify the King's subjects."
- In his work *Two Treatises on Government*, philosopher John Locke maintains the "natural" right of citizens to have arms for their individual and collective defense.

1688

- In the bloodless "Glorious Revolution," William and Mary defeat King James II, abolish the standing army, and restore—to Protestants only— the right to keep and bear arms.

1689

- The British Bill of Rights includes a condemnation of previous kings for disarming the people and specifies that henceforth "The subjects which are Protestants may have arms for their defence suitable to their conditions and allowed by law."

1698

- Philosopher Algernon Sidney in his book *Discourses Concerning Government* states that "the body of the People is the Public defense, and every man is armed and disciplined." American colonists soon put the idea in practice in the form of local militias.

1700s

- Two new kinds of long guns come into use: The smoothbore musket has a short range and can be fired about four times a minute by well-trained soldiers. The rifle with its grooved barrel takes longer to load but has greater range and accuracy. Both kinds of guns must be loaded by hand, one shot at a time.

1739

- In the British court case of *Rex v. Gardner*, the judge holds that the game laws did not forbid a person from mere possession of a gun for purposes of self-defense. Several later cases have similar verdicts.

1770

- British soldiers fire on unarmed Americans in Boston, leading to an upsurge of revolutionary sentiment. The British respond by beginning to raid colonial homes and gatherings to seize guns and ammunition.

1775

- The American War of Independence is ignited when British troops under General Gage attempt to seize guns and ammunition from colonists at Lexington and Concord. Although faced down initially by the trained British troops, the American Minutemen militia begins a relentless fire, aided by accurate long-range rifles.

1776

- In addition to declaring independence, the various states write constitutions that include bills of rights. In general they refer to the danger of standing armies, the reliance on a well-regulated militia, and the right to keep and bear arms.

1777

■ British colonial undersecretary William Knox presents a proposal concerning what to do with the colonies when they were subjugated and returned to British control. His proposals include the repeal of the militia laws, the confiscation of all arms held by the people, and the prohibition of the manufacture or importation of guns or powder in America.

1789

■ The Bill of Rights to the United States Constitution is approved. It includes the Second Amendment, which guarantees the right to keep and bear arms to maintain a strong militia as a protector of liberty.

1792

■ The Militia Act is passed. It recognizes both an unorganized ("enrolled") militia and an organized militia.

1822

■ In the Kentucky case of *Bliss v. Commonwealth*, the court holds that the state constitution prohibits any interference with the right to keep and bear arms, even concealed weapons.

1836

■ Samuel Colt's revolver is patented. Because it can fire six shots without reloading, it represents a formidable increase in firepower for close combat and helps settlers repel Indian raids.

1837

■ Georgia passes the first ban on handguns. It is later overturned in *Nunn v. State* as a violation of the Second Amendment.

1840

■ The court in the Tennessee case of *Aymette v. State* upholds some measure of gun control by letting stand a ban on carrying concealed weapons. It bases its decision on English laws that had specified conditions under which weapons could be held.

1846

■ In the Georgia case of *Nunn v. State*, the court says that the state can use its police power to ban some kinds of weapons (such as concealable handguns) but not all firearms. This marks a general trend where courts uphold gun control measures that can be justified as an exercise of the police power.

1850

■ Some southern states argue that black slaves do not have the Second Amendment right to keep and bear arms because they are "not citizens."

1857

■ In *Dred Scott v. Sanford*, Supreme Court Chief Justice Taney declared that the Bill of Rights had not been written to protect blacks and that doing so would mean that, among other things, they could "keep and carry arms wherever they went."

1865

■ Following the Civil War, Black Codes are enacted to restrict the rights of the newly freed slaves. Prohibiting them from keeping and carrying firearms is a common provision.

1866

■ The Winchester repeating rifle lets its user fire up to 15 shots by working a lever every few seconds. It will become known as the gun that won the West.
■ The Fourteenth Amendment, the Freedman's Bureau Act, and the Civil Rights Act of 1866 all include the Second Amendment right to keep and bear arms among the rights that the states are prohibited from taking from any citizen.

1871

■ The National Rifle Association is established. It initially focuses on improving marksmanship to ensure proper national defense.

1876

■ In *U.S. v. Cruikshank* a group of Ku Klux Klansmen are convicted of depriving "persons of color" their right to keep and bear arms.

The Supreme Court overturns the conviction, declaring that this right is independent of the Second Amendment and that the latter cannot be used against individuals or states, only against the federal government.

1886

■ In *Presser v. Illinois,* the Supreme Court reaffirms its ruling in the *Cruikshank* case but also says that states cannot abolish the right of citizens to keep and bear arms because it would deprive the United States of the pool of citizens who make up the "reserve militia."

1908

■ New York becomes the first state to require hunting licenses.

1911

■ New York City enacts the Sullivan Act, which becomes the prototype for handgun registration laws. The law may have been passed by the Tammany Hall political machine in response to fear of growing crime associated with Italian immigrants.

1919

■ Congress enacts the first tax that applies to weapons. It is promoted as a revenue-raising tax rather than as a gun control measure.

1920s

■ A newly developed military weapon, the Thompson submachine gun, or tommy gun, finds an unforseen application as the gangster's gun of choice. Its devastating firepower spurs demands for a federal gun control law.

1927

■ A federal law prohibits the mailing of concealable firearms in the United States.

1934

■ The National Firearms Act of 1934 is passed. The law includes a variety of taxes on the manufacture, sale, and transfer of automatic weapons and certain short-barreled weapons, as well as requiring an FBI background check and the consent of local law enforcement officials for any purchase. The law does not apply to handguns.

1938

- Congress passes the Federal Firearms Act of 1938. It requires that manufacturers, importers, and dealers in firearms (and ammunition for pistols and revolvers) obtain licenses. The law also prohibits delivery of a gun to a known criminal, to someone under indictment, or in violation of local licensing laws.

1939

- In *U.S. v. Miller* the Supreme Court rejects an appeal by stating that it could find no evidence that a sawed-off shotgun was suitable for use in a militia, and because it is not, carrying it would not be protected by the Second Amendment. Because the decision also affirms an individual right to bear arms, it would be cited by both supporters and opponents of gun control.

1958

- The Federal Aviation Act is passed. It prohibits the carrying of firearms "on or about" any passenger flying on a commercial aircraft.

1963

- The assassination of President John F. Kennedy begins what many will see as an era of heightened violence and social tension.

1966

- The nation is shocked when Charles Whitman kills 16 people with a rifle from the top of a tower at the University of Texas. He is killed by police.

1967

- As crime rates continue to increase, the President's Commission on Law Enforcement includes among its recommendations national registration of handguns and the prohibition of interstate sales of handguns.

1968

- Following the assassination of Dr. Martin Luther King, Jr., and Senator Robert Kennedy, Congress passes the Omnibus Crime Control and Safe Streets Act of 1968. It includes the Gun Control Act of 1968, which prohibits nearly all interstate gun sales, requires licensing of all gun dealers, and requires the recording of details about gun sales.

1969

■ The National Commission on the Causes and Prevention of Violence issues a report that includes recommendations for laws for the national registration of handguns and the licensing of handgun purchasers.

1972

■ Senator Birch Bayh of Indiana proposes a bill that would prohibit the manufacture and sale of "nonsporting" handguns. It passes in the Senate but dies in the House. A similar bill will be passed by the Senate in 1974.

1973

■ The National Advisory Commission on Criminal Justice Standards and Goals sets a goal of banning all private ownership of handguns by 1983.

1977

■ In *Moore v. East Cleveland* the Supreme Court states (in passing) that the right to keep and bear arms is one of the "specific guarantees" contained in the Constitution of the United States, but this ruling is not applied to gun control cases.
■ The District of Columbia imposes a ban on the acquisition, purchase, or possession of handguns.

1980s

■ The decade of the 1980s introduces deadlier weapons to America's streets, including such semiautomatic pistols as the Glock and Tec-9 and, to a lesser extent, semiautomatic ("assault") rifles such as the AK-47. Media exposure to such weapons in drug- and gang-related violence helps to spur support for gun control in general and a ban on semiautomatic assault weapons in particular.

1980

■ In *Lewis v. U.S.* the Supreme Court holds that the federal government denying felons the right to possess firearms does not infringe on the provisions of the Second Amendment right to keep and bear arms nor on the equal protection clause of the Fourteenth Amendment.

1981

- President Ronald Reagan and James Brady, his press secretary, are wounded in an assassination attempt by John Hinckley. Brady and his wife Sarah later join Handgun Control, Inc., to lobby for effective handgun control legislation.
- The village of Morton Grove, Illinois, passes an ordinance that bans individual possession of a variety of weapons including handguns, automatic weapons, and short-barreled shotguns. A United States district court holds that the ordinance is constitutional. In 1983 the United States Court of Appeals, Seventh Circuit, confirms the lower court decision in *Quilici v. Morton Grove.* The Supreme Court declines to hear the case.

1982

- California voters defeat Proposition 15, which would have imposed strict handgun controls, including registration and a freeze on the total number of guns available.

1984

- Congress passes the Armed Career Criminal Act, amending the Gun Control Act of 1968. It imposes stiff fines and prison terms for felons and other prohibited classes of persons who receive, possess, or transport a firearm. An appropriation bill passed by Congress eliminates probation or suspended sentences for persons committing a federal felony with any firearm and imposes an add-on 15-year sentence for possession of a firearm by a robber or burglar who is a repeat offender.

1986

- Writing in the *New England Journal of Medicine*, researchers Arthur Kellermann and Donald T. Reay report a survey showing that a gun kept in the home was 43 times as likely to kill a family member or friend than to kill a criminal intruder. Speaking of "an epidemic of firearms violence," a number of other medical writers begin to urge stricter gun control and education. Criminologist Gary Kleck disputes such findings, citing his own survey that says that armed citizens successfully drive off criminals more than 2 million times a year, usually without firing a shot.
- Congress passes the Firearms Owners Protection Act, a law that rolls back some provisions of earlier federal firearms legislation. For example, it reduces "paperwork" violations for firearms dealers from a felony to a misdemeanor and allows the interstate sale of long guns by dealers. However it also increases penalties for drug traffickers who possess firearms

and incorporates an amendment that essentially bans the purchase of automatic firearms by civilians if the guns were manufactured after the enactment of the law.
- The Law Enforcement Officers Protection Act is passed. It bans the manufacture or importation of so-called cop-killer bullets that can pierce officers' bulletproof vests.

1988

- Congress passes the Terrorist Firearms Detection Act. It bans firearms (such as plastic handguns) that cannot be detected by security equipment such as airport X-ray machines.

1989

- A deranged gunman opens fire on a playground in Stockton, California, killing five schoolchildren. Such school shootings will become a major spur to gun control efforts in the 1990s.
- California adopts the Roberti-Roos Assault Weapon Act. It bans many types of semiautomatic weapons and bans sales by unlicensed dealers.
- In what becomes a growing trend, Florida enacts a law requiring a background check for persons buying a gun from a dealer and a law requiring gun owners to keep their guns locked so that children cannot get access to them.

1990

- The Indiana Supreme Court rules that the mayor of Gary, Indiana, violated the state constitution when he denied gun permits to city residents. He cites the 1871 Civil Rights Act, which had been passed to counter the actions of Ku Klux Klan members.
- More states, such as California, Connecticut, and Iowa, pass tougher gun control regulations, requiring background checks and longer waiting periods for gun purchasers.
- In *United States v. Verdugo-Urquidez*, the Supreme Court notes in passing that *the people* has a consistent meaning of "individuals" when used in the Constitution, including the Second Amendment.

1991

- Twenty-three people are killed in a Texas cafeteria by George Hennard, Jr., who then kills himself. A woman named Suzanna Gratia later tells a congressional committee that she probably could have shot Hennard with her own gun if the law had allowed her to bring it into the building.

1992

- The wife and son of Randy Weaver are killed by FBI agents in a siege of his remote cabin, where he had fled after being charged with selling a sawed-off shotgun. The incident galvanizes antigovernment radicals. Weaver is later acquitted of the most serious charges and wins a settlement from the government. Congress holds hearings that question the "rules of engagement" used by the FBI.

1993

- Colin Ferguson opens fire on a Long Island Railroad commuter train, killing 5 people and injuring 19.
- Gian Ferri uses an assault weapon to kill eight and injure six people in a San Francisco office tower. Gun control activists (including some relatives of shooting victims) refer to such incidents in demanding stricter gun controls, including a ban on assault weapons. Gun rights activists suggest that armed citizens could save many lives during such incidents.
- *April:* The FBI ends its siege of Branch Davidian sect leader David Koresh and his followers by battering their compound with tanks and injecting tear gas. The building is consumed by fire, killing Koresh and most of his followers, including dozens of children. Like Ruby Ridge, this incident fuels the antigovernment militia movement and is cited by some gun rights advocates as showing the need for citizens to have guns to resist tyrannical government.
- *November:* Congress passes and President Clinton signs the Brady Handgun Violence Prevention Act. This law establishes nationwide background checks and a five-day waiting period for all handgun purchases.

1994

- In another major victory for gun control advocates, Congress also passes the Assault Weapons Ban Bill, which bans 19 semiautomatic firearms described as "assault weapons."

1995

- In *United States v. Lopez*, the Supreme Court strikes down the federal Gun-Free School Zone Act. The Court rules that Congress did not show a sufficient relationship between the gun ban and its constitutional power to regulate interstate commerce. (The Second Amendment is not mentioned.)
- *April:* Timothy McVeigh sets off a truck filled with explosives, destroying the federal building in Oklahoma City, killing 168 people, and injuring hundreds more. Although not directly involving firearms, the incident

contributed to public anxiety and promoted demands for gun control, while seeming to quiet the most radical antigovernment groups.

1998

- Veteran movie actor Charlton Heston is elected president of the National Rifle Association, in what is viewed by many gun control advocates as an attempt to rehabilitate the organization's somewhat tarnished image.
- In the case of *Dix v. Beretta* a jury refuses to hold the gun maker liable when a teenager fires a gun that he thinks is unloaded. The plaintiff had claimed that the gun was defectively designed. That same year, however, in the Brooklyn, New York, case of *Hamilton v. Accu-Tek*, a jury does find some gun makers liable for marketing and distributing guns recklessly, making it easy for guns to reach the hands of criminals.
- By the end of the year, more than 20 cities file class action suits against gun makers, adopting a strategy similar to that used successfully against the big tobacco companies.

1999

- *April:* Two students, Dylan Klebold and Eric Harris, kill 15 people (including themselves) at Columbine High School in Littleton, Colorado, with several guns and many homemade bombs. The tragedy immediately spurs a demand for new gun control measures, as well as calling into question the role of parents and the media in creating violent, disaffected teens. The uproar also stalls attempts by gun advocates to liberalize concealed-carry laws in a number of states.
- *June:* Congress fails to agree on a package of gun control measures as part of a new criminal justice bill. One sticking point is whether to impose a 24-hour or a 72-hour waiting period for purchases made at gun shows. Gun control advocates want the longer period to ensure that background checks are complete and also to serve as a "cooling off" period for possibly disturbed purchasers. Gun rights advocates believe that the instant background check now in place for dealer sales be used instead. Other proposals include a ban on importing high-capacity ammunition clips and a requirement that guns be sold with trigger locks.
- *July 29:* Mark O. Barton, apparently despondent over failed investments, kills 9 people (including members of his family) and wounds 13 at two Atlanta brokerage firms.
- *August 10:* Buford Furrow, an avowed racist, allegedly kills an Asian-American postal worker and opens fire on a Jewish community center in Los Angeles, wounding five people including three young children.

- *August 10:* A report released by the federal Department of Education says that about three-quarters of the states have experienced a decline in the number of students expelled for gun possession. At least part of the decline is attributed to stronger security measures instituted in schools following the Columbine shootings in April.

- *August 28:* California enacts some of the nation's toughest new gun laws. New safety test requirements are expected to stop the sale of most inexpensive handguns. Gun show promoters will have to obtain licenses, and all new handguns sold in California must include trigger locks. Earlier in the year, California had strengthened its assault weapons ban and limited buyers to buying one gun per month.

- *September 16:* A gunman opens fire at a church youth meeting in Fort Worth, Texas, killing 8 people including himself. He is later identified as Larry Gene Ashbrook, described as a "jobless loner" who was feared by several of his neighbors.

- *September 30:* A California appeals court rules that victims of a 1993 mass shooting in a San Francisco office building can sue gun manufacturers.

- *October 8:* An Ohio judge throws out Cincinnati's lawsuit against gun manufacturers, ruling that only the legislature has the authority to regulate product design, and that "the risks associated with the use of a firearm are open and obvious and matters of common knowledge." Instigators of a California state gun lawsuit believe that the ruling will not affect their case, which is brought on different grounds.

- *October 11:* The venerable Colt firearms company announces that it will no longer sell handguns to consumers, except as collector's items. The company is believed to have acted to reduce its potential liability in future lawsuits and because fear of lawsuits has begun to drive suppliers, lenders, and investors from the consumer firearms market.

- *October 15:* A U.S. district judge in Los Angeles overturns the county's ban on gun shows. He rules that state law preempts the county from legislating in this area, and that the county action poses an "undue hardship" to promoters who had sponsored the gun show for 22 years.

- *November 2:* A disgruntled worker alleged to be Byran Uyesugi opens fire at a Xerox office in Honolulu, killing seven people, and surrenders later to police.

2000

- *January:* In his State of the Union Address, President Clinton calls on states to register handgun owners, requiring them to have a background check, photo ID, and proof that they meet safety requirements. The

White House also announced it would seek $280 million in funding to enforce existing gun laws.

- *January:* The U.S. Conference of Mayors meets in Washington, D.C. They display a blackboard listing nearly 3,100 fatal gun victims since the Columbine shootings and call for Congress to pass the legislation on gun sales and shows that had stalled the previous year.
- *January:* Officials in the cities of San Francisco and Oakland, California, propose municipal ordinances that would ban the sale of so-called ultra-compact handguns that can be easily carried in peoples' pockets. (Due to their good quality construction, such guns are not covered under existing legislation banning "Saturday Night Specials.")
- *February:* President Clinton proposes a $30 million dollar initiative to reduce shooting deaths in public housing projects. The program would include computerized tracking of gun incidents, public education, and promotion of gun safety measures such as locked boxes and childproof safety latches.
- *February 29:* Six-year-old Kayla Rolland is shot and killed by a fellow first grader, who apparently stole a loaded gun from his chaotic, drug-ridden home and brought it to school. President Clinton renews his call for gun safety legislation (including trigger locks), while Democratic candidates in the upcoming primary election charge Republicans with being political captives of the National Rifle Association.
- *March 1:* Ronald Taylor allegedly goes on a shooting spree in suburban Pittsburgh, Pennsylvania, killing three people and wounding two. Taylor, who is black, is reported to have written racist notes about whites, Jews, and Asians (his alleged victims are all white). He is charged with "ethnic intimidation" (a hate crime).

CHAPTER 4

BIOGRAPHICAL LISTING

This chapter briefly introduces individuals who have played an important part in the gun control debate, including political leaders, researchers, writers, and activists.

Barbara Boxer, U.S. senator from California, elected to the Senate in 1992 after having served 10 years in the House. In addition to working for women's issues and health care, Boxer has been a strong advocate in the Senate for gun control, including the Brady Bill, the Assault Weapons Ban, and the attaching of gun control provisions to more recent crime bills.

James Brady, gun control activist. He had a distinguished career during the 1970s as a Republican political consultant and press secretary in a variety of political and corporate settings. In January 1981, he was appointed White House press secretary to the newly elected Ronald Reagan. On March 30, 1981, he was seriously wounded in an assassination attempt on President Reagan. While struggling to recover, he joined with his wife Sarah in gun control efforts, becoming particularly involved in the leadership of Handgun Control, Inc.

Sarah Brady, gun control activist. Starting in the 1960s, Brady was a schoolteacher and Republican Party worker. In 1981, her husband was seriously wounded (along with President Reagan) in an assassination attempt. This experience spurred Brady into becoming a full-time gun control activist. She played a key role and remains chairperson of Handgun Control, Inc. (Handgun Control, Inc., and the Center to Prevent Handgun Violence are generally considered to be the nation's largest and most effective gun control advocacy groups.) Her most significant achievement thus far has been the passage in November 1993 of the Brady Bill, named in honor of her husband. This law established waiting period and background check requirements for all handgun purchases. Brady has received numerous public service awards.

Biographical Listings

George Bush, president of the United States, 1989–1993. Bush has had a moderate stance on gun control issues, leading to some criticism from the NRA and gun rights advocates. Bush supported some controls on assault weapons, including banning further imports of such weapons. When NRA executive vice president Wayne LaPierre issued a fund-raising letter in 1995 that referred to federal agents as "jack-booted thugs," Bush resigned his NRA membership.

William Jefferson Clinton, former Arkansas governor and president of the United States, 1993–2001. Clinton has been a strong supporter for gun control measures such as the Brady Bill. Following the Littleton shootings in April 1999, Clinton called for closing loopholes in gun laws by requiring background checks for purchasers at gun shows, as well as supporting waiting periods and requiring the sale of trigger locks with guns. In his rhetoric, Clinton often distinguishes between hunting/sporting use of guns and the use of assault weapons.

John Coale, trial lawyer who has specialized in suing on behalf of children and other victims of unsafe products or practices. He has sued school boards for their overuse of drugs to treat students with Attention Deficit Disorder, sued Ford Motor Company for designing unsafe school buses, and, in his biggest case to date, played a key role in a class action suit that won a $200 billion settlement from tobacco companies for the health costs caused by their products. In October 1998 his legal consortium, the Castano Group, filed the first of what is likely to be a wave of lawsuits against gun makers, charging them with selling unsafe guns and with reckless marketing. His flamboyant style and savvy use of the media have given him a high profile.

Barbara Fass, mayor of Stockton, California, in 1989 when Patrick Purdy went on a schoolyard shooting rampage with a semiautomatic weapon, killing five children. Representing the U.S. Conference of Mayors, Fass testified before Congress in favor of banning assault weapons as a way to prevent similar tragedies in the future.

Dianne Feinstein, senator and gun control advocate. Feinstein was a member of the San Francisco Board of Supervisors during the 1970s. Although rebuffed two times in running for the office, she became the first woman mayor of San Francisco in November 1978 following the assassinations of Mayor George Moscone and Supervisor Harvey Milk by disgruntled former supervisor Dan White. During her nine years as mayor, she was credited with reducing crime and social unrest in the city. In 1992 she began her career as a senator from California. She has been a strong advocate for gun control, particularly for the successful passage of a ban on assault weapons.

Alan M. Gottlieb, prominent gun rights activist; chairman of the Citizens Committee for the Right to Keep and Bear Arms and founder of the

Second Amendment Foundation. Gottlieb has written many articles on the Second Amendment and on gun rights. He is publisher of two magazines, *Gun Week* and *Gun News Digest*. Among his books are the *Gun Owners Political Action Manual* and *The Gun Rights Fact Book*. He has also been active in the environmental "wise use" movement, a movement that promotes compromises between economic and environmental considerations.

Stephen P. Halbrook, professor of philosophy, attorney, and writer on constitutional law, specializing in the Second Amendment. His book *That Every Man Be Armed: The Evolution of a Constitutional Right* is influential in the Second Amendment debate. In support of a suit by the NRA, Halbrook argued against the California assault weapons ban in 1990.

Orrin Hatch, veteran senator from Utah. Hatch came from a working class Mormon background and has worked for labor reform and religious freedom from a generally conservative free-enterprise standpoint, though he was also a strong supporter of the Americans with Disabilities Act. He is a frequent opponent of gun control legislation. He argues from the history and original intent of the Constitution in favor of a robust interpretation of the Second Amendment that would be comparable to that generally given to the First Amendment by liberals. On the other hand, in 1997 he proposed a Criminal Justice Bill that would provide for a minimum five-year sentence for those convicted of criminal gang activity. Although gun advocates generally favor tough penalties for crime (especially gun-related crime), the bill was criticized by both civil libertarians and some gun owners for its expansive definitions of crime that could ensnare innocent gun owners and dealers.

Charlton Heston, Academy Award–winning movie actor, best known for his star roles in *Ben-Hur* and *The Ten Commandments*. Elected president of the National Rifle Association in 1998. In electing him president, the NRA probably wanted to harness Heston's appeal as a moral icon and patriarch, particularly to older and more conservative Americans. As a conservative activist, Heston goes against the generally liberal grain of Hollywood political causes.

Don B. Kates, Jr., an activist in the civil rights struggle of the 1960s while a student at Yale Law School. He later worked in legal assistance programs and then became a professor of Law and an attorney in private practice in the San Francisco area. Kates provides consultation on firearms legislation for police departments and legislative committees. He is also a prolific advocate of gun rights who has written many articles and books as well as the article on the Second Amendment in the *Encyclopedia of the American Constitution*.

Biographical Listings

Arthur R. Kellermann, director of Emory University's Center for Injury Control. In the 1980s he published a series of studies in the *New England Journal of Medicine* that supported tougher gun control, claiming that a gun kept in the home was 43 times more likely to kill a family member or friend than to kill a criminal intruder and that restricting access to guns could prevent many murders and suicides. Kellermann's writings became part of a growing body of literature created by activist physicians and medical researchers who came to view gun violence as an epidemic that should be treated as a serious public health problem. Critics such as Gary Kleck and Don Kates pointed to what they saw as serious flaws in such studies, such as their ignoring or underestimating the impact of widespread use of firearms by citizens to scare off criminals.

Gary Kleck, professor of criminology at Florida State University. A strong civil libertarian and member of the ACLU, his reexamination of the Second Amendment led him to change from being a gun control supporter to an advocate of gun rights. In 1983 he wrote an article for the Michigan Law Review that, together with the work of Stephen Halbrook and Sanford Levinson, led many scholars to support an individual rights interpretation of the Second Amendment. His books include *Point Blank: Guns and Violence in America.*

Neal Knox, director of the Firearms Coalition and First Vice President of the NRA. He is a frequent candidate for head of the NRA, leading the more radical wing of that organization while trying to soften its public image. Moderates often accuse him of heavy-handed tactics. Knox began his struggle to radicalize the NRA in 1977 when incoming president Harlon Carter appointed him head of the organization's political arm, the Institute for Legislative Action. He was ousted in 1982 in a disagreement over lobbying practices but returned to the leadership in 1991. According to opponents, his tightly organized political machine effectively controls the organization.

David B. Kopel, former Manhattan assistant district attorney and firearms law expert. Kopel has written numerous pro-gun rights works including *The Samurai, The Mountie, and the Cowboy,* a cross-cultural analysis of gun control laws that concludes that the European approach to gun control would be ineffective and incompatible with the United States's cultural roots. He has authored numerous papers challenging the premises behind proposals such as bans on semiautomatic assault weapons.

Wayne LaPierre, CEO of the National Rifle Association and a vigorous gun rights advocate. He is the author of *Guns, Crime, and Freedom,* a comprehensive attack on the opponents of gun rights and what he views as a media biased against gun owners. In recent years he has emphasized the prosecution and jailing of criminals who misuse guns, pointing out that while the Clinton Administration claims to have stopped 400,000 criminals from buying guns under the Brady Bill, virtually none have been prosecuted. Some civil libertarians have criticized LaPierre's "tough on crime" proposals as draconian and lacking in flexibility and due process.

Sanford Levinson, McCormick Professor at the University of Texas. Although he remains generally politically liberal, Levinson's studies of the Second Amendment led him to the conclusion that it did protect an individual right to keep and bear arms and that it should be taken seriously by constitutional scholars. His 1989 paper "The Embarrassing Second Amendment" helped touch off a renewed debate about the amendment's meaning and the suggestion that it should be, like the First and Fourth Amendments, incorporated into the Fourteenth Amendment and applied to the states.

John R. Lott, criminal law and economics teacher at the University of Chicago, where he is the John M. Olin Visiting Law and Economics Fellow. In 1988–1989 he was the chief economist at the United States Sentencing Commission. He has written many articles for academic journals and has recently written a book, *More Guns, Less Crime: Understanding Crime and Gun Control Laws.* Together with David Mustard, he has published studies that claim that crime decreases in proportion to the number of law-abiding citizens who carry concealed weapons.

Fernando Mateo, New York City carpet store owner who founded Goods for Guns, a private organization that sponsors programs where people can turn in guns and receive certificates for toys and sporting goods, food, and other rewards. A number of similar programs have been started by sports teams, recording companies, and celebrities such as hip-hop stars. Mateo says he got his idea when, after watching news accounts of murder and suicide victims, his son said that he would give up all of his Christmas presents if it would get one gun off the street. Some gun rights advocates have criticized such programs as being more symbolic than truly effective, with many of the guns being turned in unlikely to be involved with crime.

Carolyn McCarthy, congresswoman from Long Island and former licensed practical nurse. Her husband was killed and her son badly wounded in the Long Island Railroad shooting in 1993. She gained national attention as she devoted her efforts to her son's difficult rehabilitation. She also studied gun issues, learning that the gun Colin Ferguson (the LIRR killer) had used in the shooting had been bought in California and illegally taken to New York and that its high-capacity (15-round) magazine was legal. She began to work for tougher gun laws. When the Republican representative in her district voted to overturn the assault weapons ban, she changed parties to Democrat and ran against him, making gun control the centerpiece of her successful campaign. Her story was the basis for the TV movie *The Long Island Incident.*

Tanya Metaksa, executive director of the National Rifle Association's lobbying unit, the Institute for Legislative Action. Articulate, intense, and energetic, Metaksa is often found on the front lines of the pundit circuit when gun control legislation is being debated in Congress. Metaksa's prominent role in the NRA leadership may also reflect the organization's conscious effort in recent years to appeal to women.

Lawrence Pratt, head of the Gun Owners of America and a vigorous advocate for the right to keep and bear arms on philosophical as well as constitutional grounds. Pratt has aroused controversy because of alleged connections, which he denies, with white separatist groups.

Ronald Reagan, president of the United States, 1981–1989, former movie actor and former governor of California. Reagan began his political life espousing a generally conservative, pro-gun rights position. However on March 30, 1981, he (along with press secretary James Brady and two law enforcement officers) was wounded in an attempted assassination by John W. Hinckley, Jr. Reagan quickly recovered from his wounds, but Brady's recovery would be far more difficult. When the Bradys became involved with Handgun Control, Inc., and promoted legislation that would require background checks for gun purchasers (the Brady Bill), Reagan, along with former presidents Nixon, Ford, and Carter, endorsed the bill.

Janet Reno, attorney general of the United States, 1993– . A strong supporter of gun control, including registration of all guns and a licensing system similar to that used for motor vehicles, Reno has been criticized as being ultimately responsible for the FBI siege and assault on the Branch Davidian compound in Waco, Texas, that led to the death of sect members and their children. Although the question of whether the ultimate fire was set by Davidians or was a consequence of the FBI attack continues to be disputed, the Waco confrontation did have a strong effect in galvanizing the organization of militia groups to resist what they see as ongoing federal intrusions on civil rights. Revelations in 1999 of possible army involvement in the siege and attack on the compound, as well as the use of pyrotechnics (munitions capable of causing fires) have complicated the question of Reno's knowledge and possible culpability. Further investigations by Congress and independent investigators are likely in 2000.

J. Neil Schulman, science fiction writer, libertarian, and gun rights activist. He is active in the Libertarian Futurist Society, which gave him the Prometheus Award for *The Rainbow Cadenza,* an exploration of the meaning of individual autonomy and its relation to creativity in a collectivist society. Schulman has written several popular defenses of gun rights including *Stopping Power: Why 70 Million Americans Own Guns.*

Charles Schumer, Democratic senator from New York, former representative from the 9th District of New York and veteran on the House Judiciary Committee, where he chaired the subcommittee on Crime and Criminal Justice. Schumer is a strong advocate for gun control who helped pass the Brady Bill; he also advocates bans on armor-piercing ammunition and a limit on the number of guns a person may purchase or own without a special "arsenal license."

L. Neil Smith, science fiction writer, libertarian, and gun rights activist. Smith has written many pro-gun articles and opinion pieces that feature a crisp, hard-hitting style. His fiction emphasizes the moral dimensions of arms bearing and self-defense: For example, in *The Probability Broach*, virtually all people (even children) carry weapons, viewing it as a symbol of autonomy, responsibility, and moral health.

CHAPTER 5

GLOSSARY

AK-47 Also known as Kalashnikov, named for its orginator, it is an originally Soviet-built semiautomatic rifle that is used widely throughout the world in insurgencies and other conflicts. An AK-47 is regulated (and often banned) as an assault weapon.

ammunition Collectively, the components expended by a gun, such as primer, gunpowder, and bullet(s) usually put together in the form of cartridges.

antique firearms By most regulatory standards, firearms manufactured before 1899. They often require handmade ammunition. Generally, antique firearms are excepted from regulation.

armor-piercing ammunition Bullets designed to penetrate armor, such as a bullet-proof vest. Its effectiveness comes from a metal core (such as tungsten or depleted uranium). Civilian ownership of such ammunition has been banned in most cases.

assault weapon Technically, an automatic or select-fire rifle or handgun designed for military use. In the gun control debate, however, this term is usually applied to semiautomatic rifles, shotguns, or handguns that have a high-capacity magazine and certain military-type features such as a pistol grip or bayonet mount. Laws banning assault weapons may specify certain models (and their clones), general characteristics of banned weapons, or both.

automatic weapon A type of rifle (such as the military versions of the AK-47 or M-16; submachine gun; or machine pistol) that fires bullets continuously as long as the trigger is pulled. Automatic weapons have been regulated by the federal government since 1934, with extensive background checks required for purchasers, taxes for buyers and sellers, and other regulations.

bolt-action A firing mechanism on some rifles. The shooter turns a bolt to insert a cartridge and load the weapon.

Bureau of Alcohol, Tobacco, and Firearms (BATF)   Federal agency whose primary purpose is to enforce federal firearms laws by overseeing transactions and tracing or otherwise investigating guns used in crimes.

burst fire   A setting on some military rifles that fires a set number of bullets (often three) each time the trigger is pulled. The ability to select fully automatic or burst fire is one characteristic of true assault rifles.

caliber   The diameter of a bullet (and thus of the barrel of the gun that accommodates it). In the United States, the measurement is usually given in hundredths of an inch (thus ".45 caliber revolver"); in many other countries it is given in millimeters (thus, 9-millimeter semiautomatic pistol).

carbine   A rifle with a short barrel (often used by cavalry in earlier times). Under federal regulations, rifles with a barrel shorter than 16 inches must be registered.

cartridge   A round of ammunition consisting of primer, propellant (powder), and bullet in one container. The cartridge replaced the use of separately poured powder and ball in the 19th century.

chamber   The part of the gun barrel that holds the cartridge for firing. Rifles and pistols normally have a single chamber into which cartridges are fed; revolvers have multiple chambers that rotate into the barrel for firing. Also, the word can be used in verb form, meaning to load a round of ammunition into firing position.

clip   A mechanism that holds a number of cartridges ("a 10-round clip"). The cartridges are fed singly (semiautomatic) or continuously (automatic) into the firing chamber as the trigger is pulled. Banning of high-capacity clips (which is usually defined as having more than 10 rounds) is a common goal of gun control advocates.

collective rights interpretation   An interpretation of the Second Amendment that sees it as guaranteeing only a general right of the people to bear arms, through an official militia organization.

concealed carry   The carrying of a firearm (usually a handgun) so that it is not visible, such as in a holster beneath clothing or in a pack or other portable container. Nearly all states require a permit for concealed carry. Their policies range from the permissive (all law-abiding adults) to the highly restrictive (must show a definite need).

cop-killer bullet   Term for armor-piercing ammunition popularized by gun control advocates. The term gets its name on the basis that it especially endangers police wearing bullet-proof vests.

defensive gun use   An instance where a person uses a gun to prevent a crime such as assault or burglary. In most cases the gun is not actually fired. Gun rights and gun control advocates often differ concerning the number of defensive gun uses that take place annually in the United States, with estimates ranging from 100,000 to 2.5 million.

Glossary

double-action A firing mechanism where the same pull of the trigger both retracts and releases the hammer or firing pin, discharging the weapon.

felony A serious crime such as murder, rape, or robbery and is generally punishable by a sentence in a state or federal prison. Convicted felons are generally not allowed legally to own firearms.

firearm Any portable gun-type weapon that shoots a bullet through the explosive force generated by the burning of gunpowder or a similar propellant.

flash hider (or suppressor) A device attached to the muzzle of a gun to reduce the flash caused by the exploding powder, thus making it harder to locate the shooter. It is often included in regulations as a characteristic of banned assault weapons.

Fourteenth Amendment This amendment was passed following the Civil War; it guarantees that all citizens will be treated equally under state laws and will be given their basic rights. During the 19th century the courts did not interpret it to require that states be bound by the rights given in the First, Second, and other amendments. In the 20th century many parts of the Bill of Rights have been "incorporated" in the Fourteenth Amendment guarantees, but thus far the Second Amendment has not been so incorporated.

Glock A 9-millimeter semiautomatic pistol that holds 17 shots. Typically, this type of high-capacity semiautomatic pistol has replaced the revolver as the handgun of choice for many criminals and police.

gun control A general term for regulations affecting the ownership or use of firearms. This can include bans on certain weapons or accessories, background checks, waiting periods, and licensing for gun owners and laws regulating the storage or concealed carrying of firearms.

gun culture A term used by both gun opponents and supporters to describe the way in which firearms ownership is viewed and promoted. Generally, control advocates see gun culture as an obsessive if not pathological preoccupation with firearms. Gun rights advocates, on the other hand, see gun culture as an expression of traditional American virtues such as self-reliance.

gun permit A license or document that authorizes an individual to have a gun at home or to carry it on one's person.

handgun A small firearm such as a pistol or revolver that can be held in the hand for firing and can be easily concealed.

Handgun Control, Inc. Founded in 1974 and later led by Sarah and James Brady, it is probably the largest and most effective gun control advocacy group. It played a key role in passing the Brady Bill and the Assault Weapons Ban and supports litigation against gun manufacturers.

homicide   The killing of one human being by another. An unlawful homicide may be viewed as murder or manslaughter depending on circumstances. A killing in self-defense may be considered a "justifiable homicide."

individual rights interpretation   A view of the Second Amendment that sees it as guaranteeing an individual right to keep and bear arms, independent of any collective responsibility to the organized militia.

instant background check   A background check for firearms purchasers that involves the presenting of valid identification and verification by phone or computer to check if the purchaser has a criminal or mental health record that would preclude firearms ownership. In 1998 the Brady Bill's waiting period for most gun purchases was phased out to be replaced by a national instant background check.

lever action   A mechanism used in some rifles that loads a round into the chamber when the shooter pulls a lever.

licensing laws   Laws that specify the requirements and procedures for the purchase, sale, possession, or carrying of guns. In addition to basic federal requirements, states and localities often have their own licensing laws. Such laws can vary from being minimal to highly restrictive (such as the total ban on handguns in Washington, D.C.).

long gun   A firearm with a long barrel such as a rifle and most shotguns. It is generally fired from the shoulder. Many jurisdictions that have restrictive regulations for handguns have fewer restrictions on long guns because they are usually not concealable and are used in only a small proportion of crimes.

M-16 rifle   A fully automatic military assault rifle, similar to a machine gun. This version is generally banned for civilian use. Similar rifles configured for semiautomatic firing are subject to assault weapons regulations.

machine gun   General term for an automatic weapon that fires moderately high-caliber ammunition. Machine guns have been heavily regulated since 1934 under federal law.

machine pistol   Also called "submachine gun"; an automatic pistol (such as the Uzi) that is generally smaller than a machine gun and fires lighter pistol ammunition.

magazine   A container (which can be box-shaped, tubular, or drum-shaped) that holds cartridges and includes a spring-loading mechanism for semiautomatic or automatic fire. It can be built into the gun itself or be detachable. Banning high capacity (more than ten rounds) magazines is a major goal of gun control advocates.

mandatory sentence   A minimum or add-on sentence for persons convicted of certain crimes or circumstances, such as committing a robbery while carrying a firearm. Gun rights advocates such as the NRA often promote mandatory sentences as an alternative to further restrictions on law-abiding gun owners.

"may issue" A policy where a local jurisdiction can issue a concealed weapons carry at its discretion. This generally occurs only when the applicant can demonstrate a severe need for self-protection. Because the requirements are so strict, this policy can in practice amount to a ban on concealed-carry for the general public.

militia An organized military force consisting of nonprofessional citizen-soldiers; also, persons potentially eligible for militia service. Official state militias have been incorporated into the National Guard. In recent years unofficial militias have been organized primarily by people concerned about government threats to rights, particularly gun rights.

muzzle The opening in a gun barrel out of which the bullet emerges.

muzzle brake A device that diverts some of the expanding gas from a gun's firing, reducing recoil. It is often considered to be a military or "assault weapon" feature.

National Crime Surveys Reports of crime statistics from the U.S. Bureau of Justice Statistics. These include numbers of various types of crimes such as homicides, assaults, and burglaries and statistics on incarcerated persons.

National Rifle Association The U.S.'s oldest and largest gun rights organization with more than 2 million members. As a "gun lobby" to Congress and state legislatures, it has been extraordinarily effective, at least until recent years, in blocking new federal and many state gun control proposals.

negligence A basic component of tort liability. Gun dealers have been sued for negligence in selling firearms to intoxicated people, and gun makers have been sued for negligence in marketing guns in a way that makes them easily accessible to the criminal black market.

pistol A general term for a handgun (a gun that can be held and fired using the shooter's hands). The two main types in modern use are those with a single firing chamber, into which bullets are loaded from a clip or magazine, and revolvers, which have multiple firing chambers that rotate into place.

police power In general, the right of a jurisdiction to make regulations to promote public security and safety. Many court decisions have held that states and cities can exercise their police power in banning handguns or assault weapons.

product liability The field of tort law that considers whether the manufacturer or seller of a product can be held liable for defects in or misuse of the product. Gun manufacturers have been sued for defective product design and, more recently, for reckless marketing and distribution practices.

pump action   A mechanism by which a shell is loaded into a shotgun by the working of a "pump" or slide. This action makes a distinctive sound that is often a significant deterrent to criminal activity.

registration   The process by which identifying information about a gun purchaser and the firearm itself is recorded and filed. Under the Gun Control Act of 1968, such records are kept by gun dealers subject to examination by law enforcement officials. Many gun control advocates favor that such records be kept in a central registry by the government to make it easy to trace illegal guns. Gun rights advocates strongly oppose such a system, fearing it would make it easy for the government to confiscate all firearms at some later date.

revolver   A handgun with a revolving cylinder that contains separate chambers (usually five to nine chambers), each containing a cartridge. Each time the trigger is pulled, the cylinder revolves, bringing the next cartridge into the barrel for firing.

rifle   A long gun that has a spiral-grooved barrel. This causes the bullet to spin, improving accuracy. Rifles can have a variety of loading mechanisms such as manual (bolt or lever) or semiautomatic or automatic (magazine).

right to keep and bear arms   A right guaranteed in the Second Amendment, though there is much dispute over whether the right is absolute or limited and whether it pertains to individuals or only to the people collectively. Gun rights advocates support this right on philosophical grounds as well as believe it to be guaranteed in the Constitution as an individual right.

round   A cartridge containing everything necessary for shooting—the primer, propellant (powder), and bullet. Clips and magazines are generally rated as to the number of rounds or cartridges they hold.

safety training   A course or program intended to teach gun owners the safe handling of their weapon, such as loading, unloading, determining whether the gun is loaded, and the use of safety mechanisms. Sometimes includes instruction in the laws pertaining to firearms and their use in self-defense.

Saturday night special   A term that probably originated in a slur against African-American neighborhoods, it has been popularized by gun control advocates in referring to cheap, low-caliber handguns that are often poorly made. A number of communities have passed laws banning such guns. Gun rights advocates oppose such laws as discriminating against the poor and depriving them of the means of self-defense.

sawed-off shotgun   A shotgun whose barrel has been shortened to less than 18 inches (or, for a rifle, 16 inches). The shortness makes it possible to conceal the weapon. Such weapons are restricted under federal law in much the same way as are machine guns.

Glossary

Second Amendment This amendment states that "A well-regulated militia, being necessary to the security of a free state, the right to keep and bear arms, shall not be infringed." Gun rights advocates interpret this as guaranteeing an essentially unlimited individual right to bear arms. Gun control advocates claim that only the right of the states to have a militia is guaranteed and that the amendment has no application to the control of private weapons ownership or use. Although scholars are divided, the courts have generally (but not conclusively) followed the latter view.

selective fire A mechanism found in some military-type rifles that allows the shooter to set the gun to be fired automatically or semiautomatically as either a single shot or a "burst" of several rounds.

self-defense The right to take violent action to protect oneself, others, or one's property from violent attack. Gun rights advocates often cite self-defense as a fundamental extension of the right to life and liberty and gun ownership as a right that makes self-defense truly effective. Gun control advocates emphasize self-defense as a collective function to be handled by the police. Legally, certain standards (which vary somewhat among jurisdiction) must be met for an action to be considered legitimate self-defense, such as it being necessary to prevent imminent harm to a person, it being proportional to the threat, and there being no way to safely retreat.

sentence enhancement laws Laws that provide for an additional term of imprisonment for certain specified actions, such as being in possession of a firearm while committing a felony.

"shall issue" A policy under which a sheriff or other official must give a gun-carrying permit to any adult applicant who doesn't have a criminal or mental health record. Gun rights advocates have been trying to enact such policies because they believe that armed citizens can significantly deter crime.

shotgun A long gun that is fired from the shoulder like a rifle but that has one or two barrels that are smooth rather than rifled. It fires a shell, which is a container full of shot (small balls).

silencer A device that is attached to the muzzle of a gun to reduce the sound made when the gun is fired. Silencers are virtually prohibited by federal law.

snub-nosed A handgun with a short barrel (3 inches or shorter); it is easy to conceal in a pocket or purse but is rather inaccurate in aim.

Street Sweeper A semiautomatic 12-gauge shotgun that holds 12 rounds and can be fired quickly; a devastating weapon for close combat that was banned as an assault weapon as part of the 1994 federal Assault Weapons Ban.

submachine gun An automatic weapon that fires pistol-caliber ammunition, such as the Uzi; also called a machine pistol. Submachine guns are generally tightly regulated under federal law, as are machine guns.

substitution theory A hypothesis that suggests that if handguns are restricted or banned, criminals will substitute more dangerous weapons such as sawed-off shotguns or rifles.

TEC-9 A semiautomatic pistol that holds 36 shots and can be fired at a rate of one shot per second. It and similar pistols have been banned as assault weapons.

transfer of guns The sale, exchange, or other form of conveying of a gun from one private individual to another. Recent gun control proposals would require that all transfers be done indirectly through a federally licensed dealer.

trigger lock A lock that fits into a gun trigger so that the gun cannot be fired until the lock is unlocked. Proposals in the late 1990s in Congress called for a requirement that trigger locks be either mandatory or be made available with each new handgun sold.

undetectable firearms Handguns made primarily of plastic, making them hard to detect through a conventional metal or X-ray detectors such as those used in airports. Banning such guns is a goal of many gun control advocates. Some gun rights advocates question whether truly undetectable guns exist or constitute a real threat.

Uniform Crime Reports An annual FBI report titled "Crime in the United States." It summarizes statistics provided by state and local law enforcement agencies.

Uzi A machine pistol originally invented by Uzi Gal, an Israeli army officer. Uzis are regulated as a fully automatic weapon.

vigilantism Law enforcement organized by private citizens without official sanction, often when police protection is not available, such as in newly organized territories or during civil unrest. Depending on circumstances, it has ranged from unconscionable lynching to a necessary and restrained exercise of collective self-defense.

waiting period A period that must elapse before a gun that has been purchased can be turned over to the buyer. In some cases a waiting period is necessary to allow for conducting a full background check, but the arrival of instant-check systems has removed this justification. Gun control advocates now promote waiting periods as a cooling-off mechanism to reduce impulse killings, although gun rights advocates warn that a waiting period may prevent a victim from being able to defend her or himself from a stalker or abusive spouse.

weapon's-effect hypothesis The idea that mere exposure to a weapon may trigger aggressive behavior in susceptible individuals.

PART II

GUIDE TO FURTHER RESEARCH

CHAPTER 6

HOW TO RESEARCH GUN CONTROL ISSUES

As with other controversial issues, activists on both sides of the gun issue have created many useful web sites. Because they offer overviews and links to news and source materials, such sites provide a good jumping-off place for research. Of course, as you explore the web, you will encounter many references to books and other printed materials that are not available online. It will then be time to use the library and its catalog and other bibliographical tools. This chapter describes some of the most important and useful research tools, both online and traditional.

GUN CONTROL ON THE WEB

Handgun Control, Inc., (together with its research affiliate the Center to Prevent Handgun Violence) is the largest gun control advocacy group. Its web site http://www.handguncontrol.org/ provides many resources, including information about current state and federal gun laws, news about lawsuits against gun makers, fact sheets on gun use, a variety of research studies supporting gun control efforts, and links to other gun control and gun violence prevention groups.

The Coalition to Stop Gun Violence (and its associated Educational Fund to End Gun Violence) is the other large national gun control group. Its site is located at http://www.gunfree.org has generally the same kind of offerings as Handgun Control, but has its own research and reports, so you should explore both sites thoroughly.

A number of medically oriented groups have become involved in gun control issues. The HELP (Handgun Epidemic Lowering Plan) network site at http://www.childmmc.edu/help/helphome.htm has programs and publications. The group Physicians for Social Responsibility also has part of its site devoted to violence issues (including gun control), at http://www.psr.org/violence.htm. The Johns Hopkins Center for Gun Policy and Research at http://infosys.jhsph.edu/centers/gunpolicy/ also offers links and resources (including bibliographies.) Another site to check is the Pacific Center for Violence Prevention, which devotes part of its site at http://www.pcvp.org/pcvp/firearms/guncntn2.html to firearms-related research and issues.

GUN RIGHTS ON THE WEB

The gun rights groups have if anything been even more active on the web than the gun control advocates. The largest gun rights site is, of course, the National Rifle Association at http://www.nra.org. Its site is divided into three parts: the headquarters (for membership and other business queries), "NRA live," and the "NRA ILA" (Institute for Legislative Action). The "live" service provides interesting multimedia content, but the ILA site is best for in-depth access to research materials. Like Handgun Control, Inc., it provides information about current gun laws and news about legislative battles, but of course it approaches it from a gun rights point of view. The NRA also has its own collection of studies and papers that challenge those supporting gun control and argue the case for armed self-defense and crime deterrence.

There are a variety of other gun rights groups, many more militant than the NRA. The largest is probably Gun Owners of America (http://www.gunowners.com), which is oriented toward lobbying and direct political action.

See Chapter 8 for many other national gun-related groups. Most of them have web sites. Many sites have lists of links to like-minded groups so, as with all web research, exploration can become an ever-widening spiral.

GOVERNMENT AGENCIES AND STATISTICS

Not surprisingly, there are important government sites that have useful information for gun issues research. The Treasury's Bureau of Alcohol, Tobacco, and Firearms (http://www.atf.treas.gov/) is the source for official federal gun regulations and their interpretation. The FBI (http://www.fbi.gov/) is responsible for tracing guns involved in crime, and it gathers many statistics about gun use. And because the gun issue is so closely connected with crime trends, the Department of Justice's

Bureau of Justice Statistics home page at http://www.ojp.usdoj.gov/bjs/ is another very important resource, as is its annual compilation "Sourcebook of Criminal Justice Statistics" (available at http://www.albany.edu/sourcebook/). Note that the Bureau site also has a set of links to other crime statistics sites.

Because public opinion is very important to the future of the gun issue, it's also useful to periodically check the Gallup Organization (http://www.gallup.com/poll/) for polling data.

BIBLIOGRAPHIC RESOURCES

Bibliographic resources is a general term for catalogs, indexes, bibliographies, and other guides that identify the books, periodical articles, and other printed resources that deal with a particular subject. They are essential tools for the researcher.

LIBRARY CATALOGS

Access to the largest library catalog, that of the Library of Congress, is available at http://lcweb.loc.gov/catalog/. This page explains the different kinds of catalogs and searching techniques available.

Yahoo offers a categorized listing of libraries at http://dir.yahoo.com/Reference/Libraries/. Of course, for materials available at one's local public or university library, that institution will be the most convenient source.

Online catalogs can be searched not only by the traditional author, title, and subject headings, but also by matching keywords in the title. Thus a title search for *gun control* will retrieve all books that have that word somewhere in their title. (Of course a book about gun control may well not have that phrase in the title, so it is still necessary to use subject headings to get the most comprehensive results.)

The most important LC subject heading is, not surprisingly, "*gun control*". This heading can be subdivided by place (United States, an individual state, or a foreign country). The following primary subheads are also important:

bibliography
government policy
juvenile literature
law and legislation
political aspects

Many of these subheads can also be divided by place, for example, "*Gun Control—Government Policy—United States*". Naturally, *United States* is the most frequently used geographical subhead, and like others, it can be further divided using subheads such as:

Citizen participation
Evaluation
Handbooks, manuals
History
Public Opinion
Societies, etc.
Statistics

The broader topic "*firearms*" will also be of interest. Its subdivisions include:

government policy
history
law and legislation

which will generally overlap with "*gun control*". Other firearms-related headings include:

firearm accidents
firearm ownership
firearms industry
firearms owners
firearms theft

and, of course, particular types of firearms:

machine guns
pistols
rifles

Once the record for a book or other item is found, it is a good idea to see what additional subject headings and name headings have been assigned. These in turn can be used for further searching.

BIBLIOGRAPHIES, INDEXES, AND DATABASES

Bibliographies in various forms provide a convenient way to find books, periodical articles, and other materials. Most book-length bibliographies published before the 1990s are not very useful because there has been an explosion of materials published on this topic during the past decade.

Abstracts are brief summaries of articles or papers. They are usually compiled and indexed—originally in bound volumes but, increasingly, available online. Some examples of indexes where you might retrieve literature related to gun control include:

Criminal Justice Abstracts (1977–)
Criminal Justice Periodical Index (1978–)
GPO (1976–) (index to government publications)
Index Medicus (1960–)
Index to Legal Periodicals & Books (1981–)
National Criminal Justice Reference Service Abstracts Database (NCJRS)
Social Sciences Citation Index (1956–)
Social Sciences Index (1974–)
Sociological Abstracts (1952–)

Generally these indexes are available only through a library where you hold a card and cannot be accessed over the Internet (unless you are on a college campus).

However UnCover Web (http://uncweb.carl.org/) is generally available for searching and contains brief descriptions of about 8.8 million documents from about 18,000 journals in just about every subject area. Copies of complete documents can be ordered with a credit card.

There's also the National Criminal Justice Reference Service's Justice Information Center web page at http://www.ncjrs.org/. It offers a searchable abstract database containing 150,000 criminal justice publications, and it can be a real gold mine for the more advanced researcher.

FREE PERIODICAL INDEXES

Most public libraries subscribe to database services such as InfoTrac that index articles from hundreds of general-interest periodicals (and some moderately specialized ones). The database can be searched by author or by words in the title, subject headings, and sometimes words found anywhere in the article text. Depending on the database used, "hits" in the database can result in just a bibliographical description (author, title, pages, periodical name, issue date), a description plus an abstract (a paragraph summarizing the contents of the article), or the full text of the article itself.

Many libraries provide dial-in, Internet, or telnet access to their periodical databases as an option in their catalog menu. However, licensing restrictions usually mean that only researchers who have a library card for that particular library can access the database (by typing in their name and card number). Check with local public or school libraries to see which databases are available.

For periodicals not indexed by InfoTrac (or for which only abstracts rather than complete text is available), check to see whether the publication has its own web site (many now do). Some scholarly publications are putting all or most of their articles online. Popular publications tend to offer only a limited selection. Some publications of both types offer archives of several years' back issues that can be searched by author or by keyword.

BOOKSTORE CATALOGS

Many people have discovered that online bookstores such as Amazon.com at (http://www.amazon.com) and Barnesandnoble.com (http://www.barnesandnoble.com) are convenient ways to shop for books. A less-known benefit of online bookstore catalogs is that they often include publisher's information, book reviews, and reader's comments about a given title. They can thus serve as a form of annotated bibliography.

On the other hand, a visit to one's local bookstore also has its benefits. Although the available selection of titles is likely to be smaller than that of an online bookstore, the ability to browse through books physically before buying them can be very useful.

KEEPING UP WITH THE NEWS

It is important for the researcher to be aware of currently breaking news. In addition to watching TV news and subscribing to local or national newspapers and magazines, there are a number of ways to use the Internet to find additional news sources.

NEWSPAPERS AND NETNEWS

Like periodicals, most large newspapers now have web sites that offer headlines and a searchable database of recent articles. The URL is usually given somewhere in one's local newspaper. Yahoo! is also a good place to find newspaper links: See http://dir.yahoo.com/News_and_Media/Newspapers/Web_Directories/. Web researchers should note that many newspapers charge for reviewing archived articles on their web databases. Researchers should consider whether or not they want to pay for such services. A cheaper, albeit more time-consuming, method is to use a local library's archives.

Net News is a decentralized system of thousands of "newsgroups," or forums organized by topic. Most web browsers have an option for subscribing to, reading, and posting messages in newsgroups. The Dejanews site (http://www.deja.com) also provides free access and an easy-to-use interface to newsgroups. The general newsgroup for gun matters is *"rec.guns"*. Some other possibilities are *"info.firearms"*, *"info.firearms.politics"*, and *"talk.politics.gun"*.

MAILING LISTS

Mailing lists offer another way to keep up with (and discuss) recent developments. Some gun control and gun rights organizations maintain such lists, which you can learn about from their web site and then subscribe to by clicking on a link or by sending a specially formatted e-mail message using the instructions provided. The mailing list software automatically collates and distributes the e-mail messages. The Gunnery.net site at http://www.gunnery.net/firearm%20mailing%20lists.html provides a list of gun-related mailing lists. Some are specialized (dealing with particular models of gun or aspects of shooting), but there is also a general gun list. These are generally oriented toward the gun culture.

Net News and mailing lists are generally most valuable when they have a moderator who keeps discussions focused and discourages "flaming," or heated or personally insulting, statements.

SEARCHING THE WEB

A researcher can explore an ever-expanding web of information by starting with a few web sites and following the links they offer to other sites, which in turn have links to still other sites. But because this is something of a hit-and-miss proposition, some important sites may be missed if the researcher only "web surfs" in this fashion. There are two more focused techniques that can fill in the information gaps.

WEB INDEXES

A web index is a site that offers what amounts to a structured, hierarchical outline of subject areas. This enables the researcher to zero in on a particular aspect of a subject and find links to web sites for further exploration.

The best known (and largest) web index is Yahoo! (http://www.yahoo.com). The home page gives the top-level list of topics, and you follow them down to more specific areas. The area for gun issues can be reached by clicking on *"Society and Culture"* and then on *"Firearms"*. There are then the following topics: *"Companies"*, *"Firearms Policy"*, *"Shooting"*, and *"Smart Guns"*. (Of course, there may well be others by the time you read this.) *"Firearms Policy"* includes *"Gun Control"* and *"Gun Rights"*. Clicking on those gets links to a number of sites, some more useful than others. For example the listing as of July 1999 under *"Gun Rights"* was:

Campaign for Concealed Carry for All Law Abiding Iowans—devoted to enlisting Iowa gun owners to lobby their legislators for a change to the existing law for concealed weapons.

Canada's Universal Directory of the Recreational Firearms Community—clubs, dealers, organizations, and anything relating to recreational firearms.

Firearm Laws in Australia—Target shooter defends his sport in light of recent media attention and criticizes the Australian Medical Association and some parts of the media, including 3AW.

Firearms & Liberty Geoff's Firearms and Freedom Page—Information and resources for the pro-gun, pro-liberty citizen.

GunTruths—resource center about gun rights and responses to anti-gun propaganda.

Jeff Chan's Firearms Archive—research, statistics, commentary, court cases, letters, legislation, and more.

Second Amendment Law Library—collection of law review articles concerning the Second Amendment.

Second Amendment Stuff—Dedicated to the right to keep and bear arms.

Warning Shot—Liberty Activist Action of the Month.

Web Directory: International Firearms—links groups and individuals advocating the right to keep and bear arms worldwide.

Usenet—alt.politics.usa.constitution.gun-rights

In addition to following Yahoo!'s outlinelike structure, there is also a search box into which the researcher can type one or more keywords and receive a list of matching categories and sites.

Web indexes such as Yahoo! have two major advantages over undirected surfing. First, the structured hierarchy of topics makes it easy to find a particular topic or subtopic and then explore its links. Second, Yahoo! does not make an attempt to compile every possible link on the Internet (a task that is virtually impossible, given the size of the web); rather, sites are evaluated for usefulness and quality by Yahoo!'s indexers. This means that the researcher has a better chance of finding more substantial and accurate information (this advantage is also provided by sites like those of Handgun

Control, Inc., and the NRA of course). The disadvantage of web indexes is the flip side of their selectivity: The researcher is dependent on the indexer's judgment for determining which sites are worth exploring.

Two other web indexes are LookSmart (http://www.looksmart.com) and The Mining Company's About.com (http://home.miningco.com). These work much in the same way as Yahoo!. For example, to get to gun issues on About.com, one clicks on "*Society and Culture*", then "*Issues/Causes*", then "*Crime/Punishment*", and then on the "*NetLinks*" section on that page, click on "*Guns*". The first part of the resulting list of links read as follows on the day we checked:

Banning Saturday Night Specials Doesn't Work
This article disputes any anticrime benefit.

The Brady Bill Expired November 30, 1998
What is your state replacing it with?

Background Checks Prevent Over 11,584 Gun Sales
Among those barred from buying guns between November 30 and January 10 were 1541 very foolish people who were actively wanted by the police.

Ballistics
From Your Guide: A list of reference articles.

Buying Guns On The Internet
If you have a charge card, it's easy—no matter who you are.

Canadian Firearms Laws

Carrying Concealed Weapons
The laws by state.

Cities Suing Handgun Makers: New Orleans
Encouraged by government suits against tobacco companies, New Orleans seeks damages for homicides and accidental deaths.

Cities Suing Handgun Makers: Update: Backlash
[February 1999] This past year, a number of cities have sued gunmakers to recover gun-related costs. Lately, bowing to NRA pressure, states are beginning to prohibit cities from doing so. A proposed Florida law would make it a third-degree felony for a mayor to sue a gunmaker.

Does Gun Control Discriminate Against the Poor?
According to this article, banning Saturday night specials makes it harder for the poor to defend themselves (another article, by the same author, making pretty much the same argument).

Gun Control

Facts and Myths About Guns
As presented by gunowners.org.

The Founding Fathers and Guns
What Thomas Jefferson, Samuel Adams, et al. had to say about gun ownership (from the NRA).

Gun Control: Its Racist Origins
(from the NRA.website) Yes, this sounded bizarre to me, too. But read the article.

Gun-Free Schools Act of 1994
A federal law instructing states to mandate a minimum one-year suspension for any student bringing a gun to school.

Gun-Free Zones Around Schools
The Gun Owners of America sees this as an unconstitutional infringement of the right to bear arms.

Gun Laws By State
Purchase limitations, waiting period, current legislation, and more.

Gun Manufacturers Sued
[January 1999] Over 30 manufacturers are being sued by families of shooting victims on the grounds that they don't control distribution of guns.

As you can see, this site presents a good selection of material on many sides of the issue. Sites like Yahoo! and About.com are worth checking frequently so you will be alerted about new developments.

There are also an increasing number of specialized online research guides that are something like traditional bibliographical essays with the added bonus of having the materials discussed already linked so that they are just a click away. The Boston University Library has a research guide to gun control at http://www2.bu.edu/library/research-guides/guns.html.

SEARCH ENGINES

Search engines take a very different approach to finding materials on the web. Instead of organizing topically in a "top-down" fashion, search engines work their way "from the bottom up," scanning through web documents and indexing them. There are hundreds of search engines, but some of the most widely used include:

- Alta Vista (http://www.altavista.digital.com)
- Excite (http://www.excite.com)

How to Research Gun Control Issues

- Go (http://www.go.com)
- Google (http://www.google.com)
- Hotbot (http://www.hotbot.com)
- Lycos (http://www.lycos.com)
- Magellan (http://www.magellan.excite.com)
- Northern Light (http://www.northernlight.com)
- WebCrawler (http://www.WebCrawler.com)

Search engines are generally easy to use by employing the same sorts of keywords that work in library catalogs. There are a variety of web search tutorials available online [try *web search tutorial* in a search engine]. One good one is published by The Web Tools Company at http://thewebtools.com/searchgoodies/tutorial.htm.

Here are a few basic rules for using search engines:

- When looking for something specific, use the most specific term or phrase. For example, when looking for information about laws concerning carrying concealed weapons, use the specific term *"concealed carry"*, because this is the standard term.

- When looking for a more general topic, such as the relationship between guns and crime, use several descriptive words (nouns are more reliable than verbs), for example, *"gun crime statistics"*. Most engines will automatically put pages that match all three terms first on the results list. This search will likely get you a list that starts with statistics and then includes more general discussions of guns and crime.

- Use "wildcards" when a desired word may have more than one ending; for example, *semiauto** matches both *semiautomatic* and the more slangy *semiauto*.

- Most search engines support Boolean (*and, or, not*) operators that can be used to broaden or narrow a search.

- Use AND to narrow a search: *"youth AND violence"* will match only pages that have both terms.

- Use OR to broaden a search: *"gun OR firearm"* will match any page that has *either* term.

- Use NOT to exclude unwanted results: *"gun NOT handgun"* finds articles about guns but not handguns (of course *gun* is also used as a general term for any sort of firearm, so the filtering effect won't be complete).

Because each search engine indexes somewhat differently and offers somewhat different ways of searching, it is a good idea to use several different search engines, especially for a general query. Several "metasearch" programs automate the process of submitting a query to multiple search engines. These include:

- Metacrawler (http://www.metacrawler.com)
- Inference FIND (http://www.infind.com/infind/)
- SavvySearch (http://www.savvysearch.com)

There are also search utilities that can be run from the researcher's own PC rather than through a web site. A good example is Mata Hari, a "shareware" (try before you buy) program available for download at http://thewebtools.com/.

FINDING ORGANIZATIONS AND PEOPLE

Lists of gun control or gun rights organizations can be found on major sites such as those of Handgun Control, Inc., or the NRA and index sites such as Yahoo! If such sites do not yield the name of a specific organization, the name can be given to a search engine. Generally, the best approach is to put the name of the organization in quote marks such as "Mothers for Gun Control."

Another approach is to take a guess at the organization's likely web address. For example, the National Rifle Association is commonly known by the acronym NRA, so it is not a surprise that the organization's web site is at www.nra.org. (Note that noncommercial organization sites normally use the .org suffix, government agencies use .gov, educational institutions have .edu, and businesses use .com.) This technique can save time but doesn't always work.

There are several ways to find a person on the Internet:

- Put the person's name (in quotes) in a search engine and possibly find that person's home page on the Internet.
- Contact the person's employer (such as a university for an academic, or a corporation for a technical professional). Most such organizations have web pages that include a searchable faculty or employee directory.
- Try one of the people-finder services such as Yahoo People Search (http://people.yahoo.com) or BigFoot (http://www.bigfoot.com). This may yield contact information such as e-mail address, regular address, and/or phone number.

LEGAL RESEARCH

Gun issues inevitably become legal issues because the use (and misuse) of guns is a subject of both criminal and civil law. Because of the specialized terminology of the law, legal research can be more difficult to master than bibliographical or general research tools. Fortunately, the Internet has also come to the rescue in this area, offering a variety of ways to look up laws and court cases without having to pore through huge bound volumes in law libraries (which may not be accessible to the general public, anyway.)

FINDING LAWS

When federal legislation passes, it eventually becomes part of the United States Code, a massive legal compendium. Laws can be referred to either by their popular name or by a formal citation. For example, the Gun Free Schools Act is cited as 18 USC §921, meaning title 18 of the U.S.C. code, section 921 (actually the law amended certain subsections of section 921).

The U.S. Code can be searched online in several locations, but the easiest site to use is probably the U.S. Code database at http://uscode.house.gov/. The U.S. Code may also be found at Cornell Law School (a major provider of free online legal reference material) at http://www4.law.cornell.edu/uscode/. The fastest way to retrieve a law is by its title and section citation, but phrases and keywords can also be used.

Legislation is not immediately compiled into the U.S. Code (this is done every five years). Instead of U.S. Code numbers, one can use Public Law numbers in many databases. For example the Brady Handgun Violence Control Act is Public Law 103–159 (sometimes abbreviated P.L. 103–159).

Federal laws are generally implemented by a designated agency that writes detailed rules, which become part of the Code of Federal Regulations (C.F.R.). A regulatory citation looks like a U.S. Code citation, and takes the form *vol.* C.F.R. sec. *number.*

Regulations can be found at the web site for the relevant government agency (such as the Bureau of Alcohol, Tobacco, and Firearms, or BATF).

Many states also have their codes of laws online. The Cornell University Legal Information Institute at http://www.law.cornell.edu/ is an "all-in-one" site that has both federal and state laws.

KEEPING UP WITH LEGISLATIVE DEVELOPMENTS

Pending legislation is often tracked by advocacy groups. For example, Handgun Control, Inc., has a legislative page at http://www.handguncontrol.org/legislation.htm and the NRA has a similar service at http://www.nraila.org/.

There has been a lot of activity in Congress relating to gun control lately. The Library of Congress catalog site (telnet *locis.loc.gov*) includes files summarizing legislation by the number of the Congress (each two year session of Congress has a consecutive number: for example, the 105th Congress was in session in 1997 and 1998 and the 106th will be in session in 1999 and 2000. Legislation can be searched for by the name of its sponsor(s), the bill number, or by topical keywords.

For example, a search of the 106th Congress for the phrase "*gun control*" produced a list that included the following:

B05 GUN BUY BACK PARTNERSHIP GRANT ACT OF 1999//(STLI=1)
B06 GUN CONTROL//(LIVT)
B07 GUN CONTROL BILL//(PTTL=1)
B08 GUN CRIME PROSECUTION ACT OF 1999//(STLI=1)
B09 GUN DEALER RESPONSIBILITY ACT OF 1999//(STLI=1)
B10 GUN INDUSTRY ACCOUNTABILITY ACT//(STLI=1)
B11 GUN INDUSTRY RESPONSIBILITY ACT//(STLI=1)
B12 GUN KINGPIN PENALTY ACT//(STLI=1)

Typing "*s B09*" for the Gun Dealer Responsibility Act of 1999 displays brief information about this bill:

1. S.1101: SPON=Sen Reed, Jack; OFFICIAL TITLE: A bill to provide for tort liability of firearms dealers who transfer firearms in violation of Federal firearms law.

Note that the sponsor and title of the bill are given, along with a brief description. Typing *chrn* (for "chronology") would then display any "floor actions" that have happened to the bill, such as being referred to committee.

The Library of Congress THOMAS site (http://thomas.loc.gov/), provides a web-based interface that may be easier to use for many purposes. Under the "*Legislation*" section of the page, existing laws can be looked up by Public Law number or summaries of legislation considered by each Congress can be searched by keyword or bill number. For example, if you have read something about a major gun control bill being debated in Congress but can't remember the details, you can type in the keywords "*gun control*" and see something like the following:

1. H.R.2122: A bill to require background checks at gun shows, and for other purposes. Sponsor: Rep McCollum, Bill.—LATEST ACTION: 06/18/99 Measure failed of passage in House, roll call #244 (147-280).

Clicking on the Bill number (2122) gives a screen with links to summary, text of legislation, current status, floor actions, and so on. Of course, if one knows the number, one can go directly to this listing from the search screen by searching by number.

FINDING COURT DECISIONS

Like laws, legal decisions are organized using a system of citations. The general form is: *Party1 v. Party2 volume reporter* [optional start page] *(court, year).*
Here are some examples from Chapter 2:

> *Presser v. Illinois*, 116 U.S. 252 (1886): Here the parties are Presser and the State of Illinois. The case is in volume 116 of the U.S. *Supreme Court Reports,* and the case was decided in 1886. (For the Supreme Court, the name of the court is omitted.)
>
> *U.S. v. Warin*, 530 F.2d 130 (6th Cir.): The parties are the United States and Warin, and the case is in volume 530 of the U.S. F.2d reporter, in the 6th U.S. Circuit.
>
> *City of Salina v. Blaksley*, 72 Kan. 230 (1905): This is a Kansas State Supreme Court case (vol. 72 of the Kansas reporter).

To find a federal court decision, first ascertain the level of court involved: district (the lowest level, where trials are normally held), circuit (the main court of appeals), or the Supreme Court. The researcher can then go to a number of places on the Internet to find cases by citation and, often, the names of the parties. Some of the most useful sites are:

• The Legal Information Institute (http://supct.law.cornell.edu/supct/) has all Supreme Court decisions since 1990 plus 610 of "the most important historic" decisions.
• Washlaw Web (http://www.washlaw.edu/) has a variety of court decisions (including states) and legal topics listed, making it a good jumping-off place for many sorts of legal research.
• The following site has handily compiled a large collection of gun-related federal and state cases, criminal and civil, as well as a lot of other material on gun laws: http://www.cs.cmu.edu/afs/cs/usr/wbardwel/public/nfalist/.

LEXIS AND WESTLAW

Lexis and Westlaw are commercial legal databases that have extensive information including an elaborate system of notes, legal subject headings, and ways to show relationships between cases. Unfortunately, these services are too expensive for use by most individual researchers unless they are available through a university or corporate library.

MORE HELP ON LEGAL RESEARCH

For more information on conducting legal research, see the "*Legal Research FAQ*" at http://www.cis.ohio-state.edu/hypertext/faq/usenet/law/research/top.html. This also explains more advanced techniques such as "Shepardizing" (referring to *Shepard's Case Citations*), which is used to find at how a decision has been cited in subsequent cases and whether the decision was later overturned.

Finally, a word of caution about the Internet: It is important to critically evaluate all materials found on the Internet. Many sites have been established by well-known, reputable organizations or individuals. Others may come from unknown individuals or groups. Their material may be equally valuable, but it should be checked against reliable sources.

CHAPTER 7

ANNOTATED BIBLIOGRAPHY

This chapter provides an extensive annotated bibliography for gun control and gun rights issues. It is subdivided into the following 10 areas:

- Reference works (including other bibliographies)
- General introductions and overviews
- Gun control advocacy (general)
- Gun rights advocacy (general)
- Legal issues (Second Amendment, tort liability, etc.)
- Laws and legislation (including politics and lobbying groups)
- Guns and society (general topics that don't fit into any of the above category)
- Studies and surveys (including responses and criticisms)
- Guns, children, and schools
- International perspectives

Each area is further subdivided by type of material: books, articles and papers, and Internet documents. Note that many newspaper and magazine articles are also accessible in some way through the Internet, but if they first appeared in print, then they are listed under "articles and papers." The category "Internet documents" includes both articles whose content is fixed and pages that are regularly updated (such as those that contain current news). See Chapter 6 for more information about useful web sites.

REFERENCE WORKS

This category includes works that are primarily references or collections of resources, including bibliographies.

BOOKS

Bijlefeld, Marjolijn, ed. *The Gun Control Debate: A Documentary History.* Westport, Conn.: Greenwood Press, 1997. A collection of more than 200 primary source documents relating to gun control issues. Includes historical, constitutional, legal, and legislative aspects of gun regulation.

Casey, Verna. *Gun Control: a Selected Bibliography.* Monticello, Ill.: Vance Bibliographies, 1988. A somewhat dated bibliography but it is useful for researching classic works.

Cottrol, Robert J., ed. *Gun Control and the Constitution: Sources and Explorations on the Second Amendment.* New York: Garland Publishing, 1994. Collects historical and legal material that illuminates many facets on the gun control debate in terms of the intent and interpretation of the Constitution, original intent versus broad interpretation, and the political philosophy of republicanism.

Dizard, Jan E., Robert Merrill, and Stephen P. Andrews, ed. *Guns in America: A Reader.* New York: New York University Press, 1999. A large collection of primary sources relating to guns in American life and history.

Gun Control: Restricting Rights or Protecting People? Revised Spring 1999 edition. Wylie, Tex.: Information Plus, 1999. A concise but complete guide to gun issues, including historical origins, aspects of gun use today, court decisions, studies, and other information. The book concludes with a pro-con debate and a resource list.

Halbrook, Stephen P. *Firearms Law Deskbook: Federal and State Criminal Practice.* Deerfield, Ill.: Clark Boardman Callaghan, 1995. A reference to federal and state firearms laws for practicing attorneys.

Johns Hopkins Center for Gun Policy and Research. *Firearm Violence: An Annotated Bibliography.* Baltimore, Md.: Johns Hopkins Center, 1996. Covers resources dealing with firearms ownership and use, legal and legislative issues, the gun industry, gun control supporters and opponents, and strategies for reducing gun violence.

Kruschke, Earl R. *Gun Control: A Reference Handbook.* Santa Barbara, Calif.: ABC-Clio, 1995. A comprehensive reference guide that includes background to gun control issues, chronology, biographies, and a guide to organization and resources.

Stewart, Alva W. *Gun Control: Its Pros And Cons: A Checklist.* Monticello, Ill.: Vance Bibliographies, 1986. Useful for finding older works.

INTERNET DOCUMENTS

Bardwell, William. "NFA and Other Gun Law Related Info and Cases." Available online. URL:http://www.cs.cmu.edu/afs/cs/user/wbardwel/public/nfalist/index.html. Downloaded on July 7, 1999. Compiles a variety of laws, regulations, court decisions (at all levels) [Bureau of] Alcohol, Tobacco, and

Firearms (ATF) rulings, and links to other gun-related sites. An excellent reference source although the selection has a pro-gun rights bias.

Canadian Institute for Legal Action. "Canadian and International Firearms Organizations Links." Available online. URL: http://www.cila.org /links.htm. Updated on July 6, 1999. Gives web links to a variety of Canadian and international shooting and gun rights organizations.

"Gunindex.com." Available online. URL: http://www.gunindex. com/index.html. Updated on March 21, 1999. Online directory to firearms manufacturers, dealers, gun clubs, and other resources.

Johns Hopkins Center for Gun Policy and Research. "Firearm Injury and Public Health: A Selected Bibliography." Available online. URL: http://infosys.jhsph.edu/centers/gunpolicy/bibliography.cfm. Downloaded on July 6, 1999. List of articles and papers on epidemiology of gun violence, risks and benefits of gun ownership, gun policy, and evaluating gun laws. Appears to emphasize works that support gun control.

Mealey, Charles. "Firearms Groups and Organizations." Available online. URL: http://home.tampabay.rr.com/membercouncil/gunorgs.htm. Updated on October 17, 1998. An extensive listing of organizations involved in firearms training, education, and gun rights advocacy.

National Rifle Association. Institute for Legislative Action. "A Citizen's Guide to Federal Firearms Laws." Available online. URL: http://www.nraila.org/research/1999.1215FederalFirearmLicenses-001.shtml. Downloaded on June 5, 1999. Integrates and summarized federal firearms law by topic, such as a person's ineligible right to own firearms, laws relating to particular kinds of guns, transporting firearms, and carrying firearms.

National Rifle Association. Institute for Legislative Action. "Compendium of State Firearm. Law. S." Available online. URL: http://www.nraila.org /research/1997.716-Bill of RightsCivilRights-032.html. Downloaded on June 5, 1999. Interactive summary of state firearm laws in the form of a map of the United States.

"Rec.guns on the Web." Available online. URL: http://www.recguns.com/. Downloaded on July 7, 1999. Provides the FAQ file for the newsgroup rec.guns, which includes information on gun laws, gun use, and other techniques involving firearms. The site includes other topics such as gun safety and links to pro-gun rights groups.

GENERAL INTRODUCTIONS AND OVERVIEWS

This category includes introductions and overviews to the gun control debate, including some works written for younger readers. These works generally try to be even-handed and present arguments from both sides rather than explicitly advocating a gun control or gun rights position, though some bias is noted.

BOOKS

Aitkens, Maggi. *Should We Have Gun Control?* Minneapolis, Minn.: Lerner Publications, 1991. For young adults. Explores the opposing interpretations of the Second Amendment and the question of whether the government should regulate private access to guns.

Beckelman, Laurie. *Gun Control.* New York: Crestwood House, 1999. Introduces and gives an overview of the gun debate for young people.

Dizard, Jan E., Robert Merrill Muth, and Stephen P. Andrews, Jr. *Guns in America: A Reader.* New York: New York University Press, 1999. Provides more than 40 selections covering topics such as the origin of the gun control, the pro and con of gun ownership, minorities and guns, the militia movement, and possible compromises between gun control and gun rights advocates.

Dolan, Edward F., and Margaret M. Scariano. *Guns in the United States.* New York: Franklin Watts, 1994. An overview and collection of resources geared for junior high and high school students.

Edel, Wilbur. *Gun Control: Threat to Liberty or Defense Against Anarchy?* Westport, Conn.: Praeger, 1995. An introduction to gun control issues from a philosophical and practical viewpoint.

Fuller, Sharon. *The Gun Control Debate: An Update.* Madison, Wisc.: State of Wisconsin Legislative Reference Bureau, 1994. Summarizes legislation and related issues as of the mid-1990s.

Gottfried, Ted. *Gun Control: Public Safety and the Right to Bear Arms.* Brookfield, Conn.: Millbrook Press, 1993. For teens. A balanced but vividly written account of gun control that includes legal issues (such as the meaning of the Second Amendment) and social issues as well as the thoughts and feelings of teens themselves.

Hofstadter, Richard, and Michael Wallace. *American Violence: A Documentary History.* New York: Alfred A. Knopf, 1970. Presents a historical context for violence in the United States, including a discussion of the U.S.'s "gun culture." The authors favor gun control.

Nisbet, Lee, ed. *The Gun Control Debate: You Decide.* Buffalo, N.Y.: Prometheus Books, 1990. Addresses the "gun culture" in the United States, the Second Amendment, the effectiveness of gun legislation, and the use of guns for self-defense. For each topic, there is a selection of articles written by historians, legal experts, criminologists, or social thinkers. A good resource for students and debaters, though statistics are now somewhat outdated.

O'Sullivan, Carol. *Gun Control: Distinguishing Between Fact and Opinion.* Teacher's Guide Edition. San Diego, Calif.: Greenhaven Press, 1990. Useful for leading class discussions and sharpening critical thinking skills in sorting out facts, anecdotes, opinions, and scientific conclusions.

Pontonne, S., ed. *Gun Control Issues.* Commack, N.Y.: Nova Science Publishing, 1997. Introduces the key facts and issues in the gun control debate including the Brady Law, assault weapons, and statistics on gun use.

Roleff, Tamara L., ed. *Gun Control: Opposing Viewpoints.* San Diego, Calif.: Lucent Publishing, 1997. Articles and position papers from a variety of experts, arranged in a pro-and-con format to cover issues such as the relation between guns and crime, guns as a health problem, and the nature of the constitutional right to bear arms.

Siegel, Mark. *Gun Control: An American Issue.* Wylie, Tex.: Information Plus, 1997. Presents charts and statistics on many aspects of gun use; also includes pro-and-con statements and a summary of gun laws.

Spitzer, Robert J. *The Politics of Gun Control.* 2nd edition. New York: Chatham House, 1998. An account of gun-related issues, including the interpretation of the Second Amendment and the relationship between guns and crime. This book contains a generally pro gun control slant.

Zimring, Franklin E. *The Citizen's Guide to Gun Control.* New York: Macmillan Publishing, 1987. An introduction to the many aspects of gun control issues, the gun control movement, and activism. The book presents research, discussion, statistics, and surveys of public opinion.

———. *Gun Control.* Washington, D.C.: U.S. Dept. of Justice, National Institute of Justice, 1988. An introduction and study guide to the issue.

ARTICLES AND PAPERS

Buchsbaum, Herbert. "Guns R Us." *Scholastic Update*, vol. 126, February 11, 1994, p. 18ff. General introduction to the gun debate. The article is written for young people but may be useful for all readers.

Dreyfuss, Robert. "Good Morning, Gun Lobby!" *Mother Jones*, vol. 21, July–August 1996, pp. 38ff. Describes the politics of Neal Knox, the NRA vice president, as accommodating militialike radicals internally while trying to create an outward image of the NRA as mainstream. The article recounts the progressive radicalization of the NRA since the late 1970s and claims that Knox now has an iron grip on the organization's governance.

"Firing Line." *Mother Jones*, vol. 19, March–April 1994, pp. 5ff. Contains rebuttals by gun advocates such as Wayne LaPierre of the NRA to the magazine's earlier article "Life Without Guns," which advocated a total gun ban. The article also contains responses by gun control advocates including Josh Sugarmann and Senator Bill Bradley of New Jersey and other viewpoints from readers.

"Gun Control: Across the United States, Gun-Control Supporters, Opponents 'Shoot' It Out." *Current Events*, vol. 97, November 6, 1997, pp. 1ff. Introduces the U.S. gun control debate with pro-and-con views, background, statistics, and public opinion polls.

Leddy, Edward F. "Guns and Gun Control." *The Reader's Companion to American History*, 1991, edition, pp. 477ff. Gives a brief historical introduction to the gun issue in the United States.

"Other Voices on Gun Control." *Playboy*, vol. 41, May 1994, p. 47. Collection of opinions on gun control from various celebrities and experts.

Rosenberg, Merri, Sarah Brady, and Tanya Metaksa. "Up in Arms." *Scholastic Update*, vol. 131, November 2, 1998, pp. 10ff. Presents a panel discussion/debate between Handgun Control, Inc.'s Sarah Brady and the NRA's Tanya Metaksa. Brady argues for a variety of measures to restrict access to guns and make them safer. Metaksa says that gun owners should be held responsible for their actions, not deprived of their rights.

Stasio, Marilyn. "Gun Crazy: Are We a Country Out of Control?" *Cosmopolitan*, vol. 216, March 1994, pp. 180ff. Describes violent shooting incidents and their depressing consequences for the United States and then provides quotes and arguments on both sides of the gun debate, introducing topics such as assault weapons, gun buy-back programs, and the growing interest of women in gun ownership.

Witkin, Gordon. "Should You Own a Gun?" *U.S. News & World Report*, vol. 117, August 15, 1994, pp. 24ff. Uses the question of gun ownership to introduce the overall debate about gun control. The article features a debate between Gary Kleck, whose research shows that gun owners use their guns for defense up to 2.5 million times a year (seldom shooting them) and that criminals are deterred by their fear of armed citizens, and Arthur Kellermann, whose equally provocative study found that guns in the home were 43 times more likely to kill a resident or friend than an armed intruder.

Witkin, Gordon, and Katia Hetter. "The Fight to Bear Arms." *U.S. News & World Report*, vol. 118, May 22, 1995, pp. 28ff. An overview of the gun issue, including a discussion of legal developments and a chronology of firearms developments and gun legislation.

Worsnop, Richard L. "Gun Control: Will It Help Reduce Violent Crime in the U.S.?" *CQ Researcher*, vol. 4, June 10, 1994, pp. 507ff. Introduces the debate over gun control as it focuses on the assault weapons ban debated in Congress in 1994. The article also includes discussion of political, social, and criminological aspects, as well as sidebars on specific gun topics.

INTERNET DOCUMENTS

ABC News. "The Great Debate." Available online. URL: http://abcnews. go.com/sections/us/DailyNews/guns_ends.html. Downloaded on June 8, 1999. Introduces the gun control debate. The first of a series of news features that can be accessed from this page, this series includes historical background, legislation, pro-and-con essays, and surveys of public opinion.

GUN CONTROL ADVOCACY (GENERAL INFORMATION)

This section presents works that take a definite position in favor of gun control but present a variety of arguments or address a variety of issues. Works that focus on particular legislation will be found under "Laws and Legislation"; works that rely on scientific surveys or statistics will be found under "Studies and Surveys."

BOOKS

Anderson, Jack. *Inside the NRA: Armed and Dangerous, An Exposé.* Beverly Hills, Calif.: Dove Books, 1996. Takes on the National Rifle Association, which prize-winning investigative reporter Jack Anderson believes has become an extremist group that lobbies against reasonable gun control measures.

Clise, Michele Durkson, and Marsha Burns (illustrator). *Stop the Violence Please.* Seattle: Allied Arts Foundation and University of Washington Press, 1994. For young readers. The book begins with a tragic gun accident and then gives facts about youths and gun violence and suggests steps young people and parents can take to reduce it. It includes a list of books, films, and organizations.

Diaz, Tom. *Making a Killing: The Business of Guns in America.* New York: New Press, 1999. Attacks the gun industry for irresponsibility in the manufacture and marketing of its products and advocates a legal strategy similar to that successfully used against the tobacco industry.

Landau, Elaine. *Armed America: The Status of Gun Control.* Julian Messner, 1991. Uses anecdotes about crime and violence and the arming of the United States to build a case for gun control.

Larson, Eric. *Lethal Passage: The Story of a Gun.* New York: Vintage Books, 1995. Works backward from a 1988 murder rampage by a disturbed teenager to unravel how the weapon used was obtained by the shooter.

The book exposes irresponsible practices of the gun industry, resulting in a powerful argument for gun control.

ARTICLES AND PAPERS

"An Outrage That Will Last: The Public Has Had Its Fill of Politicians Who Won't Touch the Gun Problem." *Time*, vol. 153, May 10, 1999, p. 35. Argues that the Littleton shootings have led to a new resolve for gun control that can be seized by Democratic presidential candidates such as Al Gore. The article argues for age limits for gun ownership, registration, a ban on semiautomatic weapons, and requirements for trigger locks.

Adler, Karl P. "Firearm Violence and Public Health: Limiting the Availability of Guns." *JAMA, The Journal of the American Medical Association*, vol. 271, April 27, 1994, pp. 1281–1282. Argues that firearm violence "has reached epidemic proportions in this country and is now a public health emergency." Adler recommends a variety of tax, gun control, and gun education measures.

Bogus, Carl T. "NRA: Money, Firepower, and Fear." *Tikkun*, January/February 1994, pp. 79ff. Autobiographical article that tells the story of a prominent attorney who became a convert to the cause of gun control after he was shot by a disturbed client. At first he tries to mediate between gun control supporters and the NRA, but he concludes that gun supporters are intransigent and that only a massive political mobilization of gun control advocates will achieve the necessary objective of restricting guns to only a few categories of people.

Drinan, Robert F. "America Needs Gun Control If It Is to Call Itself a 'Civilized Society.'" *National Catholic Reporter*, vol. 27, May 24, 1991, p. 11. A passionate moral argument for gun control from noted liberal Catholic priest and social commentator Robert Drinan.

Keller, Barbara L. "Frontiersmen Are History." *Newsweek*, August 16, 1993, p. 10. Recounts a break-in at the author's home and her decision not to buy a gun for self-defense. Keller argues that Americans need to abandon the frontier mentality and accept a ban on assault weapons and strict controls on other firearms.

Kelley, Ken. "Surgeon General's Warning: Guns Are Hazardous to Your Health." *Mother Jones*, vol. 19, January–February 1994, p. 55. Interview with Surgeon General Joycelyn Elders. She says that guns are a major health issue and that they are too accessible; she attacks the NRA. Elders, supports a tax to make guns less affordable, to issue safety warnings on guns, and to enforce training requirements for gun owners.

Sugarmann, Josh. "Reverse Fire: The Brady Bill Won't Break the Sick Hold Guns Have on America. It's Time for Tougher Measures." *Mother Jones*, vol. 19, January–February 1994, pp. 36ff. Argues that halfway measures such as the Brady Bill with its background check and waiting period won't really stop violence. The government should ban the new, deadlier types of guns (especially handguns and assault weapons) that are creating a serious public health problem. This would be in keeping with the way other dangerous products are regulated.

INTERNET DOCUMENTS

Center to Prevent Handgun Violence. "ProjectLifeline: Health Professionals Educating the Public About Handgun Violence." Available online. URL: http://www.handguncontrol.org/protecting/D3/d3prlife.htm. Updated on February 14, 1999. Describes a program cosponsored by Handgun Epidemic Lowering Plan (HELP) Network and Physicians for Social Responsibility. Its purpose is to mobilize health professionals to provide public education and work for preventative measures for reducing handgun violence.

Handgun Control, Inc. "State Organizations and Other Links." Available online. URL: http://www.handguncontrol.org/action.asp. Updated on June 17, 1999. Provides links to national, state, and local gun control and gun violence prevention groups.

GUN RIGHTS ADVOCACY (GENERAL INFORMATION)

This section presents works that take a definite position in favor of gun rights (and thus against gun control) but presents a variety of arguments or addresses a variety of issues. Works that focus on particular legislation will be found under "Laws and Legislation"; works that rely on scientific surveys or statistics will be found under "Studies and Surveys."

BOOKS

Gottlieb, Alan M. *Gun Rights Fact Book.* Bellevue, Wash.: Merril Press, 1988. A guide to federal and state firearms laws and gun-related issues from a pro-gun viewpoint. Succinct, but some facts relating to laws may be outdated.

———. *Politically Correct Guns: Please Don't Rob or Kill Me.* Bellevue, Wash.: Merril Press, 1996. Takes on the gun control advocates by deploying humor and sarcasm but also provides a useful (though one-sided) overview. Gottlieb is chairman of the Citizens Committee for the Right to Keep and Bear Arms.

———. *The Rights of Gun Owners: A Second Amendment Foundation Handbook.* Bellevue, Wash.: Merril Press, 1991. A reference and advocacy handbook for gun rights activists.

Hornberger, Jacob G., and Richard M. Ebeling, ed. *The Tyranny of Gun Control.* Fairfax, Va.: Future of Freedom Foundation, 1997. A collection of essays opposing gun control; includes philosophical discussion of the right to armed self-defense from a libertarian standpoint.

Kates, Don B., with John K. Lattimer and James R. Bowen. *The Great American Gun Debate.* San Francisco: Pacific Research Institute for Public Policy, 1997. Discusses all aspects of the gun debate including defensive gun use, guns as a public health problem, media bias in coverage of gun issues, and the Second Amendment and the philosophy of self-defense. Generally, the book has a pro gun rights perspective.

LaPierre, Wayne R. *Guns, Crime, and Freedom.* Washington, D.C.: Regnery Publishing, 1994. A vigorous defense of gun rights by the CEO of the National Rifle Association; emphasizes the constitutional right to bear arms, on the one hand, and the ineffectiveness of gun control against criminals, on the other.

Mack, Richard I., and Timothy Robert Walters. *From My Cold Dead Fingers: Why America Needs Guns.* Safford, Ariz.: Rawhide Western Publishing, 1994. Presents an unabashed case for gun rights.

Quigley, Paxton. *Armed & Female.* New York: E. P. Dutton, 1989. A combination of gun advocacy and a "how to" manual for women who want to obtain a gun for self-defense. Quigley covers both practical and legal considerations for gun use and includes real-life accounts of crime incidents to illustrate tactical problems.

Schulman, J. Neil. *Self Control, Not Gun Control.* Santa Monica, Calif.: Synapse-Centurion, 1995. Presents a forceful pro-gun viewpoint based on both philosophical arguments for self-defense rights and practical arguments against the effectiveness of proposed gun control measures.

———. *Stopping Power: Why 70 Million Americans Own Guns.* Santa Monica, Calif.: Synapse-Centurion, 1994. Similar to the preceding book; a gun advocacy book that attempts to confront the gun control advocates head on.

Simkin, Jay, Aaron S. Zelman, and Alan M. Rice. *Lethal Laws: "Gun Control" Is the Key to Genocide.* Milwaukee, Wisc.: Jews for the Preservation of Firearms Ownership, 1994. Argues that gun control has been a key step in the process of mass murder conducted by the Nazis, Soviets, and other dictatorships of the 20th century. The authors claim that the drafters of U.S. gun laws adopted much of their language from Nazi gun laws.

Tonso, William R., ed., and the Second Amendment Foundation. *The Gun Culture and Its Enemies*. Bellevue, Wash.: Merril Press, 1990. Presents two collections of essays. The first part deals with the gun culture that has developed around the use of guns in many parts of the United States. The second part deals with persons and groups that are determined to destroy, or at least marginalize, the gun culture.

ARTICLES AND PAPERS

Hornberger, Jacob G. "Gun Control, Patriotism, and Civil Disobedience." *Freedom Daily*, 1991, n.p. in Hornberger, Jacob G., ed. *The Tyranny of Gun Control*. (Fairfax, Va.: Future of Freedom Foundation, 1997. Also available online. URL: http://www.fff.org/freedom/0591a.htm. Downloaded on November 8, 1999. Asserts that resistance to gun control is an aspect of the civil disobedience that is often needed to preserve liberty against government encroachment.

Polsby, Daniel D. "The False Promise of Gun Control." *Atlantic Monthly*, March 1994, n.p. Argues that gun control laws don't work and actually increase the disadvantage between law-abiding citizens and criminals. Social problems such as poor education, lack of jobs, and broken families, rather than guns, are the root cause of crime that must be addressed.

Snyder, Jeff. "An Argument for Assault Weapons." *Insight on the News*, vol. 10, October 3, 1994, pp. 34ff. Argues against the Clinton administration's claim that assault weapons should not be allowed to citizens because they have become the "weapon of choice for criminals." The actions of criminals should not constrain the rights of citizens, and the very fact police also use such weapons belies the argument that they are of no use for self-defense.

Wollstein, Jarret. "Will You Be Safer If Guns Are Banned?" *Freedom Daily*, July and August 1994 n.p., in Hornberger, Jacob G. *The Tyranny of Gun Control*. Fairfax, Va.: Future of Freedom Foundation, 1997. Also available online. URL: http://www.fff.org/freedom/0794c.htm and http://www.fff.org/freedom/0894c.htm. Both pages downloaded on November 8, 1999. Marshals evidence that the availability of guns is not the key factor in the increase in violent crime, that armed self-defense works in most cases, and that gun laws only hurt potential crime victims.

Wright, James D. "Ten Essential Observations on Guns in America." *Society*, vol. 32, March–April 1995, pp. 63ff. Spells out the facts and factors that must be understood in order to address the problem of gun violence. Because guns are misused by a small, criminally inclined minority, measures that mainly address legal gun sales and use are unlikely to affect crime very much. The gun culture's point of view is not bizarre and deserves some respect.

INTERNET DOCUMENTS

Botsford, David. "The Case Against Gun Control." Available online. URL: http://www.netside.com/~lcoble/2ndamend/control.txt. Posted on April 17, 1997. A historical and philosophical essay on individuals, weapons ownership, and the history of gun regulation from a strongly pro gun rights viewpoint.

Laughlin, Mark A. "The Philosophy in Defense of Firearms." Available online. URL: http://www.eoffshore.com/root/pofad.html. Updated on August 5, 1999. A systematic philosophical and historical argument in defense of gun rights that is based on Ayn Rand's philosophy of objectivism.

National Rifle Association. Institute for Legal Action. "The War Against Handguns." Available online. URL: http://nraila.org/research/19990729-HandGuns-001.html. Downloaded on June 11, 1999. Summarizes statistics and arguments against handgun control and discusses legal cases and attacks strategies of handgun control groups.

Polsby, Daniel D., and Dennis Brennen. "Taking Aim at Gun Control." Available online. URL: http://www.vixpy.demon.co.uk/gun/articles/GCPS.HTM. Posted on October 30, 1995. Analyzes gun-related issues such as whether gun owners are more violent than the general population, the true relationship between perpetrators and victims of homicide, and the utility of waiting periods and laws targeting drive-by shootings. The site presents what it calls 10 "myths" favored by gun control advocates, reviews the effects of existing gun control laws, and challenges studies supporting gun control.

LEGAL ISSUES

This section covers legal issues that underlie the gun control debate, such as the meaning of the Second Amendment and the applicability of tort law (theories of liability) to firearms manufacturers.

BOOKS

Carmer, Clayton E. *For the Defense of Themselves and the State: The Original Intent and Judicial Interpretation of the Right to Keep and Bear Arms.* Westport, Conn.: Praeger Publishers, 1994. Explores the conflict between the original intent of the Second Amendment, well established by scholarship as conferring an individual right to keep and bear arms, and the judicial interpretation of the Supreme Court and most other courts that have preferred a collectivist interpretation and that have avoided a direct confrontation with the language of the Constitution.

Halbrook, Stephen P. *That Every Man be Armed: The Evolution of a Constitutional Right.* Albuquerque, N.M.: University of New Mexico Press, 1984. Traces the right to bear arms through common law, the colonial experience, and the framers of the U.S. Constitution. Continues with survey of cases and interpretations in the post–Civil War period and later, as well as Supreme Court decisions.

———. *Freedmen, the Fourteenth Amendment, and the Right to Bear Arms, 1866–1876.* Westport, Conn.: Praeger, 1998. Discusses the gun laws passed to disarm blacks in the South and the failure to use the Fourteenth Amendment to guarantee the rights of these citizens, and the consequences for the modern gun control issue.

Kates, Don B. *Handgun Prohibition and the Original Meaning of the Second Amendment.* Bellevue, Wash.: Second Amendment Foundation, 1984. Discusses whether the prohibition of handguns (as opposed to rifles and other weapons of a more military application) is compatible with the original understanding of the Second Amendment.

Kruschke, Earl R. *The Right to Keep and Bear Arms: A Continuing American Dilemma.* Springfield, Ill.: Thomas, 1985. Explores the legal history of firearms law and cases in the United States.

Malcolm, Joyce Lee. *To Keep and Bear Arms: The Origins of an Anglo-American Right.* Cambridge, Mass.: Harvard University Press, 1994. Explores the evolution of the right to keep and bear arms in the English common law and colonial experience. Malcolm concludes that the Second Amendment, arising out of that tradition, was intended to guarantee an individual right.

Rand, Kristen. *Lawyers, Guns, and Money: The Impact of Tort Restrictions on Firearms Safety and Gun Control.* Washington, D.C.: Violence Policy Center and Public Citizen, 1996. Discusses the effects of civil court decisions in shaping the practices of the firearms industry, including the use of safety devices, as well as the impact on the overall gun control movement.

ARTICLES AND PAPERS

Allen, Mike. "Colt's to Curtail Sale of Handguns, Hoping to Limit Liability." *New York Times.* URL: http://www.nytimes.com/library/national/101199ct-colt.html. Posted on October 11, 1999. Reports that Colt, one of America's oldest gun manufacturers, is pulling out of the consumer gun market and will concentrate on manufacturing military weapons. A senior executive is quoted as saying that fear of future liability judgments is making it very hard for firearms manufacturers to obtain financing from lenders.

Arrow, Paul S. "Kelley v. R.G. Industries: California Caught in the Crossfire." *Southwestern University Law Review*, vol. 17, 1988, n.p. Argues that the court in the Kelley case should not have required that the gun in question have an actual defect in its design before determining whether it posed an excessive or unreasonable risk.

Barrett, Paul M. "Jumping the Gun? Attacks on Firearms Echo Earlier Assaults on Tobacco Industry; But Contrasts Are Big, Too; No Leaked Memos Yet, Nor Same Sums at Stake; 'Cigarettes Can Only Kill You.'" *The Wall Street Journal*, March 12, 1999, p. A1. Suggests that although comparing gun makers to tobacco companies may be good public relations strategy, there are many key differences between the two industries and the outcome of the legal assault is not certain.

Batey, Robert. "Techniques of Strict Construction: The Supreme Court and the Gun Control Act of 1968." *American Journal of Criminal Law*, vol. 13, Winter 1986, n.p. Discusses Supreme Court cases involving the Gun Control Act of 1968, pointing out ways that a case for reasonable doubt can be construed from the language, intent, or history of the law.

Bogus, Carl T. "Pistols, Politics, and Products Liability." *University of Cincinnati Law Review*, vol. 59, Spring 1991, n.p. Discusses the early approach of courts to questions of product liability for firearms. Suggests that courts have been remarkably reluctant to apply strict liability standards to guns, possibly because judges are afraid that gun groups would then push for tort reform.

———. "Race, Riots, and Guns." *Southern California Law Review*, vol. 66, May 1993, n.p. Counters arguments by gun rights advocates that the history of gun control is bound up with the use of gun laws to suppress minorities. Bogus suggests that the Second Amendment and other gun rights statements might be themselves construed as a means for controlling minorities and that at any rate the connection between race and violence is very complex.

Bowen, Scott. "Gunmakers on Trial." *Outdoor Life*, vol. 203, May 1999, p. 22. Reports on the February 1999 Brooklyn court verdict (*Hamilton v. Accu-Tek*) that held some gun makers liable for negligent marketing, as well as other cases and upcoming litigation.

Boyer, Peter J. "Big Guns." *The New Yorker*, vol. 75, May 17, 1999, pp. 54ff. Describes the efforts of Dennis Henigan and the Castano group of lawyers who, fresh from their victory over Big Tobacco, are organizing the legal assault on the firearms industry. They believe that public reaction to the Littleton shootings may aid their cause considerably.

Annotated Bibliography

Brazil, Jeff, and Steve Berry. "Federal Safety Law Targets 15,000 Items, But Not Guns." *Los Angeles Times*, vol. 117, February 1, 1998, p. A1. Points out the fact, surprising to many people, that guns are not subject to the federal regulations governing most products. The authors explain the legal and political history that led to this situation.

Brown, Wendy. "Guns, Cowboys, Philadelphia Mayors, and Civic Republicanism: On Sanford Levinson's 'The Embarrassing Second Amendment.'" *Yale Law Journal*, vol. 99, December 1989, pp. 661–667. A rebuttal to Levinson's influential article that suggested that the Second Amendment needs to be taken seriously as a guarantee of an individual right to keep and bear arms. Brown criticizes Levinson's appeal to "republicanism" in the arming of the individual against the state. She also criticizes the image of the armed citizen, noting that it is, from the feminist viewpoint, an armed male.

Burger, Warren E. "The Right to Bear Arms." *Parade Magazine*, January 14, 1990, n.p. Recounts the history of the militia in America and argues that the Second Amendment, although a valid expression of the framers' concerns, is no longer relevant. Burger (the renowned retired Supreme Court justice) thus believes that the keeping and bearing of arms should be subject to the same sorts of regulations as, for example, the owning and driving of automobiles. He considers, though, that screening, licensing, and identification of gun owners and their firearms are appropriate.

Carney, Dan. "Brady Decision Reflects Effort to Curb Congress' Authority." *Congressional Quarterly Weekly Report*, vol. 55, June 28, 1997, p. 1524. Explains the U.S. Supreme Court decision *Printz v. U.S.*, where the court struck down the part of the Brady Bill that required local sheriffs to perform background checks on gun purchasers. The justices ruled that the provision extended beyond Congress's power to regulate interstate commerce.

Chiang, Harriet, and Kevin Fagan. "Gunmakers Can Be Sued by Victims." *San Francisco Chronicle*, September 30, 1999, p. A1, A19. Reports that a California state court of appeal has, for the first time in American legal history, ruled that a gunmaker can be held liable for the criminal use of its products. The case arose from a 1993 mass shooting in a San Francisco office building.

Cohen, Adam. "When There's Smoke" *Time*, vol. 153, February 22, 1999, p. 65. Describes the results of a Brooklyn lawsuit that found some gun makers liable for shootings. Plaintiffs hailed the decision as a breakthrough in holding the gun manufacturers liable, although defendants pointed to the fact the jury cleared 10 of 25 defendants and found no damages against six others. Although the outcome of future cases remains uncertain, gun makers may now be themselves under the gun.

Cole, Thomas B., and Franklin E. Zimring. "On Law and Firearms." *JAMA, The Journal of the American Medical Association,* vol. 275, June 12, 1996, p. 1709. Interviews legal scholar Franklin E. Zimring, who explains that the new emphasis on firearms as a public health issue is encouraging legal scholars to reexamine the role of firearms and approaches to risk reduction.

Colford, Stephen W. "Suit Targets TEC-9 Gun Ad Claims." *Advertising Age,* vol. 65, July 11, 1994, p. 14. Describes a lawsuit filed by victims of a San Francisco high-rise shooting spree against IntraTec, the makers of the Tec-9 assault pistol. The most damning evidence may be advertising that touts the weapon's resistance to fingerprints.

Cottrol, Robert J., and Raymond T. Diamond. "The Second Amendment: Toward an Afro-Americanist Reconsideration." *Georgetown Law Journal,* vol. 809, December 1991, pp. 309–361. Suggests that while African-American intellectuals have generally followed the pro-gun control stance of modern liberals, the authors suggest that in the light of the historical failure of the government to protect African Americans, the Second Amendment's concept of an armed citizenry may still be valid.

"D.C. Law Makes Innocent Pay For Crime." *American Rifleman,* vol. 140, May 1992, p. 63. Criticizes a new District of Columbia ordinance that holds gun makers liable for direct and indirect damages caused by misuse of their products, without requiring that the product actually have any defects.

"Does the Brady Bill Violate States' Rights?" *CQ Researcher,* vol. 6, September 13, 1996, p. 809. Gives pro and con arguments on whether the Brady Bill violates states' rights in imposing an unfunded mandate to perform background checks. (The Supreme Court later overturned this provision on interstate commerce grounds.)

Dowlut, Robert. "Federal and State Guarantees to Arms." *Dayton Law Review,* vol. 15, 1989, pp. 59–89. Suggests that the right to keep and bear arms be treated in a way similar to other fundamental rights such as freedom of speech. This would mean that there can be narrowly tailored restrictions, such as prohibiting the bringing of arms into public buildings, but not the peaceful bearing of arms at home or in the street. Dowlut criticizes the courts' ignorance of the Second Amendment and argues that an armed populace is still important to a free society.

Ehrman, Keith A., and Dennis A. Henigan. "The Second Amendment in the Twentieth Century: Have You Seen Your Militia Lately?" *University of Dayton Law Review,* vol. 15, 1989, pp. 5–58. Argues that the Second Amendment guarantees an individual right to keep and bear arms only to the extent it is necessary for the maintenance of an effective militia. Because the federally directed National Guard has replaced the old state militias, it is no longer necessary for private individuals to have firearms, and there is no obstacle to prohibiting them.

Annotated Bibliography

Fedarko, Kevin. "A Gun Ban Is Shot Down." *Time*, vol. 145, May 8, 1995, p. 85. Describes the Supreme Court decision *U.S. v. Lopez*, where the justices overturned the Gun Free Schools law, saying that the federal government's power to regulate interstate commerce did not extend to banning guns around schools.

"Gun Decision Puts a Check on Federal Authority." *Congressional Quarterly Weekly Report*, vol. 53, April 29, 1995, pp. 119ff. Gives excerpts from the *U.S. v. Lopez* decision, in which the Supreme Court rules that the Gun Free School Zones Act was an impermissible use of the power of Congress to regulate interstate commerce.

Halbrook, Stephen P. "To Keep and Bear Their Private Arms: The Adoption of the Second Amendment 1787–1791." *Northern Kentucky Law Review*, vol. 10, no. 1, 1982, n.p. Argues that for the framers of the Bill of Rights, the term *the people* as used in the Second Amendment means the same thing as it does in the First, Fourth, Ninth, and Tenth amendments—"each and every free person."

Henigan, Dennis, and Bob Barr. "Symposium [on gun lawsuits]." *Insight on the News*, vol. 15, April 26, 1999, p. 24. A debate by Dennis Henigan, director of the Legal Action Project of the Center to Prevent Handgun Violence and pro-gun Congressman Bob Barr. Henigan describes the pioneering suits and says they are justified by the damage guns do to society and the costs imposed on taxpayers and are in accordance with basic principles of tort law such as the obligation not to create hazardous products. Barr, who is sponsoring federal legislation to ban such suits, argues that they amount to an assault on constitutional rights that would not be tolerated if similar arguments had been raised against books that can contain harmful ideas but are protected by the First Amendment.

Hewitt, Bill. "Retribution: Not Forgiving or Forgetting, a Shooting Victim's Family Takes a Pair of Gunmakers to Court." *People Weekly*, vol. 49, March 23, 1998, pp. 81ff. Reports on the lawsuit filed by the family of gun victim Aaron Halberstam against Wayne and Sylvia Daniel, the makers of the Cobray semiautomatic pistol. The gun is sold as a mail-order kit (except for one part); the makers are accused of inflammatory advertising ("the Drug Lord's choice") and negligent marketing and distribution. (The jury later found the gun maker not to be liable.)

Horwitz, Joshua M. "Kelley v. R.G. Industries, Inc.: A Cause of Action for Assault Weapons." *University of Dayton Law Review*, vol. 15, 1989, pp. 125–139. Argues that the legal theory used against manufacturers of Saturday night specials (cheap, easily concealable handguns) could also be applied to makers of assault weapons. In both cases the weapons are not designed for traditional sporting uses, and their design makes them unreasonably dangerous.

"John Coale's Next Case." *The Economist (U.S.)*, vol. 350, February 27, 1999, p. 32. Describes the efforts of attorney John Coale to organize legal action against gun makers. Coale has won a large judgment on behalf of victims of Attention Deficit Disorder, successfully sued Ford for defects in its school buses, and played a large part in the record-breaking state tobacco settlement. Now he's used his media contacts to help turn public attention to negligent marketing by gun companies—the main grounds for the upcoming civil trials.

Jost, Kenneth. "The States and Federalism; Should More Power Be Shifted to the States?" *CQ Researcher*, vol. 6, September 13, 1996, pp. 795ff. Places the challenge of local sheriffs to the Brady Bill in the context of a resurgent movement toward "federalism" or recognition of states' rights.

Kinsley, Michael. "Second Thoughts." *The New Republic*, vol. 202, February 26, 1990, p. 4. Argues that the Second Amendment remains disturbing for thoughtful liberals, despite their advocacy for gun control. Liberals would never accept for the First Amendment the narrow parsing they are willing to mete out to the Second, while conservatives who defend gun rights often disregard freedom of speech. Kinsley favorably reviews Don Kates's arguments for a right to keep and bear arms subject to certain limitations.

Lee, Henry K. "Gunmaker Not at Fault in Slaying, Jury Says." *San Francisco Chronicle*, November 17, 1998, pp. A17, A19. Reports the finding of a Berkeley, California, jury that the Beretta company was not liable for a teenager's accidental shooting. In the case *Dix v. Beretta*, the plaintiff had argued that the gun lacked reasonable safety features, and the gun company argued that they had provided adequate safety warnings.

Lenzi, John C. "The Second Amendment—A Decade in Review." *American Rifleman*, vol. 138, March 1990, p. 56. Summarizes Second Amendment jurisprudence and scholarship during the 1980s from a gun rights point of view.

Levin, Myron. "Legal Claims Get Costly for Maker of Cheap Handguns." *Los Angeles Times*, vol. 116, December 27, 1997, p. A1. Reports that Lorcin Engineering, a major maker of Saturday night specials, has filed for bankruptcy, largely because it faces $4 million or more in claims for personal injury or wrongful death arising from use of its products.

Levinson, Sanford. "The Embarrassing Second Amendment." *Yale Law Journal*, vol. 99, 1989, pp. 637–659. Signals a major shift of scholarship from the collectivist to the individualist interpretation of the Second Amendment. Levinson argues that the right to keep and bear arms should be acknowledged, even though, like many other fundamental social rights, it can have considerable costs.

Lott, John R. Jr., "Gun Shy: Cities Turn from Regulation to Litigation in their Campaign Against Guns." *National Review*, December 21, 1998, p. 46. Reports that the success of states in suing tobacco companies has inspired a similar effort by cities against gun makers. But unlike tobacco companies, gun makers can point to a social benefit: evidence showing that guns have also saved lives and money by deterring criminals.

Ma, Kenneth. "Crusading to Bring Big Gun Makers to Justice." *The Chronicle of Higher Education*, vol. 45, March 19, 1999, p. A10. Describes efforts by David Kairys, a law professor at Templeton University, to develop legal theories for suing gun makers. These include assessing the full costs of gun killings and accidents to cities in the form of police and medical services and showing that gun makers are marketing their product in a reckless or negligent manner, such as by focusing on high crime areas where their products are most likely to be abused.

Malcolm, Joyce Lee. "The Right of the People to Keep and Bear Arms: The Common Law Tradition." *Hastings Constitutional Law Quarterly*, Winter 1983, pp. 313–314. Argues that the Second Amendment must be understood in terms of how the English common law was understood by the Constitution's framers. This law saw the militia as springing from all citizens and was kept strong by maintaining their individual right to keep and bear arms.

McArdle, Elaine. "Lawyers, Guns, and Money: Firearms Litigation Ready to Explode." *Lawyers' Weekly USA.* November 30, 1998. Reports on the first wave of class action suits against gun makers, the legal strategies, and the confidence of proponents that they are on the winning side.

McClurg, Andrew J. "Handguns as Products Unreasonably Dangerous Per Se." *University of Arkansas at Little Rock Law Journal*, vol. 13, Summer 1991, n.p. Argues that gun makers should be held strictly liable for firearms injuries, primarily because of the destructiveness of firearms. (This article was presented as a debate with Philip D. Oliver—see Oliver's article below.)

Metaksa, Tanya K. "Constitutional Quake Rocks California Gun Ban." *American Rifleman*, vol. 146, May 1998, p. 44. Reports on a California district court decision that prevents the state attorney general from adding new firearms to the state assault weapons ban. The court said the existing procedure was arbitrary and failed to provide due process.

Metaksa, Tanya K., and Dennis A. Henigan. "At Issue: Does the Second Amendment Guarantee an Individual Right to Keep and Bear Arms?" *CQ Researcher*, vol. 7, December 19, 1997, p. 1121. A debate between the NRA's chief lobbyist and a leading pro gun control litigator over whether the Second Amendment guarantees an individual right to bear arms, or only the right of the state to keep a militia. The authors give opposing citations from scholars of the "individualist" camp and former Chief

Justice Warren Burger, who considered statements made by the NRA about the Second Amendment to be deceptive.

Murray, Frank J. "Gun Makers Tough Target." *Insight on the News*, vol. 15, April 26, 1999, p. 38. Reports that the coordination of large-scale lawsuits against gun makers by cities and others has resulted in a counterattack by the NRA and gun makers, who are pushing for state bills that would limit liability. Nevertheless, the industry remains vulnerable and the future is uncertain.

Murray, Frank J., and George Archibald. "Constitution Scholars Divided over Issues of Self-Defense." *Insight on the News*, vol. 11, May 29, 1995, p. 32. Discusses the applicability of constitutional protections to privately organized militias, such as those that came into prominence in the late 1980s and early 1990s. The Clinton administration and many scholars say that the "well-regulated militia" of the Second Amendment refers only to official organizations such as the National Guard. However, other scholars and some court decisions support the right of individuals to keep and bear arms, and the First Amendment allows people to "peacefully assemble" for redress of grievances.

Newbart, Dave. "Made to Kill." *Scholastic Update*, vol. 131, April 12, 1999, p. 4. Describes the arguments being used in negligence suits against gun makers. Written for young people, but is a good, detailed introduction suitable for all readers.

"Ohio Judge Dismisses Gun Suit." Associated Press, in *San Francisco Chronicle*, October 8, 1999, p. A5. Reports that an Ohio judge has dismissed one of the growing wave of lawsuits brought against gun manufacturers by states and municipalities. The judge ruled that the legislature, not the court was the proper body for regulating gun design, and that the risks of gun usage had not been concealed by manufacturers.

Oliver, Philip D. "Rejecting the 'Whipping-Boy' Approach to Tort Law: Well-Made Handguns are not Defective Products." *University of Arkansas at Little Rock Law Journal*, vol. 14, Fall 1991, n.p. Response to an article by Andrew McClurg (see above). Oliver argues that well-made handguns are neither defective nor unreasonably dangerous and that attempting to hold gun makers liable distorts basic principles of tort law.

Olson, Walter. "Firing Squad." *Reason*, vol. 31, May 1999, p. 58. Warns that negligence suits against gun makers may erode the right to obtain firearms by forcing restrictions. A major court victory in any state could have the effect of "legislating" for all. Conservatives may have to suspend their belief in federalism and support national legislation to protect gun makers from lawsuits.

Overstreet, Mark H. "Warren Burger vs. The Founding Fathers." *American Rifleman*, vol. 140, February 1992, p. 53. Criticizes statements by former

Chief Justice Warren Burger, who said that the Second Amendment referred only to the collective right to maintain an organized militia.

Reynolds, Glenn Harlan. "A Critical Guide to the Second Amendment." *Tennessee Law Review*, vol. 62, Spring 1995, pp. 461ff. Asserts that a "standard model" of interpreting the Second Amendment has emerged from recent scholarship. In this model, the right to keep and bear arms is an individual right but as such is subject to limitations such as the prohibition of weapons of mass destruction. Reynolds also reflects on the difference between the scholarly consensus and the views that seem to dominate the popular media.

Rosen, Jeffrey. "Dual Sovereigns: Who Shall Rule—Congress or the Court?" *The New Republic*, vol. 217, July 28, 1997, p. 16. Reports on recent Supreme Court decisions (such as the *Lopez* decision, which overturned the Gun Free School Zones Act and part of the Brady Law) that seem to be giving greater weight to state sovereignty. Rosen argues that the conservative majority on the court may be applying the same sort of "judicial activism" that conservatives generally oppose when employed by liberals. The effects of any attempt to restore something like the pre Civil War balance between federal and state powers are likely to be subtle and complex, with unintended consequences.

Schulz, Max. "Smoking Guns: A Big-City Mayor Trains His Sights on Weapon Makers." *Reason*, vol. 30, July 1998, pp. 56ff. Reports on Philadelphia mayor Ed Rendell's organization of a legal campaign against gun makers, in which he is seeking an effective legal theory to overcome the lack of direct causation between the manufacture and misuse of a firearm. Rendell's style combines tough-talking conservative rhetoric about crime and liberal "feel-good" language.

Shalhope, Robert E. "The Ideological Origins of the Second Amendment." *Journal of American History*, vol. 69, 1982, pp. 613–614. Acknowledges that the framers of the Second Amendment intended to guarantee an individual right to keep and bear arms while suggesting that the destructiveness of modern weapons and the considerable changes in social organization may still be powerful arguments for gun control.

Shulman, J. Neil. "The Text of the Second Amendment." *Journal on Firearms and Public Policy*, Summer 1992, n.p. The author asked Roy Copperud, an expert on English grammar, to interpret the language of the Second Amendment. Copperud concludes that the amendment specifies a preexisting, unconditional right of the people. The "militia clause" may describe the reason for guaranteeing the right, but the right does not depend on the existence of (or membership in) the militia.

Sprigman, Chris. "This is Not a Well-Regulated Militia." *Open Forum*, Winter 1994, n.p. Reviews Supreme Court cases and concludes that the

Court has interpreted the Second Amendment as protecting state militias, not as an individual right to bear arms. Sprigman cites *United States v. Miller* (1939) and argues that the militia concept is probably not relevant to modern America.

Stevens, Susan M. "Kelley v. R.G. Industries: When Hard Cases Make Good Law." *Maryland Law Review*, vol. 46, Winter 1987, n.p. Argues that the court in the *Kelley* case was justified in extending liability law to cover a product (cheap handguns) that the legislature had concluded serves no socially useful purpose. The court was making legitimate social policy in cooperation with the legislature, and the policy may well save lives by curtailing the distribution of dangerous weapons.

"Supreme Court Cases of Gun Owner Interests." *American Rifleman*, vol. 146, September 1998, p. 24. Summarizes aspects of Supreme Court rulings that may affect gun owners, such as the question of what it means to "willfully" violate a law and the definition of "carrying" a weapon.

"Taking Aim." *Current Events*, vol. 98, February 26, 1999, p. 1. Describes the upcoming legal "shoot-out" between a group of cities and major gun manufacturers. The cities are taking a legal approach similar to that used against tobacco companies. The NRA is mobilizing and pressuring legislatures and Congress to pass laws banning such suits.

U.S. Congress. Committee on the Judiciary. Subcommittee on the Washington, D.C. [Hearings], U.S. G.P.O., 1982. Transcript of Congressional hearings on the Second Amendment and the right to keep and bear arms. These hearings are of historical importance as they represent ascendancy of a generally conservative (or libertarian) viewpoint that supports the individual rights interpretation of the Second Amendment.

Weatherup, Roy G. "Standing Armies and Armed Citizens: An Historical Analysis of the Second Amendment." *Hastings Constitutional Law Quarterly*, Fall 1975, pp. 1000–1001. Argues that the sole effect of the Second Amendment is collective, affirming the right of the states to maintain National Guard units and confers no individual right to keep and bear arms.

INTERNET DOCUMENTS

Center to Prevent Handgun Violence. Legal Action Project. "Selected Editorials" Available online. URL: http://www.handguncontrol.org/. Downloaded on July 8, 1999. A selection of recent editorials, often commenting on proposed gun legislation and current litigation.

Fezell, Howard. "2nd Amendment Home Page." Available online. URL: http://www.2ndamendment.net/. Updated on July 18, 1999. Resources and essays by the author on the Second Amendment from an individual rights point of view.

Glaberson, William. "Right to Bear Arms: A Second Look." Available online. URL: http://www.nytimes.com (search archive). Posted on May 30, 1999. Describes recent trends in legal scholarship that seem to be strengthening the viewpoint that the Second Amendment guarantees an individual right to bear arms. A Texas judge has recently ruled that the Second Amendment does guarantee the right to carry some kinds of weapons. The case is undergoing appeal.

"The Intent of the Second Amendment to the Constitution of the United States of America." Available online. URL: http://www.the-summit-group.com/rec/firearms/quotes.html. Posted on September 20, 1996. Quotes from the framers of the Constitution (and their contemporaries) on the right to keep and bear arms as an exposition of the historical intent of the Second Amendment.

Legal Action Project, Handgun Control, Inc. "Litigation Docket." Available online. URL: http://www.handguncontrol.org/legalaction/dockets/docket.htm. Updated on June 13, 1999. Describes pending litigation in which the Legal Action Project of Handgun Control, Inc., is involved. The site includes class action suits being brought by cities against gun makers.

National Center for Policy Analysis. "NCPA Policy Report No. 223." Available online. URL: http://www.cila.org/NCPA%20Policy%20Report%20No.%20223.htm. Posted in March 1999. Provides arguments in defense of gun manufacturers who are increasingly being sued for negligence. Web site includes sections on the effectiveness of armed citizenry for self-defense and crime reduction, the economic benefits of defense with firearms, legal arguments, and a summary of recent cases.

Policy.com. "Gun Control Under Fire." Available online. URL: http://www.policy.com/issuewk/1999/0329_65/detail398.html. Posted on March 29, 1999. A large collection of links to news and arguments involving the growing number of liability suits filed against gun makers. Gives a good representation of both sides of the issue.

Polsby, Daniel B. "Treating the Second Amendment as Normal Constitutional Law." Available online. URL: http://www.reason.com/ 9603/fe.POLSBY guns.text.html. Posted on December 13, 1997. Explores how the Second Amendment would be applied if it were treated like other "first class" provisions of the Bill of Rights, such as the First Amendment. Polsby suggests that, like speech, the "time, place and manner" of bearing arms could be regulated, but the right itself would have to be respected.

Reynold, Glenn Harlan, and Don B. Kates. "The Second Amendment and States' Rights: A Thought Experiment." Available online. URL: http://www.sirius.com/~gilliams/second.html. Posted on October 27, 1995. Unfolds logical possible consequences of accepting the premise of many gun control advocates that the Second Amendment guarantees only the right of states to have a militia. The resulting possibilities may be surprising: independent state military forces, a different view of the National Guard, and a radically different form of federalism.

Second Amendment Foundation. "Federal Court Upholds Second Amendment as an Individual Right!" Available online. URL: http://www.saf.org/SummEmerson.html. Posted on May 25, 1999. Reports on a startling decision by Judge Sam Cummings of the Northern District of Texas, who dismissed a gun case on Second Amendment grounds, finding that said amendment guaranteed an individual right to keep and bear arms. The decision is sure to be appealed.

Shade, Gary A. "The Right to Keep and Bear Arms: The Legacy of Republicanism vs. Absolutism." Available online. URL: http://www.ideasign.com/chiliast/pdocs/repabso.htm. First published on January 10, 1993. Concludes that history has shown that the right to keep and bear arms is integral to the duties of the citizens of a republic.

"Suing Gun Makers." Available online. URL: http://www.reason.com/bi/guns.html. Updated on July 11, 1999. Summarizes recent developments in suits against gunmakers, with links to organizations involved in the litigation and to articles previously published in *Reason* magazine.

Volokh, Eugene. "Sources on the Second Amendment and Right to Keep and Bear Arms in State Constitutions." Available online. URL: http://www.law.ucla.edu/faculty/volokh/2amteach/sources.htm. Updated on July 7, 1999. Collection of texts, cases, and commentaries relating to the Second Amendment, including provisions in state constitutions and bills of rights. An interesting inclusion is state provisions that are grammatically similar to the Second Amendment in that they have an introductory clause, but that they also refer to such provisions as the freedoms of speech and expression.

LAWS AND LEGISLATION

This section covers discussion of specific gun laws and proposed legislation, as well as the political process and the activities of lobby groups.

BOOKS

Argiriou, Stephen L. *Concealed Handgun Carry.* Noblesville, Ind.: P.O.L.I.C.E. Training Systems, 1998. An illustrated, practical guide to obtaining and legally using a permit to carry a concealed weapon.

Briggs, Doug. *A Matter of Personal Protection: The Weapons and Self-Defense Laws.* 3rd ed. Houston: Beverly Book Co., 1995. Extensive guide to Texas laws on gun ownership and self-defense.

Annotated Bibliography

Bruce, John M., and Clyde Wilcox, editors. *The Changing Politics of Gun Control.* Lanham, Md.: Rowman & Littlefield, 1998. A collection of essays that explores the growing passion on both sides of the gun debate and the changes in political alignment since the wounding of James Brady gave gun control advocates a new focus for their efforts. The book also charts developments in Congress, the state legislatures, and the courts.

Davidson, Osha Ray. *Under Fire: The NRA and the Battle for Gun Control.* Expanded ed. Iowa City: University of Iowa Press, 1998. A balanced, detailed "report from the trenches" detailing the operation of the National Rifle Association. Describes the evolution of the NRA from an organization oriented toward promoting marksmanship to the U.S.'s most powerful gun lobby in battles against gun control proposals in Congress.

Edel, Wilbur. *Gun Control.* Westport, Conn.: Praeger Publication, 1995. A history of the development of gun control laws in the United States.

Thomas, Lee O., and Jeffrey Chamberlain. *Gun Control in New York: A Guide to New York's Firearms and Weapons Laws.* Guilderland, N.Y.: Gunlock Press, 1990. A detailed reference to New York's complicated firearms laws.

United States. Congress. House. Committee on the Judiciary. *Gun Laws and the Need for Self-Defense: Hearing Before the Committee . . .* Washington, D.C.: Government Printing Office, 1996. Hearings on the impact of gun control laws on the ability of people to defend themselves against criminals.

U.S. General Accounting Office. *Gun Control: Implementation of the Brady Handgun Violence Prevention Act.* Washington, D.C.: Goverment Printing Office, 1996. Evaluates the effectiveness of the Brady Law and concludes that the law is of limited effectiveness because it applies only to guns sold by federally licensed dealers, not those sold by private individuals (such as at gun shows). The law also neither provides funds to help local law enforcement officers conduct background checks nor imposes penalties for their failure to do so.

Voit, William K. *Common Elements of State Gun Control Laws.* Lexington, Ky.: States Information Center, Council of State Governments, 1987. A compilation of features found in state firearms legislation. This book is now somewhat outdated.

ARTICLES AND PAPERS

"Al Gore's Lucky Break: Gore's First Weapon Against George W. Bush Is a Freebie from the G.O.P. Can Gun Control Jump-Start His Campaign?" *Time,* vol. 153, June 28, 1999, pp. 38ff. Reports that Republican backpedaling on the gun issue following the Littleton shootings may have given Democratic presidential candidate frontrunner Al Gore a jump start on the 2000 campaign.

Gun Control

Barry, Dan. "An Icon Goes to Washington: Representative Carolyn Mc-Carthy Finds Herself Grappling With the Burden of Her Saintly Image and the Pressure to Become an Ordinary Politician." *The New York Times Magazine,* June 22, 1997, p. 20. Reports on Carolyn McCarthy's adjustment to practical politics as a newly elected member of congress. (After her husband was killed and her son was wounded in a shooting spree, Mc-Carthy became a gun control advocate and congressional candidate.)

Becker, Gary S. "Stiffer Jail Terms Will Make Gunmen More Gun-Shy." *Business Week,* n. 3360, February 28, 1994, p. 18. Argues that high taxes on guns and ammunition will only prevent law-abiding citizens from purchasing guns, while criminals buy most of their guns on the illegal market and pay no tax. However, a study by James Q. Wilson and Richard H. Herrenstein suggests that "add-on" sentences for using a gun in a crime do deter criminals from choosing to carry a gun.

Bovard, James. "The Assault-Weapons Scam." *Freedom Daily,* March and April 1996, in Hornberger, Jacob G. *The Tyranny of Gun Control,* Fairfax, Va.: Future of Freedom Foundation, 1997. Argues that the 1994 ban on assault weapons is poorly written, confusing, arbitrary, and ineffective.

Bowman, Catherine. "Alameda County Moves Against Gun Shows." *San Francisco Chronicle,* July 28, 1999, pp. A1, A16. Reports that Alameda County supervisors approved an ordinance that prohibited people from possessing firearms on county property, in effect banning gun shows from the Alameda County Fairgrounds.

Broadwell, Laura, and Colleen D. Gardephne. "Susan Kenney: Guns Away." *Parenting,* vol. 6, May 1992, p. 24. Describes a crusade launched by Susan Kenney, whose 12-year-old son was killed by a friend's father's gun. She successfully lobbied for a Connecticut law that will punish parents whose children misuse unlocked guns.

Broder, John M. "Clinton to Impose a Ban on 58 Types of Imported Guns; Fresh Blow to the N.R.A.; Assault Weapons Fail to Meet Exemption for Sports Use, Treasury Review Finds." *The New York Times,* vol. 147, April 6, 1998, p. A1. Reports on President Clinton's order that added 58 models of assault weapons to the list of banned imports. The NRA had opposed the "sporting use" criterion as vague and arbitrary.

Bruni, Frank, and James Dao. "Gun-Control Bill Rejected in House in Bi-partisan Vote; Too Much for Some, Too Little for Others After a Fierce Debate." *The New York Times,* June 19, 1999, p. A1. Reports what appeared to be a stalemate in Congress: The House rejected a bill containing gun provisions that had been weakened by gun rights advocates (mainly Republicans). As a result, no gun control laws were able to be passed in 1999.

Bruning, Fred. "Decency, Honor and the Gun Lobby." *Maclean's,* vol. 108, June 12, 1995, p. 9. Reports with approval on former president George Bush's resignation from the NRA after it issued a fund-raising letter that referred to federal agents as "jack-booted thugs." Bruning portrays the NRA as increasingly extreme, taking on characteristics of the radical right-wing militias.

Buckley, Gail Lumet. "The Gun Cult." *America,* vol. 175, October 19, 1996, p. 8. Argues that the NRA represents a quasi-religious "gun cult" and that Catholics should reject religious arguments for gun ownership and instead support gun control efforts.

Buckley, William F., Jr. "Heston to the Rescue." *National Review,* vol. 49, June 2, 1997, pp. 62ff. Suggests that Charlton Heston, newly elected president of the NPA, may be able to improve the image of the beleaguered organization but that the NRA will also need to accept some compromises on gun rights issues.

"Caught in the Cross-Fire: How Gun Control Turned Into a Casualty of the Capital Wars." *Newsweek,* June 28, 1999, p. 31. Describes the outcome of the Spring 1999 battle over gun control in Congress. Rep. John Dingell's compromise proposal, viewed by gun control advocates as a sellout to the NRA gun lobby, dies under fire from both sides. The article suggests that Dingell was motivated by the need to shore up political support in the South and the West, while President Clinton and Vice President Gore have been pushing a national gun control agenda to take advantage of strong overall popular support for gun laws.

Chew, Sally. "Shotgun Wedding." *Lear's,* vol. 6, January 1994, pp. 30ff. Argues that the NRA is using feminist rhetoric to lure women to obtain guns for self-defense and that this is not really in the interests of women.

"Clinton Calls for Quick Passage of Gun Laws." Associated Press in *San Francisco Chronicle,* July 16, 1999, p. A3. Describes President Clinton's appearance before a group of students from Columbine High School, the scene of school shootings in April 1999. The article also reports on students who have organized to lobby for gun control.

Cramer, Clayton E., and David B. Kopel. "'Shall Issue': The New Wave of Concealed Handgun Permit Laws." *Tennessee Law Review,* vol. 62, Spring 1995, pp. 679ff. Describes the movement to reform concealed handgun laws so that permits would be available to all law-abiding citizens rather than issued at the discretion of a sheriff or other official. Considering Florida as a test case, the authors point out that contrary to the prediction of opponents, only a tiny number of permit owners lost their permit later because of a gun-related crime. At the same time, crime rates were reduced considerably.

D'Agnese, Joseph. "Smart Guns Don't Kill Kids." *Discover,* September 1999, pp. 90–93. Describes emerging and proposed technologies for making guns safer. Examples include guns that fire only when they recognize their authorized user by means of fingerprint sensors, magnetic locks, or radio-activated locks. Skeptics are concerned that glitches in oversophisticated systems might cause guns to fire without authorization or failure to fire when needed.

Dao, James. "Congressman's Gun Votes: Consistency or Calculation? Differing Views of a Republican's Choices." *The New York Times,* June 21, 1999, p. A15. Explores the topsy-turvy battle over gun control in Congress in mid-1999, where a vote may not really mean what it seems to mean. Representative Rick A. Lazio's political calculations are used as an example.

Daughtry, Sylvester, Jr., and John M. Snyder. "Will Gun Control Laws Help Reduce Crime in America?" *CQ Researcher,* vol. 4, June 10, 1994, p. 521. Debates philosophically and practically whether gun control laws will actually reduce the crime rate.

Elvin, John. "The Thinning Ranks of America's Gun Dealers." *Insight on the News,* vol. 13, April 7, 1997, p. 23. Reports that there are 100,000 fewer gun dealers, and argues that ever more strict gun laws are the reason. Elvin describes a number of proposals that would go beyond the Brady Bill in increasing paperwork and expense for gun dealers and that could lead to a national registration system that would facilitate gun confiscation.

"Faces of Violence: Lobbyists, Politicians and Haters, Guns Are the Tie That Binds." *Rolling Stone,* n. 710, June 15, 1995, pp. 57ff. Gives profiles of 45 people and companies active in lobbying for gun rights, generally portraying them as extremist and insensitive to social needs.

Fagan, Kevin. "Gun Group Modeled After MADD." *San Francisco Chronicle,* May 17, 1999, pp. A13, A16. Reports that a group of survivors and relatives of gun violence victims is organizing a national campaign to lobby for gun control. The group plans to ring bells once a year to commemorate gun victims. It was inspired by the example of MADD (Mothers Against Drunk Driving).

Feinstein, Dianne. [Response to Overturning of Gun Free Schools Zones Act by the Supreme Court]. *Congressional Record,* April 27, 1995, n.p. Explains that the 1990 version of the act was overturned because the federal government did not show a convincing relationship between education and its power to regulate interstate commerce. The 1994 version of the law, however, remains intact. It does not rely on the interstate commerce power but simply requires the gun policy as a condition for schools receiving federal funding.

Feinstein, Dianne, and Dan Gifford. "Q: Is the Federal Ban on Assault Weapons Working?" *Insight on the News*, vol. 12, February 26, 1996, pp. 26ff. A debate between Senator Feinstein (D-Calif.) and Dan Gifford, a gun rights advocate, about whether the national assault weapons ban has worked. Feinstein argues that the number of such weapons used in crime as well as the killing of police officers has been reduced. Gifford, however, argues that assault-type weapons play only a minor role in crime and that gun control advocates have cynically used factoids and scare-mongering tactics.

Fineman, Howard, Matt Cooper, and Daniel Pedersen. "Under Fire." *Newsweek*, May 31, 1999, p. 24. Suggests that in the wake of Littleton and other shootings President Clinton, Vice President Gore, and other Democratic leaders have become emboldened to use the gun control issue as wedge issue against the Republicans. They believe the polls and demographic shifts are on their side.

Ford, Liam T. A. "Gunning for Change." *Reason*, vol. 26, August–September 1994, pp. 48ff. Describes the efforts of Chicago alderman William Beavers, who takes an unusual position among his peers: He wants to end the city's ban on handguns. The Democratic establishment and its wealthy backers support gun control; Beavers and his working class constituency believe that people should be able to own guns to defend themselves from criminals.

"Gender Gap on Gun Control: Women Want Tougher Laws." Associated Press, in *San Francisco Chronicle*, September 8, 1999, p. A6. Reports on an Associated Press poll that shows that 52 percent of women but only 33 percent of men believe that tougher gun laws are more likely to decrease gun violence than better enforcement of existing laws.

Gest, Ted. "Little Think Tank; Big Impact." *U.S. News & World Report*, vol. 115, December 6, 1993, p. 26. Describes the efforts of Josh Sugarmann, founder of the Violence Policy Center. The organization has issued research reports that zero in on emerging controversies such as those over assault weapons and gun dealer licensing.

Gledhill, Lynda. "'Copycat' Gun Bill Gets State Senate OK." *San Francisco Chronicle*, June 2, 1997, pp. A1, A13. Reports that the California Senate has passed legislation that would close a loophole in the state's assault weapons laws by banning guns that are similar to models already specifically banned. The quick passage was aided by public outcry following the Littleton shootings.

Glick, Susan, and Josh Sugarmann. "Why Johnny Can Shoot." *Mother Jones*, vol. 20, January–February 1995, p. 15. Criticizes the National Shooting Sports Foundation for using a government grant to produce and distribute new gun instruction videos to schools. The organization appears to be targeting future voters to get them to be favorable toward guns.

Goode, Stephen. "A Mainstream Freedom Fighter Defends the Right to Bear Arms." *Insight on the News*, vol. 13, February 3, 1997, pp. 22ff. Interviews Wayne LaPierre, who became CEO of the National Rifle Association in 1991. LaPierre rebuts criticisms that the NRA has become an extremist group, saying that the organization is mainstream and stands for fundamental American values of freedom and responsibility.

———. "NRA: Exposed or Demonized?" *Insight on the News*, vol. 13, February 3, 1997, pp. 8ff. Compares the "demonization" of the NRA by outspoken gun control advocates and the organization's own image of itself as being in the U.S. mainstream. Goode quotes gun control advocate Josh Sugarmann of the Violence Policy Center, the NRA's Wayne LaPierre, and pro-gun criminologist Gary Kleck on various gun-related issues.

"GOP Governors Embrace Gun Control Measures: Action Comes in Wake of Horrific Mass Shootings" *New York Times*, in *San Francisco Chronicle*, September 4, 1999, p. A2. Reports that under pressure from public reaction to recent mass shootings many Republican governors who had received campaign contributions from the NRA are now supporting gun control measures and refusing to sign concealed-carry reform laws endorsed by gun rights advocates.

Gunnison, Robert B. "Davis to Sign Get-Tough Bills on Guns, Pistol Restrictions, Locks on Triggers among Items OKd." *San Francisco Chronicle*, August 27, 1999. pp. A1, A3. Reports on the signing by Governor Gray Davis of tough new California gun legislation that would virtually halt sales of inexpensive handguns, impose waiting periods on purchasers at gun shows, and require that trigger locks be included with all new guns sold. Gunnison suggests that the timing of the combined signings on a Friday afternoon may be designed to minimize news coverage and thus reaction by gun rights advocates.

Hafner, Katie. "Mobilizing On Line for Gun Control." *The New York Times*, May 20, 1999, p. D5. Describes Move On, a web site that specializes in creating "flash campaigns" mobilizing voters online to lobby and back selected candidates. The organization started as a way to get back at politicians viewed as dragging out the Clinton investigation and impeachment but has now "moved on" to gun control and other issues.

Hammer, Marion P. "NRA's Friendly Face Draws Hateful Fire." *American Rifleman*, vol. 146, February 1998, pp. 10ff. Complains that Josh Sugarmann's Violence Policy Center unfairly attacks the NRA's Eddie Eagle gun safety program because he doesn't want gun safety but the complete banning of firearms.

Annotated Bibliography

Hamond, Jeff. "License to Fail." *The New Republic*, vol. 210, March 21, 1994, p. 16. Argues that a plan by Treasury Secretary Lloyd Bentsen and other Clinton administration officials to shrink the number of gun dealers by hiking dealer license fees by 900 percent won't work. Dealers can pass on at least part of the added costs to gun buyers.

Harrison, Barbara Grizzuti. "Cease Fire." *Mother Jones*, vol. 22, March–April 1997, pp. 32ff. Interviews Tanya Metaksa, the NRA's chief lobbyist. Harrison paints a vivid and not entirely unsympathetic portrait as she recounts her life and the personal experiences that shaped her attitude toward the right of self-defense and gun ownership.

"He Shot Back: Gun Control." *The Economist*, vol. 331, April 9, 1994, p. A29. Reports that David Roberti, state senator and coauthor of California's assault weapons ban, is likely to defeat a recall attempt organized by the gun lobby. (He would later prove to be successful.)

Hemenway, David. "Regulation of Firearms." *The New England Journal of Medicine*, v. 339, September 17, 1998, pp. 843ff. Argues that regulators should focus on imposing safety requirements and tightening controls on gun distribution to keep firearms out of the hands of criminals.

Henderson, Andre. "Gun Control's Costly Ammunition." *Governing*, vol. 7, May 1994, pp. 23ff. Argues that the Brady Act will impose large unfunded costs on states, particularly those that have not yet automated their criminal justice records.

Heston, Charlton. "My Crusade to Save the Second Amendment." *American Rifleman*, vol. 145, September 1997, pp. 30ff. Heston, newly elected president of the NRA, explains why he came out of retirement to participate actively in the fight for gun rights.

Hilts, Philip J. "The New Battle Over Handguns." *Good Housekeeping*, vol. 224, June 1997, pp. 110ff. Discusses proposals to limit handgun purchases to one gun per month. Hilts argues that the only private parties who need to buy large numbers of guns are those acting as "straw purchasers" who will resell the guns to criminals who are not eligible to buy firearms. Gun control advocates point to a study showing that Virginia's gun purchase limits have taken that state off the list of sources of guns used in major crimes. Gun rights advocates such as the NRA oppose the law as being ineffective because most criminals obtain guns by stealing them or by buying them from individuals on the black market. The article includes sidebars with information about other legislative proposals and current state laws.

Hinz, Greg. "Arms and the Legislature." *Chicago*, vol. 42, August 1993, pp. 27ff. Recounts gun control battles in Illinois, where the NRA maintained a tenacious control of the legislature, unlike states such as Virginia and New Jersey, where gun control measures were passed.

Gun Control

"In Waco's Wake: Gun Ownership." *The Economist*, vol. 327, May 1, 1993, p. A29. Gives a British viewpoint on the 1993 NRA convention. Suggests that the NRA is as militant as ever, though it is adapting to trends in public opinion by creating a more politically correct image. The siege and fire at the Branch Davidians' Waco compound seems not to have fazed the gun rights activists.

Jacobs, James B., and Kimberly A. Potter. "Keeping Guns out of the 'Wrong' Hands: The Brady Law and the Limits of Regulation." *Journal of Criminal Law and Criminology*, vol. 86, Fall 1995, pp. 93–120. Argues that the results of the Brady Act have fallen far short of the expectations of its proponents. An unknown but probably large number of persons denied firearms under the Brady background check were able to obtain them through illegal means. The authors suggest that gun control proponents will soon view the Brady Act only as a "small step" toward more comprehensive regulations.

"James Brady: Felled by a Bullet Intended for Ronald Reagan, He Inspired the First Federal Handgun-Control Law." *People Weekly*, March 15, 1999, p. 106. Profiles James Brady, who fought his way to recovery from severe injury at the hands of an assassin to join his wife Sarah in a successful campaign for federal handgun control.

Johnson, Bryan R. "Concealed Weapons: Congress Can Pass a Law Banning an Arbitrary List of Firearms, But It Can't Make Americans Obey It." *National Review*, vol. 46, September 26, 1994, pp. 54ff. Suggests that the assault weapons ban passed by Congress will prove ineffective because the weapons are not often used in crime, and otherwise law-abiding citizens who own such guns see no reason to obey an arbitrary law that they have reason to believe is a prelude to confiscation. Johnson cites previous experience with New York and California gun registration laws.

Kiefer, Francine. "Clinton's Legacy: Gun-Control President?" *The Christian Science Monitor*, April 29, 1999, p. 9. Recounts President Clinton's history of standing toe-to-toe against the NRA through the struggles to pass the Brady Bill and an assault weapons ban. Kiefer suggests that Clinton may face tough going if he wants to make more gun legislation part of his legacy.

LaPierre, Wayne R. "Bending Second Amendment Will Put Clinton Under the Gun." *Insight on the News*, vol. 13, November 24, 1997, p. 30. Reports on the Clinton administration's adding a new list of semiautomatic firearms to the list of banned imports. LaPierre, the CEO of the NRA, argues that it is a cynical first step to banning all other semiautomatic weapons and that the banned weapons are no different from those used by the hunters Clinton claims to respect.

———. "Standing Guard" (Column). *American Rifleman*, vol. 145, May 1997, pp. 10ff. Argues that the lack of actual enforcement of federal gun control laws should be addressed. Without enforcement of existing laws, any justification for new laws is suspect.

Lacayo, Richard. "A Small-Bore Success." *Time*, vol. 145, February 20, 1995, pp. 47ff. Suggests that the Brady handgun control law has had only limited success in keeping criminals from buying guns. Problems include the selling of many guns through private channels, not dealers; confidentiality laws that prevent many mental problems from showing up in background checks; and a loophole that exempts guns claimed from pawnshops.

Leo, John. "The Coming Shootout Over Guns." *U.S. News & World Report*, vol. 114, January 25, 1993, p. 27. Argues that halfway measures, such as screening and waiting periods, will fail to stop the growing wave of gun violence. People must be forthright and work to ban handguns completely.

Lloyd, Jilian. "For Real Gun-Control Action, Watch the States." *The Christian Science Monitor*, May 28, 1999, p. 3. Suggests that even though gun control efforts may be stalling in Congress, the tide may have turned in favor of gun control in the state legislatures. The NRA says it will recover its power, but other observers suggest that there may be a permanent change in the balance between pro-control and pro-gun groups.

Marinucci, Carla. "Most in State Want Stronger Gun Control, Poll Finds." *San Francisco Chronicle*, September 2, 1999, p. A3. Reports that Californians support stronger gun control by a 2 to 1 margin, and that gun control is more important than the right to bear arms. Public perception that Democrats are stronger on gun control may pose a dilemma for Republican candidates in upcoming elections.

Marwick, Charles. "A Public Approach to Making Guns Safer." *JAMA, The Journal of the American Medical Association*, vol. 273, June 14, 1995, pp. 1743–1744. Points out that handguns are not subject to most of the regulations that protect consumers from other hazardous products. Suggests a variety of safety measures from the mechanical to the high-tech "smart gun" that can only be fired by the authorized user.

McIntyre, Thomas. "Lines in the Sand." *Sports Afield*, vol. 214, October 1995, pp. 16ff. Argues that hunters should reject both the inflammatory rhetoric and appeals to patriotism of the NRA and the bogus facts and arguments offered by gun control advocates. McIntyre urges that the NRA pay more attention to hunting and other mainstream uses of guns and accept some rational regulation on gun sales.

Metaksa, Tanya K. "Banning Guns & Taxing Your Rights." *American Rifleman*, vol. 146, June 1998, pp. 38ff. The NRA chief lobbyist writes in opposition to proposed fees that the Clinton administration would impose on all gun sales, even private ones. The administration considers them to be service fees, but Metaksa sees them as a punitive tax on gun ownership.

———. "The Clinton War on Guns." *American Rifleman*, [March?] 1996– n.p. A monthly series of articles analyzing President Clinton's gun control agenda and strategy in both domestic and international politics.

———. "'Home Safety' by Government Mandate." *American Rifleman*, vol. 146, September 1998, pp. 42ff. Argues that lawmakers are using technicalities (such as those relating to the trigger pull and the pistol grip) to fashion a gun ban disguised as safety legislation.

"Missouri Keeps Ban on Hidden Firearms." *San Francisco Chronicle/Associated Press*, April 7, 1999, p. A3. Reports that Missouri voters defeated an attempt to liberalize concealed gun carry laws by a close vote. This represents a setback to the NRA's national effort to reform such state laws. The NRA had spent heavily on the campaign, while the opponents were backed by Hillary Clinton, who made public service spots.

Mitchell, Alison. "Politics Among Culprits in Death of Gun Control." *The New York Times*, June 19, 1999, p. A11. Analyzes Congress's failure to pass gun control legislation in spring 1999. Outrage over the Littleton shootings was apparently insufficient to break the logjam caused by competing political interests.

Novak, Viveca. "Picking a Fight with the N.R.A." *Time*, vol. 153, May 31, 1999, p. 54. Reports on the TV confrontation between actor Tom Selleck and host Rosie O'Donnell. Selleck, who had recently appeared in an NRA ad, is lambasted on O'Donnell's show in a scene that seems emblematic of the NRA's hard times since the Littleton shootings. But the NRA is fighting back and can't be counted out.

"On the Defensive: Sensing Disaster, a Littleton-Addled G.O.P. Tries to Fix Its Fumble on Gun Control." vol. 153, *Time*, May 24, 1999, p. 52. Reports on the Republicans' flat-footed response to the Littleton shootings, after which they first passed a proposal making background checks at gun shows voluntary rather than required and then reversed themselves. Democrats seem poised to take advantage of the situation in the 2000 election campaign.

"Operators Are Standing By." *U.S. News & World Report*, December 14, 1998, p. 32. Criticizes the new "instant check" system for gun purchasers because it often has technical problems that delay processing. This can lead to premature gun sales, so gun control advocates demand minimum waiting periods such as three days. Meanwhile, the NRA is criticizing the system because it may be used to surreptitiously maintain a list of gun owners.

Otero, Juan. "Congress Aims at Preempting State and Local Gun Control Measures." *Nation's Cities Weekly*, vol. 21, August 31, 1998, p. 12.

Discusses proposed federal legislation that would overrule state gun laws by requiring states to honor gun carry permits issued by other states. Gun control advocates decry the measure as a loss of local control and an invitation for, at best, marginally suitable applicants to get a permit in the most permissive state.

———. "Senator Seeks to Close Foreign Ammo Clip Loophole." *Nation's Cities Weekly*, vol. 22, March 15, 1999, p. 12. Describes the National League of Cities' support for Senator Dianne Feinstein's efforts to close a loophole that allows importing of high capacity ammunition clips, which are banned from domestic manufacture.

Perlaman, Ellen. "Living with Concealed Weapons: Police Are Learning That It May Be More Prudent to Help Write a Weapons Law Than Try to Keep It off the Books." *Governing*, vol. 9, February 1996, pp. 33ff. Discusses the approach of police to policies and legislation regarding citizens carrying guns. Although police are divided over the desirability of an armed citizenry, they need to become involved in the legislative process.

Pianin, Eric, and Juliet Eilperin. "House Defeats Gun Control Bill; Angry Democrats, Republicans Blame Each Other for Stalemate." *The Washington Post*, June 19, 1999, p. A01. Describes the acrimonious collapse of the attempt to add gun control provisions to the 1999 juvenile justice bill. When Republicans and some conservative Democrats weakened the gun show purchase waiting period requirement to 24 hours, many gun control proponents no longer supported the bill. Some form of the legislation may be revived later in the year, however.

Polsby, Daniel D. "The False Promise of Gun Control." *The Atlantic Monthly*, vol. 273, March 1994, pp. 57ff. Argues that new gun laws designed to make guns more expensive and harder to get can have perverse consequences, feeding the illegal market. It is necessary to understand the "rational" motives of criminals and others who seek guns to maximize their chance of achieving their goals. To reduce gun violence, one should try to change the social conditions that make criminal choices attractive.

Ponnuru, Ramesh. "Target Practice." *National Review*, vol. 51, June 14, 1999, p. 18. Suggests that congressional Republicans did not anticipate the depth of public anxiety over the Littleton shootings and responded ineptly when confronted by renewed challenges by gun control advocates. Republicans should have been willing to embrace sensible gun laws that did not affect the basic right to bear arms.

Quist, Janet. "NLC, Police Chiefs Oppose House Bills on Concealed Weapons Law." *Nation's Cities Weekly*, vol. 20, July 28, 1997, p. 5. Explains why the National League of Cities and International Association of Chiefs of Police oppose a federal bill that would require states to allow law enforcement officers to carry concealed weapons across state lines.

Reasons include advocacy of local control and fear of liability for misuse of guns by "visiting" officers.

Rand, Christen. "Gun Shows in America: Tupperware Parties for Criminals." *Violence Policy Center Studies*, July 1996, n.p. [Executive summary available online. URL: http://www.vpc.org/studies/tupstudy.htm. Posted on March 3, 1999.] Describes the ways in which people at gun shows circumvent gun laws and carry on a large illegal traffic, such as through "straw purchases." Rand recommends a variety of restrictions to cut off the flow of illegal guns.

Reibstein, Larry, and John Engen. "One Strike and You're Out." *Newsweek*, vol. 128, December 23, 1996, p. 53. Explains that a 1996 law, intended to cut down domestic violence by banning gun ownership by persons convicted of even relatively minor violent acts, may result in many law enforcement officers being no longer able to carry guns. Police unions oppose the law, and critics suggest that it may violate the constitutional ban against ex post facto laws that punish acts retroactively.

"Report by GAO Batters Brady." *American Rifleman*, vol. 144, April 1996, pp. 18ff. Describes the Government Accounting Office's (GAO's) report of shortcomings of the Brady Law. The article suggests that the main problem is that the law targets law-abiding citizens but does little to prevent criminals from getting guns.

"Rusty Got His Gun." *The New Republic*, vol. 219 August 17, 1998, p. 8. Agrees with the NRA that more gun laws couldn't have stopped gunman Rusty Weston from stealing his parents' revolver and using it in a shooting spree in the U.S. Capitol. However, the answer is to get serious about drying up the huge supply of guns that is available to criminals and the insane.

"The Same Old NRA; Its Policies Are Harmful, Even with 'Moses' as Leader." *Los Angeles Times*, vol. 117, June 9, 1998, p. B6. Suggests that the election of Charlton Heston as head of the NRA does not change the harmful activities of the organization in blocking reasonable gun control efforts.

Sawicki, Stephen. "Revolutionary Gun Laws." *U.S. News & World Report*, vol. 126, February 15, 1999, p. 32. Reports that historical reenactors are encountering a problem with new gun laws in Massachusetts and some other states whose trigger lock and locked box requirements don't make an exception for antique weapons such as Revolutionary War muskets, for which no such devices are available.

Shapiro, Bruce. "Running Against the Gun: McCarthy on Long Island." *The Nation*, vol. 263, November 11, 1996, pp. 15ff. Discusses the promising congressional campaign of Carolyn McCarthy, who ran for Congress after her representative refused to do anything about the kind of guns Colin

Ferguson used to kill her husband and wound her son on the Long Island Railroad.

Sollum, Jacob. "Waco's Wake." *Reason*, vol. 25, May 1993, pp. 8ff. Argues that the aftermath of the Waco raid has been used by gun control advocates and politicians to further promote a crusade against "assault weapons," which are mistakenly defined and which play little part in crime.

———. "Wait a Minute." *National Review*, vol. 46, February 7, 1994, pp. 48ff. Argues that waiting periods for gun purchasers (such as that in the Brady Bill) are ineffective at reducing crime and only inconvenience law-abiding citizens.

Stanglin, Douglas. "Backfire." *U.S. News & World Report*, vol. 121, December 16, 1996, pp. 19ff. Reports that although law enforcement organizations support prohibiting gun ownership to persons convicted of relatively minor domestic violence offenses, they want an exception for police and other security personnel, fearing that too many police would end up being relegated to desk jobs.

Sugarmann, Josh. "More Gun Dealers Than Gas Stations: A Study of Federally Licensed Firearms Dealers in America." *Research Report, Violence Policy Center*, 1992. Describes the "ecology" involving the different classes of firearms dealers, how they compete with one another, and how they can circumvent gun laws (such as by a class I dealer paying an annual tax and becoming a class III dealer able to deal in fully automatic weapons).

"Texas Forbids Cities to Sue Gun Firms." *The Washington Post*, June 20, 1999, p. A14. Reports that Texas governor (and presidential candidate) George W. Bush has signed legislation that would prevent cities from suing gun makers; only the legislature could bring such suits. Bush said that manufacturers should not be held liable for the selling of a legal product.

Thurman, James N. "Disconnect Between Gun Crime and Gun-Control Laws." *The Christian Science Monitor*, May 19, 1999, p. 2. Suggests that the most popular proposals among gun control activists bear little relationship to the actual problem of gun-related crime. Neither foreign-made assault weapons nor high-capacity clips play much role in crime, which generally involves ordinary U.S.-made revolvers and pistols. Some gun control advocates believe systematic product regulation for all firearms would be a more effective approach.

———. "NRA's New Aim: To Soften Its Edges and Re-Enlist Moderates." *The Christian Science Monitor*, vol. 90, June 10, 1998, p. 5. Suggests that the National Rifle Association, in electing Charlton Heston as its head, is trying to reposition itself in the mainstream and bring back members who had left after incidents (such as the "jack-booted thugs" remark about federal agents) made the organization appear extreme.

Gun Control

—————. "Rethinking Gun Laws—Once Again." *The Christian Science Monitor*, April 28, 1999, p. 1. Reports that gun control advocates struggled to catch up with popular opinion in the wake of the Littleton shootings. Bills to liberalize concealed gun carry laws have been shelved in Colorado, Alabama, and Michigan, although California passed a "one gun a month" law. Nevertheless, even some control proponents question whether just laying down another layer of laws upon existing gun legislation will really address the causes of violent outbursts among youth.

"Time for a Change?" *U.S. News & World Report*, vol. 121, August 19, 1996, p. 18. Reports that Handgun Control, Inc., is retooling its public image by hiring a public relations consultant. The group is considering adopting a new name because it thinks the public may react negatively to the word *control*.

"Time to Aim Our Outrage at the Gun Lobby." *National Catholic Reporter*, vol. 34, April 3, 1998, p. 36. Recites the sad litany of school shootings such as those at West Paducah, Kentucky, and Jonesboro, Arkansas. The article says that it is time to react as Americans would react to deaths in a senseless war or as they have reacted to the tobacco companies—and take on the gun lobby.

Tyson, Anne Scott. "Tale of Two Lawmakers' Shift on Gun Control." *The Christian Science Monitor*, May 24, 1999, p. 3. Describes how two conservative, pro-gun senators—Max Cleland of Georgia and Gordon Smith—of Oregon changed their positions after confronting school shootings in their home districts. Their conversion may be indicative of a pro gun control trend in the wake of the Littleton shootings.

Van Biema, David. "License to Conceal." *Time*, vol. 145, March 27, 1995, pp. 26ff. Reports on the many states that are reforming gun-carry laws to make it easier to get a permit to carry a concealed weapon. Van Biema discusses the facts and arguments used by both sides.

VandeHei, Jim. "On the Hill: Gun 'n' Poses." *The New Republic*, June 28, 1999, p. 15. Points out the little recognized fact that about 50 House Democrats follow the National Rifle Association's lead and usually vote with Republicans against gun measures. The Democratic leadership often doesn't push hard for gun control for fear of alienating these members, who are generally Southern conservatives, or causing them to lose their seats.

Walker, Paulette V. "Scientists Decry Lawmakers' Decision to Slash Support for Firearms Research: House Members Say Study Was a Blatant Attempt to Raise Sympathy for Gun Control." *The Chronicle of Higher Education*, August 2, 1996, vol. 42, pp. A19ff. Reports objections by researchers studying gun violence to the House cutting their funding at the instigation of the NRA. Gun advocates, however, claim that the research is biased in favor of a gun control agenda.

Weisberg, Jacob. "The Guns of August: Schumer Saves the Crime Bill." *New York Magazine*, vol. 27, September 12, 1994, pp. 30ff. Describes the successful efforts of Charles Schumer, Democratic congressman from Brooklyn, who was able to get enough Republican votes to pass the assault weapons ban while retaining its list of banned weapons.

Weiss, Philip. "A Hoplophobe Among the Gunnies." *The New York Times Magazine*, September 11, 1994, pp. 64ff. Recounts the experiences of a reporter who was unenthusiastic about guns (*hoplophobe* means a "person who is afraid of weapons") at a National Rifle Association event.

Whitlock, Craig. "Delays in FBI Checks Put 1,700 Guns in the Wrong Hands; System Failed to Detect Banned Buyers Within Time Limit." *The Washington Post*, June 25, 1999, p. A01. Reports that technical problems prevented the FBI from completing background checks in three days as required. As a result, some applicants who were not eligible to receive guns got them. ATF agents are attempting to retrieve the guns.

"Whose Thugs, Whose Jack-Boots? The Gun Culture." *The Economist*, vol. 335, May 20, 1995, pp. A27ff. Describes the aftermath of the NRA's letter that referred to BATF agents as "jack-booted thugs," George Bush's resignation from the NRA, and the organization's continuing political clout.

Wright, James D. "Second Thoughts on Gun Control." *The Public Interest*, no. 91, Spring 1988, pp. 23–29. Suggests that gun control proposals may have unintended consequences; for example, a ban on lower-power Saturday night specials might simply lead criminals or assassins to use guns more likely to kill their victims.

INTERNET DOCUMENTS

Handgun Control, Inc. "Gun Laws by State." Available online. URL: http://www.handguncontrol.org/gunlaws.htm. Downloaded on July 7, 1999. Provides an interactive map—click on any state to get a summary of provisions of its gun laws.

Morgan, Eric, and David Kopel. "The Assault Weapon Panic: 'Political Correctness' Takes Aim at the Constitution." Available online. URL: http://shadeslanding.com/firearms/assault.weapon.html. First published on October 10, 1991. Analyzes the rhetoric of the campaign against assault weapons as a species of political correctness. The authors argue that the campaign's goals are ill-defined and deceptive and would result in diminishing freedom without having a beneficial effect on public safety. The authors believe that action directed at actual criminals is the answer.

Violence Policy Center. "Information on Pro-Gun Special Interests." Available online. URL: http://www.vpc.org/pgtopic.htm. Downloaded on July

8, 1999. Collects links to articles that seek to expose the agenda of pro-gun groups such as the National Rifle Association.

GUNS AND SOCIETY

This section covers a variety of issues, including those of a more personal or philosophical nature, that don't fit into one of the more specific categories.

BOOKS

Brown, Richard Maxwell. *No Duty to Retreat: Violence and Values in American History and Culture.* Reprint ed. Norman: University of Oklahoma Press, 1994. A study of the social values involving the appropriate use of violence from frontier days to the present. Brown emphasizes the history of the American West. He also provides an important historical context for the development of gun regulations.

Clarke, R. V. G., and David Lester. *Suicide: Closing the Exits.* New York: Springer Verlag, 1989. Advocates gun control (among other measures) as a way to reduce suicide by removing the means for easy, impulsive suicide.

Kennett, Lee B., and James L. Anderson. *The Gun in America: The Origins of a National Dilemma.* Westport, Conn.: Greenwood Press, 1975. Describes the many roles that firearms have played in U.S. culture and how the United States can indeed be said to be the "arsenal of democracy" with both positive and negative consequences.

Kleck, Gary, and Don B. Kates. *The Great American Gun Debate: Essays on Firearms and Violence.* San Francisco: Pacific Research Institute for Public Policy, 1997. Essays exploring criminological issues, the social utility of firearms, and the biased role of the media in covering the gun debate.

Kopel, David B., ed. *Guns: Who Should Have Them?* Amherst, N.Y.: Prometheus Books, 1995. Presents opinions by experts in law, criminology, medicine, psychiatry, and feminist studies; suggests that the emphasis on gun control is misplaced and that the real causes of crime lie in social factors such as the breakdown of the family.

McGrath, Roger D. *Gunfighters, Highwaymen, and Vigilantes: Violence on the Frontier.* Berkeley: University of California Press, 1997. Discusses the violent culture of the American West and the interaction between roles such as robber, professional gunfighter, and vigilante. Because this period created many gun-related images in our culture, exploring it is useful background for the gun issue.

Waters, Robert A. *The Best Defense: True Stories of Intended Victims Who Defended Themselves with a Firearm.* Nashville, Tenn.: Cumberland House,

1998. A collection of vivid accounts of ordinary people who used guns to defend themselves against attackers. Waters explores both their thoughts and feelings and the response of police and society in general; the book leans to strong gun rights advocacy.

Weir, William. *A Well-Regulated Militia: The Battle over Gun Control.* North Haven, Conn.: Archon, 1997. For young adults. Takes on both gun control and gun rights advocates. Weir criticizes their statistics and arguments and concludes that both sides are ignoring more fundamental social issues that must be addressed if violence is to be reduced.

ARTICLES AND PAPERS

Alter, Jonathan. "Curb Violence by Targeting Bullets." *Washington Monthly,* vol. 26, January–February 1994, p. 45. Argues that although gun control can and should be strengthened, the huge number of existing guns will limit its effectiveness. Therefore, the author suggests imposing strict control on the sales of bullets, as well as marking bullets for identification, perhaps with embedded microchips; making bullets both more expensive and easier to trace should cut down on gun-related crimes. He also suggests that conservatives may be willing to accept more methods of gun control in exchange for more certain and effective punishment for criminals.

———. "On the Cusp of a Crusade." *Newsweek,* May 10, 1999, p. 59. Suggests a range of reasonable responses to the Littleton tragedy, including requiring "smart guns" that can only be fired by their owner, along with economic boycotts to force media moguls to act more responsibly concerning violent content in movies and video games.

Anderson, George M. "Gun Control: New Approaches." *America,* vol. 172, March 11, 1995, pp. 26ff. Describes emerging groups such as the Violence Policy Center and the HELP Network that are recasting gun control as a public health, child safety, or suicide prevention issue. The groups hope to counter gun advertising targeted at women and other groups as being deceptive in its claims about the utility of guns for self-protection.

Baker, James J. "Second Amendment Message in Los Angeles." *American Rifleman,* vol. 140, July 1992, pp. 32ff. Argues that the 1992 Los Angeles riots demonstrated that police cannot protect citizens under all circumstances and that the right of citizens to keep arms for self-protection is essential.

Barnett, Randy E. "Guns, Militias, and Oklahoma City." *Tennessee Law Review,* vol. 62, Spring 1995, pp. 443ff. Explores the emergence of the militia movement and its social and cultural roots. Suggests that one source of the movement is frustration with the refusal of the courts to enforce the Second Amendment.

Barone, Michael. "A Dangerous Gun Show." *U.S. News & World Report*, vol. 126, May 31, 1999, p. 30. Argues that gun control advocates, like other advocates of far-reaching reform (abortion, campaign finance, etc.), don't pay enough attention to the practical difficulties and consequences of any truly serious program. Millions of gun owners won't give up their rights any more easily than millions of women would give up their right to choose abortion. Defenders of the Second Amendment are as passionate as those who stand up for the First, and they have some impressive scholarship on their side.

"The Battle Over Gun Control: The Black Community Has the Greatest Stake in the Outcome of the Gun Control Debate." *Black Enterprise*, vol. 23, July 1993, p. 27. Reports that black elected public officials are making a concerted effort to help pass gun control legislation. Blacks have a special interest in this struggle because it is their communities and youth who have suffered the most from gun violence.

Bershers, Khris. "Rendell Shares Experimental Plan to Curb Gun Violence." *Nation's Cities Weekly*, vol. 21, June 29, 1998, p. 7. Reports on Philadelphia's Mayor Edward Rendell's suggestion to the U.S. Conference of Mayors that cities work with the NRA and gun makers to incorporate safety devices such as trigger locks on guns voluntarily and to improve security at gun manufacturing plants to stop the diversion of guns to the criminal black market. But more coercive measures such as lawsuits and new regulations may overtake any voluntary efforts.

Blackman, Paul H. "Buy-Backs/Amnesties Merely Fanciful Gun Control Gimmicks." *American Rifleman*, vol. 140, April 1992, p. 52. Argues the NRA position that amnesties and "goods for guns" programs are ineffective, squander resources, and do little to keep guns away from true criminals.

Burns, Robert E. "It's Time to Stop Living Under the Gun." *U.S. Catholic*, vol. 59, January 1994, p. 2. Argues that Catholics, together with other Christians, Jews, and Muslims, should begin a crusade to eliminate the guns that are killing so many innocent people. As a moral issue, it is comparable to abortion.

Cartwright, Gary. "Fear and Loading." *Texas Monthly*, vol. 23, May 1995, pp. 114ff. Looks at the attitudes of Texans toward guns on the eve of passage of a new law making it easier to carry concealed weapons. Cartwright describes the conflicting experiences of people involved in shooting incidents, such as the pro-gun testimony of Suzanna Gratia, who watched in horror as a crazed gunmen killed 23 people in a cafeteria. She had left her own gun behind, in accordance with the law. However, critics of the proposed law believe that concealed weapons will just add to the violence and make it harder for police to deal safely with citizens.

Annotated Bibliography

Casey, Kathyrn. "Up in Arms." *Ladies Home Journal*, vol. 112, August 1995, pp. 89ff. Discusses whether women should arm themselves for their self-defense. Casey includes facts, anecdotes, advertising campaigns, and women's opinions on both sides of the issue.

Cohn, Jonathan. "Guns 'n' Moses." *The New Republic*, vol. 218, June 22, 1998, p. 42. Reports on the efforts of Aaron Zelman, founder of Jews for the Preservation of Firearms Ownership. Although the majority of Jews tend to support gun control and other liberal positions, Zelman calls upon Jewish people to reject gun control as an invitation to genocide. He finds the right and duty of self-defense to be at the core of the Jewish tradition.

"The Combat Zone: Once More Into the Breach of Gun Control." *Playboy*, vol. 41, May 1994, pp. 43ff. Laments that acrimony and inflexibility characterize both sides of the gun debate. Invites nine experts with varying perspectives to offer their points of view on a series of gun-related questions. Participants include Michael Beard, President of the Coalition to Stop Handgun Violence; Roy Innis of the NAACP; Sarah Brady of Handgun Control, Inc.; criminologist Don Kates; and constitutional scholar Sanford Levinson.

D'Agnese, Joseph. "Smart Guns Don't Kill Kids." *Discover Magazine*, September 1999, pp. 90–93. Describes and illustrates advanced prototype handgun safety devices, including fingerprint sensors, electronic rings, magnetic locks, and other systems that might make it impossible for persons other than the gun owner to fire the weapon.

Davis, Riccardo A. "Gun Exchange Strikes Nerve: Reebok Joins Toys 'R' Us to Support Cause." *Advertising Age*, vol. 65, January 3, 1994, pp. 3ff. Describes growing support for New York's Toys-for-Guns program, started by carpet store owner Fernando Mateo, Sr., and embraced by such big names as Toys 'R' Us and Reebok.

Diamond, Edwin. "Gun and Poses: Hollywood Takes on Violence." *New York Magazine*, vol. 26, December 6, 1993, pp. 32ff. Describes efforts of Dr. J. Winsten of Harvard University to get television producers to include material that portrays the dangers of guns in a way similar to that previously used with regard to driving and drinking.

"Don't Withhold Treatment on This Epidemic." *U.S. Catholic*, vol. 63, September 1998, p. 25. Points out that homicide is the second leading cause of death for youths 15–24, and that the U.S. homicide rate is far higher than that of other countries. The article reports on efforts of the Centers for Disease Control and others to treat gun violence as an epidemic and ponders whether other social problems might be better dealt with if people treated them as seriously as physical diseases.

Fletcher, Jeff. "Phoenix Gun Meltdown Heats Up Fight Against Crime." *Nation's Cities Weekly*, vol. 17, February 7, 1994, p. 11. Describes a new policy by the city of Phoenix, Arizona, which will now melt down guns that it seizes from criminals. Most cities sell the guns to dealers, where they can get back into the hands of criminals.

Garbarino, Steve. "A Farewell to Arms." *Interview*, vol. 24, March 1994, p. 108. Notes that although movies, TV, and the recording industry have created cultural icons of violence such as Dirty Harry, the Terminator, and gangsta rap, media people are becoming increasingly involved in gun control campaigns. These include public service ads targeted at youth and programs to exchange guns for concert tickets and other goodies. The article includes interviews with store owner Fernando Mateo Sr., country singer Reba McEntire, and rapper B-Real.

Gest, Ted. "Firearms Follies: How the News Media Cover Gun Control." *Media Studies Journal*, Winter 1992, n.p. Depicts widespread media bias against gun owners and the National Rifle Association, combined with ignorance of basic facts about guns on the part of media professionals.

"Gunman Kills 7 in Texas Church." *Fort Worth Star-Telegram*, in *San Francisco Chronicle*, pp. A1, A16. Reports on a gunman opening fire at a church youth meeting at Wedgwood Baptist Church in Fort Worth, killing eight people including himself.

Hewitt, Bill. "A Separate Peace: Dismayed by Violence on the Streets, A New York Businessman Offers to Swap Toys for Guns and Starts a Disarmament Crusade Across the Country." *People Weekly*, vol. 41, January 17, 1994, pp. 84ff. Tells the story of carpet store owner Fernando Mateo Sr. Dismayed by media reports of violent deaths just before Christmas in 1993, Mateo hit upon the idea of organizing a program to swap toys for guns. He believes the program provides some Christmas cheer for poor families while making homes and streets a little safer.

Idelson, Holly, and Paul Nyhan. "Waco Tragedy Sparks New Look at Guns and Law Enforcement." *Congressional Quarterly Weekly Report*, vol. 51, May 1, 1993, pp. 1085ff. Describes issues arising out of the federal raid on the Branch Davidians in Waco, Texas, including the ability of private individuals to stockpile weapons and apparent confusion and ineffectiveness in federal law enforcement.

Kates, Don B. "Shot Down." *National Review*, vol. 47, March 6, 1995, pp. 49ff. Suggests that criminologists, cops, and criminals themselves have a justified skepticism about the effectiveness of gun control laws. Studies by Gary Kleck suggest that gun bans mostly hurt law-abiding citizens who might otherwise use guns effectively to deter crime.

Katz, Jon. "The War at Home: How the Media Miss the Story on 34,000 Gun Deaths Each Year." *Rolling Stone*, n. 660, July 8, 1993, pp. 37ff. Argues that the media is biased in not focusing on gun deaths that usually occur in poor or minority neighborhoods and instead focuses on the statements of privileged gun owners.

King, Sue. "Now That We Have Running Water in the Kitchen . . ." *American Rifleman*, vol. 146, November–December 1998, p. 60. Argues that gun enthusiasts should reach out and help more women become involved in shooting and hunting.

Kopel, David. "The Federal Government Should Set a Better Example: Militias and Gun Control." *Vital Speeches*, vol. 62, March 1, 1996, pp. 315ff. Suggests that the right-wing militia activities of recent years should be seen in the historical context of violent dissent and government overreaction, citing such examples as the repression of abolitionists and labor organizers. Policy makers should try to avoid hysteria and distortion when assessing the real nature of threats. Local rather than federal action is usually better at providing precisely tailored responses.

LaPierre, Wayne. "Standing Guard" (Column). *American Rifleman*, vol. 146, November-December, 1998 p. 10. Describes Project Exile, the NRA-promoted program, first adopted in Richmond, Virginia, to enforce gun laws against felons strictly. Claims this approach has deterred many criminals from obtaining guns.

Lacayo, Richard, and Zed Nelson. "Still Under the Gun." *Time*, vol. 151, July 6, 1998, pp. 34ff. Revisits a cover story *Time* ran 30 years ago. The authors find that the United States is still struggling to control the eruption of violence, this time in the schools. Prospects for passing more effective gun control are dim because many Americans fiercely cling to the idea of gun ownership.

Landburg, Stephen E. "Psst! Wanna Buy a Gun?" *Forbes*, vol. 153, May 23, 1994, p. 112. Suggests that "amnesty" programs where police pay money for guns turned in by citizens may have the unintended effect of creating an incentive for thieves to steal and sell firearms.

Little, Christopher C. "Communitarianism, Clinton & Congress: A New Threat Emerges for Gun Owners." *American Rifleman*, vol. 141, October 1993, pp. 30ff. Discusses the philosophy of communitarianism, which seeks to balance collective and individual rights but is often accused of being excessively authoritarian. Suggests that the communitarian impulse will be seen in the Clinton administration's emerging gun control agenda.

Lowell, Piper. "A .38-caliber plowshare." *Christianity Today*, vol. 39, October 2, 1995, pp. 38ff. Describes sculptor Esther Augsberger's sculpture of a plowshare (as in the biblical "swords into plowshares") made from 3,000 guns turned in during a Washington, D.C., amnesty. The guns are melted and twisted but still recognizable in what Augsberger describes as "a symbol of hope."

Lucas, Robert A. "Hunting Rhinos." *National Review,* vol. 47, May 1, 1995, pp. 70ff. Suggests that public hysteria over armor-piercing "cop-killer" bullets such as the Black Rhino is misplaced. Tests reveal the bullets are not nearly as effective as advertised. The issue reveals sloppy thinking and garbled facts in Congress and the media.

"Maker of Tiny Pistol Denies It Is Deadly." *The New York Times,* vol. 147, May 8, 1998, p. A8. The Milex company, makers of the tiny Osa pistol (about the size of a key chain), denies that it is unusually deadly or hazardous.

"Man Charged in Supremacist Gun Sale." *Associated Press Online.* July 7, 1999. Available online. URL: http://www.nytimes.com/aponline/a/ AP-Chicago-Shootings.html. Reports that an unlicensed gun dealer sold several guns to Benjamin Nathaniel Smith, the white supremacist gunman who went on a racist killing spree. Such revelations are likely to heighten concern about the illegal gun market that is not directly affected by laws such as the Brady Bill.

Maranz, Matthew. "Guns 'R' Us: So You Want to Buy a Machine Gun." *The New Republic,* vol. 200, January 23, 1989, pp. 12ff. Describes a reporter's efforts to buy a fully automatic weapon. Although the federal requirements are complicated and expensive, he finds that it's quite possible to do so.

McClurg, Andrew J. "The Rhetoric of Gun Control." *American University Law Review,* vol. 42, Fall 1992, n.p. Discusses the use (and abuse) of rhetorical techniques in the gun control debate, including fallacies in reasoning, emotional appeals, and disreputable argument techniques such as ad hominem, "straw man," and "slippery slope."

McConnell, Joe. "Firearms: No Right Is an Island." *Whole Earth Review,* no. 77, Winter 1992, pp. 40ff. Suggests that the problem with gun control is not so much the need for guns but the need to prevent the unraveling of constitutional protections, which are interdependent. The same kinds of emotional appeals used to promote gun control could be used to promote censorship, harsher drug laws, or many other attempts to address social problems by limiting rights. McConnell explains the technicalities of assault weapons and Saturday night specials and suggests that gun education and training requirements for gun ownership are a better approach than gun bans.

Murray, Frank J. "Despite Risks, Americans Use Guns in Self-Defense." *Insight on the News,* vol. 15, June 14, 1999, p. 42. Argues that despite the uproar over guns in the United States, thousands of Americans continue quietly to arm themselves and use their guns to drive away criminals. Because actual shootings are rare, the media tends to ignore this phenomenon as not being newsworthy. Accurate numbers about defensive gun use are hard to come by, however. Includes anecdotes, such as a citizen successfully taking on cop-killing drug traffickers.

Norquist, Grover G. "Have Gun, Will Travel: GOP Concealed Gun Laws Are Spreading Like Wildfire." *The American Spectator*, vol 31, November 1998, pp. 74ff. Reports that gun rights activists, inspired by studies by John Lott and others who say that concealed weapons deter crime, are promoting laws in many states that would make it easier to carry a gun legally. (This trend seems to have been reversed following the Littleton high school shootings in April 1999, however.)

Paige, Sean. "Industries Become Ideological Targets." *Insight on the News*, vol. 14, April 27, 1998, pp. 12ff. Argues that in the wake of the Jonesboro, Arkansas, shootings, opportunistic politicians are demonizing the gun industry. Paige compares this trend to attacks on the alcohol, tobacco, and snack food industries.

Petzal, David E. "Rot and Evil." *Field & Stream*, West ed., vol. 104, May 1999, p. 112. Gives a part humorous/part serious look at problems or trends that are causing problems for gun owners, ranging from careless hunters and airlines to greedy lawyers and the NRA (for not endorsing George Bush in 1992 despite the alternative being Bill Clinton).

Polsby, Daniel D. "Equal Protection." *Reason*, October 1993, n.p. Argues that gun control leads to the disarming of groups of people who then fall prey to criminals, aggressive neighbors, or tyranny. On the other hand, an armed citizenry actually led to a relatively low rate of violence in the so-called Wild West and could have a similar deterrant effect today.

Post, Tom. "Farewell to Arms." *Newsweek*, vol. 123, January 10, 1994, pp. 20ff. Discusses some of the growing number of programs that offer goods or other incentives in return for people turning in their guns. Points out that women return about 80 percent of the guns collected.

Rosenberg, Joel. "Protecting Home and Hearth with Guns." *Minneapolis-St. Paul Star-Tribune*, January 23, 1994, n.p. Gives anecdotes about how people used firearms to defend themselves and their families successfully from burglars.

Rothenberg, Elliot C. "Jewish History Refutes Gun Control Activists." *American Rifleman*, vol. 136, February 1988, pp. 30ff. Argues the experience of millions of disarmed Jews being killed by the Nazis as well as the heroic resistance of those who chose to arm themselves and fight back in the Warsaw ghetto is a powerful argument against gun control.

Sack, Kevin. "9 Slain in Brokerage Massacre." From *The New York Times* in *San Francisco Chronicle*, July 30, 1999, pp. A1, A8. Reports on a killing rampage by failed Atlanta securities day-trader Mark O. Barton who killed 9 people, wounded 12, and finally killed himself when cornered by police.

Scheer, Robert. "Guns 'N' Poses." *Playboy*, vol. 41, March 1994, p. 45. Argues that although the NRA is wrong in its constitutional argument against gun control, it is right that gun control is unlikely to reduce crime. Crime results from a violent subculture that is fueled by social problems such as poverty and racism.

Stern, Gary M. "Guns for Toys." *Hispanic*, vol. 7, April 1994, p. 40. Describes Hispanic businessman Fernando Mateo, Sr., and his pioneering development of a gun exchange program that is sweeping the nation.

"Squirt, Squirt, You're Dead." *Time*, vol. 139, June 22, 1992, p. 35. Describes incidents where children shooting new high-power water guns sometimes get shot by people with real guns. One solution? Ban the water guns.

Sugarmann, Josh. "Reverse Fire." *Mother Jones*, January/February 1994, pp. 36ff. Points out that guns are the "second most deadly consumer product" (after cars); yet the gun industry has none of the safety regulations that are imposed on manufacturers of automobiles and other products. Sugarmann argues that guns must therefore be considered a public health issue.

Sullum, Jacob. "Voodoo Social Policy: Exorcizing the Twin Demons, Guns and Drugs." *Reason*, vol. 26, October 1994, pp. 26ff. Argues that the gun control movement, like the war on drugs, is tainted by racism, elitism, and the demonization of offenders. Both policies have badly eroded fundamental civil liberties.

Tharp, Mike. "The Rise of Citizen Militias: In Montana and Other States, Fury at Gun Control and Government Sparks a Call to Arms." *U.S News & World Report*, vol. 117, August 15, 1994, pp. 34ff. Reports the growth in militia groups that are organizing in response to what they see as government aggression and totalitarianism. They see the passage of new gun laws such as the Brady Act as being particularly ominous, along with the Ruby Ridge and Waco incidents.

Tucker, Ken. "Gunning for Attention." *Entertainment Weekly*, no. 230, July 8, 1994, p. 44. Describes new antigun public service announcements being aired by MTV, HBO, Black Entertainment Television, and other cable channels. (One announcement says "Peace: Live It or Rest in It.")

Van Derbeken, Jaxon, and Erin Hallisy. "L.A. Gunman Wounds 5—Suspect Named." *San Francisco Chronicle*, August 11, 1999, pp. A1, A13. Reports on the wounding of five people at a Jewish community center in Los Angeles with the suspect identified as Buford Furrow. The shootings sent a tremor of fear through other Jewish organizations. The article includes a chronology of mass shootings during 1999.

"Wife-Abusing Cops?" *off our backs*, vol. 27, February 1997, p. 3. Describes new regulations that will take away guns from persons convicted of domestic violence crimes—even law enforcement officers.

Wilson, James Q. "Just Take Away Their Guns." *Reader's Digest*, vol. 145, July 1994, pp. 49ff. Argues that efforts to further restrict the lawful purchase of guns will miss the mark. Lawmakers and law enforcers should focus on the illegal side of the gun trade.

Yost, Mark. "Gun Racket." *The American Spectator*, vol. 27, June 1994, p. 46. Suggests that gun buyback or exchange programs, although popular and good for public relations, have had no discernable effect on crime. The guns turned in are seldom those used by criminals but are instead those that people may need to defend themselves against crime.

INTERNET DOCUMENTS

Cramer, Clayton E. "The Racist Roots of Gun Control." Available online. URL: http://www.magi.com/~freddo/racist.html. Downloaded on June 17, 1999. Argues that gun control has been used since colonial times as a tool to subdue African Americans. Many gun laws were passed in the Reconstruction era to prevent newly freed black citizens from having access to arms. Modern laws that give police "discretion" about issuing gun permits can result in discrimination against minorities.

National Rifle Association. Institute for Legislative Action. "Armed Citizens and Police Officers." Available online. URL: http://www.nraila.org/research/19990716-LawEnforcement-001.html. Downloaded on June 6, 1999. Compilation of incidents where armed citizens helped police officers subdue criminals.

STUDIES AND SURVEYS

This section covers criminological, medical, and other studies on gun violence and the effectiveness of gun control laws, as well as critiques of such studies. Note: for studies focusing specifically on children and guns, see also the section on "Guns, Children, and Schools."

BOOKS

Coalition to Stop Handgun Violence. *The Unspoken Tragedy: Firearm Suicide in the United States*. Washington, D.C.: Educational Fund to End Handgun Violence and Coalition to Stop Gun Violence, 1995. Reports that firearms are being increasingly used in suicides by females, who had previously preferred poison. Because firearms are more often lethal than other means, the fatality rate for female suicide attempts has increased.

Kleck, Gary. *Point Blank: Guns and Violence in America*. New York: Aldine de Gruyter, 1991. Describes gun owners as a remarkably normal group, socially and psychologically, with only a small percentage of inappropriately violent individuals. Kleck suggests that the value of guns for self-defense outweighs the dangers, as well as providing an important deterrent effect. He develops a methodology for understanding the interaction between aggressor and victim and the role played by the presence of a weapon.

————. *Targeting Guns: Firearms and their Control.* New York: Aldine de Gruyter, 1997. Reviews and critiques studies of gun violence, from a generally pro-gun rights viewpoint. Updates his previous book *Point Blank.*

Wright, James D. *Armed and Considered Dangerous: A Survey of Felons and Their Firearms.* Expanded ed. New York: Aldine de Gruyter 1994. Revision of a classic study that looked at the attitude of hardened criminals toward their use of guns—and the possibility of their victims being armed.

Zimring, Franklin E., and Gordon Hawkins. *Crime Is Not the Problem: Lethal Violence in America.* New York: Oxford University Press, 1997. Argues that it is violent, often lethal, crime that is the U.S.'s distinctive problem. (Rates of nonviolent, property crimes are comparable to other nations.) Authors argue that it is necessary to focus on what facilitates this violence, including the availability of guns.

ARTICLES AND PAPERS

Adler, Karl P., et al. "Firearm Violence and Public Health: Limiting the Availability of Guns." *JAMA, The Journal of the American Medical Association*, vol. 271, April 27, 1994, pp. 1281ff. Cites statistics that indicate that firearm violence has reached "epidemic proportions." Urges tough federal gun control laws to bring the epidemic under control, including requiring that prospective gun owners be tightly screened, undergo training, and have to "rigorously" show they have a good reason to have a gun. An expansion of the assault weapons ban and higher taxes to discourage gun purchases are also recommended.

Anderson, David C. "Assault Rifles: Dirt Cheap . . . and Legal!" *The New York Times Magazine*, May 24, 1998, p. 36. Reports on a 1996 study by the Violence Policy Center that finds that gun shows are a common source of assault weapons, which are legal to purchase if they were imported prior to the ban.

Annest, Joseph L. et al. "National Estimates of Nonfatal Firearms-Related Injuries: Beyond the Tip of the Iceberg." *JAMA, The Journal of the American Medical Association*, vol. 273, June 14, 1995, pp. 1749–1754. Estimates the total number of nonfatal firearms-related injuries (of all types) and concludes there are about 2.6 nonfatal injuries for each fatal one. Nonfatal injuries were severe enough to require hospitalization in 57 percent of the cases.

Annotated Bibliography

Blackman, Paul H., et al. "Firearms and Fatalities." *JAMA, The Journal of the American Medical Association*, vol. 275, June 12, 1996, pp. 1723ff. Criticizes epidemiological approaches to firearms violence, focusing on a study by Stephen W. Hargarten on characteristics of firearms involved in fatalities. Argues that analogies between intentional gun injuries and unintentional injuries (such as auto accidents) may be flawed and that small-caliber handguns focused on by the Hargarten study are actually declining as a factor in crime. Another letter defends the importance of addressing firearms violence.

Blendon, Robert J., John T. Young, and David Hemenway. "The American Public and the Gun Control Debate." *JAMA, The Journal of the American Medical Association*, vol. 275, June 12, 1996, pp. 1719ff. Breaks down public opinion in a detailed analysis of attitudes toward guns, nature of gun ownership, and responses to a variety of specific proposals. Although some of their data is becoming stale, the approach and organization are instructive.

Bogus, Carl T. "The Strong Case for Gun Control." *The American Prospect*, no. 10, Summer 1992, pp. 19–28. Reviews studies and concludes that gun laws work, guns in the hands of citizens do not deter crime, guns are seldom used for self-defense, and people would not substitute other deadly weapons if guns were not available.

Bronars, Stephen G., and John R. Lott, Jr. "Criminal Deterrence, Geographic Spillovers, and the Right to Carry Concealed Handguns." *American Economic Review*, vol. 88, May 1998, pp. 475ff. Argues that when communities adopt laws that allow more citizens to carry guns, criminals tend to migrate to neighboring areas where stricter laws make it less likely that citizens have guns to defend themselves or their property.

Butterfield, Fox. "Gun Violence May Be Subsiding, Studies Find." *The New York Times*, October 14, 1996. Available online. URL: http://www.nytimes.com(search archive). Reports that surveys suggest that gun violence may have peaked (as of 1995) and is now declining.

———. "New Data Point Blame at Gun Makers." *The New York Times*, vol. 148, November 28, 1998, p. A9. Reports a recent study that suggests many criminals may be getting guns through legal dealers (via "straw purchasers") rather than through theft, as had been previously assumed. This may reinforce plaintiff lawyers' claims that gun makers are deliberately distributing guns into markets that they should know are being used to supply criminals.

———. "Study Finds Unsafe Practices by People Trained in Firearms." *The New York Times*, vol. 144, January 20, 1995, p. A12. Reports that although many people on both sides of the gun debate advocate firearms safety training, a study by the Harvard School of Public Health found that people who had taken safety courses are actually more likely to keep a gun loaded and unlocked at home.

Callahan, Charles M., Frederic P. Rivara, and Thomas D. Koepsell. "Money for Guns: Evaluation of the Seattle Gun Buy-Back Program." *Public Health Reports*, vol. 109, July–August 1994, pp. 472ff. Evaluates a Seattle gun buyback program. The mean age of people turning in guns was 51 years, and about 25 percent were women, suggesting that the people most likely to use guns for crime (young adult males) responded only minimally. There were no statistically significant changes in firearms-related crimes and deaths in the months before and after the program.

"Can Hidden Guns Cut Crime? Concealed Weapons Laws." *The Economist*, vol. 347, May 30, 1998, pp. 24ff. Summarizes John Lott's studies that claim to show crime reduction as a consequence of liberalization of concealed-carry laws, and recounts opposing views of critics such as Franklin Zimring. The latter claims that Lott does not account for other possible causes of lower crime, nor for intermediate causality (such as whether the change in law actually led to more people carrying concealed guns). Lott in turn replies to his critics in his new book *More Guns, Less Crime*.

Caplan, David L. "Firearms Registration and Waiting Periods: New York City's Lesson." *American Rifleman*, vol. 141, October 1993, p. 67A. Studies the effects of gun legislation passed in New York City in 1967 and claims that it has been ineffective in reducing crime.

Carlson, Tucker. "Handgun Control, M.D." *Weekly Standard*, April 15, 1996, n.p. Argues that the characterization of gun violence as a public health problem is based on flawed reasoning. Guns are passive and do not infect people the way germs do, and crime, rather than being of epidemic proportions, has actually been declining. Carlson also criticizes the New *England Journal of Medicine's* 1986 study on guns in the home.

Cheng, Vicki. "Firearms Injure 3 for Every 1 They Kill, New Research Finds." *The New York Times*, vol. 144, June 14, 1995, p. A15. Reports on Centers for Disease Control research that highlights the underemphasized extent to which firearms injure as well as kill people.

Cole, Thomas. "Extending Brady Background Checks Opposed." *JAMA, The Journal of the American Medical Association*, vol. 280, December 23, 1998, p. 2065. Reports on a conference held by a group called Academics for the Second Amendment. Speakers at the conference argued that gun control laws have been shown to have no significant effect on homicide rates. New, tougher laws are likely to discourage law-abiding citizens from acquiring the means to defend themselves, while having little or no effect on criminals who do not bother with paperwork in their gun transactions. Researchers Don B. Kates, Chester L. Britt, David B. Mustard, and others present their conclusions.

Cook, Philip J., Stephanie Molliconi, and Thomas B. Cole. "Regulating Gun Markets." *Journal of Criminal Law and Criminology*, vol. 86, Fall 1995, pp. 59–92. Suggests that regulators and policy makers must pay more attention to the complicated role that guns play in the criminal "economy" and that the ease with which guns are stolen and transported tends to make regulations centered on legitimate dealers less effective. The authors urge a police focus on stolen guns and the regulation or abolition of gun transactions that don't involve a licensed dealer.

Donohue, John J. III, and Stephen D. Levitt. "Guns, Violence and the Efficiency of Illegal Markets." *American Economic Review*, vol. 88, May 1998, pp. 463ff. Analyzes the role of guns in economic planning by criminals such as drug gangsters. The authors conclude that their decisions are based more on who is likely to win a confrontation than on the lethality of the weapons used.

Easterbrook, Greg. "Load and Lock: Making Guns Safer." *The New Republic*, May 31, 1999, p. 13. Suggests that there is no reason not to bring guns into the normal system of product safety regulations. By applying the modern engineering principles used for other products, guns can be equipped with trigger locks, loaded-round indicators, magazine safeties, and internal safeties (to prevent dropped guns from firing).

Feldman, Richard J., and Garen Wintermute. "Firearm Design and Firearm Violence." *JAMA, The Journal of the American Medical Association*, vol. 276, October 2, 1996, p. 1035. Begins with criticism by Feldman of Wintermute's approach to relating firearms design to violence and severity of injury. Feldman argues that the study ignores the likelihood that banning some types of handguns would lead to the substitution of more lethal firearms such as shotguns and rifles and that criminals prefer more expensive "quality" handguns, not cheap Saturday night specials. Wintermute replies that cheap handguns show up disproportionately in guns recovered from crimes and that lack of safety regulations make the weapons a danger even to their owners.

Glaeser, Edwin L., and Spencer Glendon. "Who Owns Guns? Criminals, Victims, and the Culture of Violence." *American Economic Review*, vol. 88, May 1998, pp. 458ff. Analyzes the distribution of gun ownership and suggests that guns are concentrated in groups whose values and experiences make gun ownership a normal thing. The authors also correlate gun ownership with income, ethnicity, and other factors.

Golden, Frederic. "Drop Your Guns!" *Time*, vol. 150, Fall 1997, pp. 56ff. Reports on Dr. Garen Wintermute's efforts to treat the "epidemic" of gun violence by establishing the Violence Prevention Research Program in 1991. His studies show that gun violence is far more likely to cause fatal or serious injuries as other forms of attack. Golden reports on Wintermute's 1994 "Ring of Fire" study that identified a small group of California gun makers as being responsible for the spread of Saturday night specials.

Goldsmith, Marsha F. "Epidemiologists Aim at New Target: Health Risk of Handgun Proliferation." *JAMA, The Journal of the American Medical Association*, vol. 261, February 3, 1989, pp. 675ff. Reports on the call of Paul Stolley, head of the American College of Epidemiology, for research into gun violence, the findings of Garen Wintermute, and other efforts. Some critics oppose the approach of likening gun use to a disease, while others fear that pursuing such a public health society may politicize medical care.

Gun Ownership. "Tied to Higher Risk for Women's Murder, Suicide." *American Medical News*, vol. 40, April 21, 1997, p. 18. Reports a study that identified risk factors for death of women by murder or suicide. Guns are the most common cause of death, and mental illness, substance abuse, and domestic violence are all important factors. The article recommends encouraging people to store guns safely or to remove them from the household and supports laws that forbid gun purchase by convicted batterers.

"Guns at Home—Do They Protect?" *U.S. News & World Report*, vol. 100, June 23, 1986, p. 9. Reports on Arthur Kellermann's now famous study that claims that guns in the home are 43 times more likely to kill a family member or friend than to kill a criminal intruder. Critics argue that the study ignores many defensive gun uses where no one is killed.

"Guns, Bias and the Evening News." *American Rifleman*, vol. 143, January–February 1995, p. 50. Presents a study and analysis of the media coverage of the Brady Bill debate. The article claims that there is a strong anti-gun bias in the reporting.

Hargarten, Stephen W. "Characteristics of Firearms Involved in Fatalities." *JAMA, The Journal of the American Medical Association*, vol. 275, January 3, 1996, pp. 42–45. Study breaks down firearms fatality by type of gun. Eighty-nine percent of firearm homicides were caused by handguns. Guns are broken down further by caliber and model.

Headden, Susan. "Guns, Money & Medicine: The Proliferation of Powerful New Weapons Has Sent the Cost of Crime Spiraling. Here's Why You Pay." *U.S. News & World Report*, vol. 121, July 1, 1996, pp. 30ff. Analyzes the health costs caused by gun crime, using a variety of example cases. The costs are increasing due to the proliferation of more powerful weapons. All consumers end up paying more for these health costs because tax money must be used to care for the majority of victims, who are uninsured.

Hemenway, David, Sara J. Solnick, and Deborah R. Azrael. "Firearm Training and Storage." *JAMA, The Journal of the American Medical Association*, vol. 273, January 4, 1995, p. 46. Found that gun owners who participated in firearms training courses were more likely to store their guns in unlocked containers, as were handgun owners in general and those who stated self-defense as their main reason for having a gun.

————. "Firearms and Community Feelings of Safety." *Journal of Criminal Law and Criminology*, vol. 86, 1995, pp. 121–132. Reports a survey that finds that about 85 percent of non gun owners would feel less safe if more people in their community owned guns, while for gun owners, about 50 percent would feel safer, and 50 percent less safe.

Kalousdian, Sona, and Sharon B. Buchbinder. "Assault Weapons as a Public Health Hazard in the United States." *JAMA, The Journal of the American Medical Association*, vol. 267, June 10, 1992, pp. 3067–3070. Argues that although actual data is hard to come by, assault weapons are a significant health hazard in the United States due to the penetrating wounds caused by their "high-velocity" rounds and the tendency of bullets to hit bystanders.

Kates, Don B., et al. "Guns and Public Health: Epidemic of Violence or Pandemic of Propaganda?" *Tennessee Law Review*, vol. 62, Spring 1995, pp. 513ff. Argues that studies purporting to show an "epidemic" of gun violence are heavily propagandistic and filled with errors of fact and reasoning. Suggests that many such studies fail to differentiate among firearms users by not employing well-established criminological and sociological factors.

Kellermann, Arthur L., and Donald T. Reay. "Protection or Peril?" *New England Journal of Medicine*, vol. 314, June 12, 1986, pp. 1557–1560. Highly influential study of the risks of keeping firearms in the home. Concludes that there are 43 suicides, criminal homicides, or accidental gunshot deaths for every case of homicide for self-protection.

Kellermann, Arthur L., et al. "Weapon Involvement in Home Invasion Crimes." *JAMA, The Journal of the American Medical Association*, vol. 273, June 14, 1995, pp. 1759ff. Analyzes home invasion crimes. Found that homeowners seldom used guns against intruders. Persons who resisted in some way were less likely to lose property but more likely to be injured. Security measures such as locks are likely to be more useful than firearms for deterring such invasions.

Kent, Christina. "Fight Over Federal Agency Pits Medicine vs. NRA; Funding for Research on Firearms Injuries at Issue." *American Medical News*, vol. 39, August 5, 1996, pp. 3ff. Reports that the National Rifle

Association is trying to stop funding for the National Center for Injury Prevention and Control's research on firearms injuries. Gun rights advocates charge that the research is misguided and biased in favor of gun control. The research is supported by the American Medical Association and other medical groups and is defended as being peer reviewed.

Kizer, Kenneth W., et al. "Hospitalization Charges, Costs, and Income for Firearm-Related Injuries at a University Trauma Center." *JAMA, The Journal of the American Medical Association*, vol. 273, June 14, 1995, pp. 1768–1773. Studies the costs to the University of California, Davis, Medical Center of treating firearms injuries. The authors use the results to estimate a national annual cost of $4 billion.

Kleck, Gary, and Marc Gertz. "Armed Resistance to Crime: The Prevalence and Nature of Self-Defense with a Gun." *Journal of Criminal Law and Criminology*, vol. 86, no. 1, 1995, n.p. [Also available online. URL: http://www.guncite.com/gcdgklec.html. Posted on January 30, 1999.] Argues that use of guns for self-defense is underreported in surveys by government agencies because of fear of prosecution. Kleck's own survey finds an estimated 2.2 to 2.5 defensive gun uses per year.

Kopel, David B. "The Untold Triumph of Concealed-Carry Permits." *Policy Review: The Journal of American Citizenship*, no. 78, July–August 1996, n.p. Argues that liberalization of concealed-carry laws did not substantially affect homicide rates and that the previous study by David McDowall, Colin Loftin, and Brian Wiersema suffers from methodological flaws. Kopel reiterates that the rate of crime by permit holders is very low.

Krug, E. G. "Firearm-Related Deaths in the United States and 35 Other High- and Upper-Middle-Income Countries." *JAMA, The Journal of the American Medical Association*, vol. 280, August 5, 1998, p. 401. Reports that the 49th World Health Assembly has declared violence a worldwide public health problem. Using data provided by health officials, a study concludes that firearms death rates are much higher in the United States and that types of death (murder or suicide) as well as rates vary with national income.

LaPierre, Wayne. "Standing Guard" (Column). *American Rifleman*, vol. 144, May 1996, p. 7. Argues that statistics show that states that jail more criminals for a longer time have lower crime rates and that incarceration is more effective in fighting crime than gun control legislation.

Lewis, Bobbie. "Preventing Firearm Violence: A Public Health Imperative." *Annals of Internal Medicine*, vol. 122, February 15, 1995, pp. 311ff. Points out that the United States has the world's highest rates of firearms-related injury and death. Strong action is needed to address this public health problem, including gun owner training, safety, and storage requirements.

Lott, John R., Jr. "Gun Show." *National Review*, vol. 51, May 31, 1999, p. 32. Argues that new gun laws proposed in the wake of the Littleton shootings would have little effect on preventing such shootings in the future. Although the media seldom mentions it, armed adults in schools have been more successful in stopping some shootings, such as the one in Pearl, Mississippi, in 1997. Lott's studies conclude that of all proposed policies, only giving law-abiding citizens (and school officials) the right to carry guns has any actual effect on reducing the number and severity of mass shootings.

———. "How to Stop Mass Public Shootings." *Los Angeles Times*, vol. 117, May 25, 1998, p. B5. Asserts that studies show that allowing qualified citizens to carry concealed weapons is the best way to prevent multiple-victim shootings.

———. "Trigger Happy." *National Review*, vol. 50, June 22, 1998, p. 49. Recounts author's personal experience dealing with gun control advocates who responded to his studies linking concealed weapons to lower crime by unleashing a barrage of distortions and attacks on his professional integrity. When accusations were shown to be false, the media was generally not interested in running corrections.

Marwick, Charles. "Help Network Says Firearms Data Gap Makes Reducing Gun Injuries More Difficult." *JAMA, The Journal of the American Medical Association*, vol. 218, March 3, 1999, p. 784. Reports surveys conducted by the Handgun Epidemic Lowering Plan (HELP) that tried to measure accuracy and completeness in the reporting of gun-related deaths and injuries. The study found that the reporting of nonfatal injuries was "spotty" and that reports often lacked needed information about the type of firearm involved and the circumstances of the injury.

———. "A Public Health Approach to Making Guns Safer." *JAMA, The Journal of the American Medical Association*, vol. 273, June 14, 1995, pp. 1743ff. Reports on a conference titled "Guns—A Public Health Approach: Making Changes in Making Guns," sponsored by the Association of Trial Lawyers of America and the Johns Hopkins Center for Gun Policy and Research. Participants said their goal was not banning guns but making them safer by applying commonly accepted product regulatory standards to firearms, just as medicines now come with childproof safety caps.

McDowall, David, Colin Loftin, and Brian Wiersema. "Easing Concealed Firearms Laws: Effects on Homicide in Three States." *Journal of Criminal Law and Criminology*, vol. 86, Fall 1995, pp. 193–206. Studies the effects of the liberalization of concealed-carry gun permit laws in Florida, Mississippi, and Oregon. Points out that firearms homicides increased in four out of the five areas studied. The authors conclude that liberalized concealed carry does not reduce gun crime and may increase it.

"Medical Costs for Gunshot Victims Estimated at $2.3 Billion Annually." Associated Press, in *San Francisco Chronicle*, August 4, 1999, p. A2. Reports on a study by researchers at the Sanford Institute of Public Policy at Duke University, based on 1994 data gathered from hospitals. The average cost per injury was $17,000.

Mitka, Mike. "Good News on Guns—But Not for Everyone." *JAMA, The Journal of the American Medical Association*, vol. 280, August 5, 1998, p. 403. Points out that Centers for Disease Control studies show that firearms deaths and injuries peaked in 1993 and have declined since, though they are still on track to become the U.S.'s leading cause of injury death by 2001. Mitka gives various points of view on the significance of this trend and whether studies are ignoring the large number of defensive gun uses.

Nelson, David E. "Population Estimates of Household Firearm Storage Practices and Firearm Carrying in Oregon." *JAMA, The Journal of the American Medical Association*, vol. 275, June 12, 1996, pp. 1744–1748. Gives a percentage breakdown of households with firearms stored in various ways (such as loaded and unlocked) and of firearm carrying. Nelson also gives correlation with alcohol use.

Orr, Daniel L., II, et al. "Regulating Firearm Advertisements." *JAMA, The Journal of the American Medical Association*, vol. 278, September 3, 1997, pp. 701ff. Includes responses to a paper arguing that firearms ads that tout guns for self-protection should be banned as deceptive. Critics argue that the evidence of the prevalence of successful defensive gun use is strong and that the paper mischaracterizes accepted interpretation of the Second Amendment and the language of the advertisements in question. The paper's authors offer rebuttals, critiquing the gun defense studies of Gary Kleck and others, and pointing out that the courts have had the last word on the Second Amendment.

Ottaway, David B. "A Boon to Sales, or a Threat? Safety Devices Split Industry." *The Washington Post*, May 20, 1999, p. A1. Discusses the uncertainty in the gun industry about whether adding safety devices such as trigger locks will help sales by offering added security or will hobble the industry by encouraging mandatory federal standards.

Peterson, Iver. "'Smart Guns' Set Off Debate: Just How 'Smart' Are They?" *The New York Times*, vol. 148, October 22, 1998, p. A1. Discusses development of "smart gun" features by Colt and other companies and debates the effectiveness of devices that would make guns usable only by their owner. Although the idea is attractive, the devices still have technical problems.

Pratt, Larry. "Health Care and Firearms." *Journal of the Medical Association of Georgia*, vol. 83, March 1994, pp. 149–152. The executive director of

Gun Owners of America argues that any study of the health costs of firearms must take into account the deaths and injuries prevented by defensive uses of firearms, including many incidents during which the gun is never fired.

Ratnesar, Romesh. "Should You Carry a Gun? A New Study Argues for Concealed Weapons." *Time*, vol. 151, July 6, 1998, p. 48. Reports on John Lott's latest book, *More Guns Less Crime*. The most extensive study on concealed-carry laws and crime rates yet undertaken, it concludes that areas with more liberal gun-carry laws have lower crime rates. The book has touched off fierce controversy, and gun control advocates dispute some of Lott's statistical methods.

"Ready, Aim, Fire: A Census of Guns." *U.S. News & World Report*, vol. 122, May 19, 1997, p. 32. Briefly reports a study by the Police Association that reports on the distribution of gun ownership in the United States. It is rather concentrated, with 10 percent of adults owning 77 percent of the nation's guns. Other statistics are included.

Rubin, Paul H., and Hashem Dezhbakhsh. "Lives Saved or Lives Lost? The Effects of Concealed-Handgun Laws on Crime." *American Economic Review*, vol. 88, May 1998, pp. 468ff. Suggests that any crime reductions due to concealed-carry laws are much smaller than suggested by John Lott and David Mustard's work. Some crime rates may even increase. Lawmakers should take these patterns into account.

Schulman, J. Neil. "Medical Malpractice." *National Review*, vol. 46, May 2, 1994, pp. 50ff. Argues that Arthur Kellermann's study that claims guns are 43 times more likely to kill a family member or friend than a criminal is misleading. Schulman notes that Kellermann himself cautioned that his original study did not take nonlethal defensive gun use (such as simply brandishing the gun) into account. Schulman also examines fallacies in more recent studies.

Sloan, John Henry, et al. "Handgun Regulations, Crime, Assaults, and Homicide: A Tale of Two Cities." *The New England Journal of Medicine*, vol. 319, November 10, 1988, pp. 1256ff. Presents an influential study that concludes that Vancouver, British Columbia, has a much lower crime death rate than the neighboring U.S. city of Seattle because Canada has much tougher gun control laws.

Smith, Tom W., and Robert J. Smith. "Changes in Firearms Ownership among Women, 1980–1994." *Journal of Criminal Law and Criminology*, vol. 86, Fall 1995, pp. 133–149. Criticizes polls and surveys by pro-gun groups that have reported a great increase in the number of female gun owners or prospective gun owners. Proponents of these surveys have generally not made their methodology clear. The authors cite the General Social Surveys by the National Opinion Research Center to suggest that there has been no statistically significant trend in the ownership of firearms by females.

Suter, Edgar A. "'Assault Weapons' Revisited—An Analysis of the AMA Report." *Journal of the Medical Association of Georgia*, vol. 85, May 1994, n.p. Criticizes the AMA report "Assault Weapons as a Public Health Hazard in the United States." Suter argues that the high ammunition capacity of such weapons is usually irrelevant because only a few shots are fired in most incidents other than well-publicized mass shootings. Suter also accuses the report for relying only on unsubstantiated anecdotal data.

———. "Guns in the Medical Literature—A Failure of Peer Review." *Journal of the American Medical Association of Georgia*, vol. 83, March 1994, pp. 133–147. Also available online. URL: http://www.netdepot.com/~donnybob/medlit.htm. Criticizes the new wave of studies of gun violence by medical researchers. Suter suggests that political biases and ignorance of basic principles of criminology and social science are leading to flawed results.

Suter, Edgar A., James J. Fotis, and Arthur L. Kellermann. "Weapons for Protection in Home Invasion Crimes." *JAMA, The Journal of the American Medical Association*, vol. 275, January 24, 1996, pp. 280ff. Suter argues that Kellermann's study of home invasions was skewed by being based only on police reports and trauma admissions and that what it really looked at was stealth crimes (burglaries), not true home invasions. Homeowner use of firearms is often not reported to police. Even under such circumstances, however, guns proved to be the safest method of resistance. Kellermann defended his data sources and questioned the objectivity of his critics.

Suter, Edgar A., et al. "Firearm Training and Storage." *JAMA, The Journal of the American Medical Association*, vol. 273, June 14, 1995, pp. 1733ff. Criticizes a previous study on this topic for focusing only on how a gun is stored and not on the specific circumstances and for not considering that in some households the risk of criminal attack may outweigh the risk of accident. The authors point out that despite the new focus on the topic, gun accidents in the United States are at an all-time low. The study authors rebut, saying that they did consider relevant variables and that keeping loaded guns is risky even when safety rules are followed.

"Talk to Your Patients About Gun Safety." *American Medical News*, November 9, 1998, p. 19(1). Urges doctors to discuss gun safety issues with their patients. The AMA has a new publication, "Physician Firearm Safety Guide," which can be helpful.

Taubes, Gary. "Violence Epidemiologists Test the Hazards of Gun Ownership." *Science*, vol. 258, October 9, 1992, pp. 213ff. Summarizes a variety of studies on gun violence and crime funded by the Centers for Disease

Control (CDC). The studies and the CDC effort itself has been attacked by the NRA as slipshod and biased against gun rights.

Teret, Stephen P., et al. "Making Guns Safer." *Issues in Science and Technology*, vol. 14, Summer 1998, pp. 37ff. Describes various technologies that can make guns "personalized" and able to be fired only by their owner. Besides reducing accidents involving children, such guns would be virtually useless to thieves.

Tonso, William R. "Guns and the Media: An Examination of the Major Media's Coverage of the Firearm Owners Protection Act Removes All Doubt About Media Bias Aimed at Guns and Law-Abiding Gun Owners." *American Rifleman*, vol. 134, April 1986, pp. 42ff. Gives analysis that claims that media coverage of the 1986 gun law reform bill reveals a significant and pervasive antigun bias.

Van Biema, David. "Peekaboo: The New Detector." *Time*, vol. 145, March 27, 1995, p. 29. Describes a Justice Department project to develop a device that can detect a concealed weapon up to 12 feet away. The device would enable police to find armed people without frisking everyone.

Vernick, Jon S., Stephen P. Teret, and Daniel W. Web. "Regulating Firearm Advertisements That Promise Home Protection: A Public Health Intervention." *JAMA, The Journal of the American Medical Association*, vol. 277, May 7, 1997, pp. 1391ff. Reports that the American Academy of Pediatrics has joined other organizations in petitioning the Federal Trade Commission to regulate firearms advertisements. Such ads often tout the benefits of guns for self-protection, but studies show that guns have more risks than benefits for their owners. The advertising is therefore deceptive.

Voelker, Rebecca. "Taking Aim at Handgun Violence." *JAMA, The Journal of the American Medical Association*, vol. 273, June 14, 1995, pp. 1739ff. Interviews Dr. John P. May. He suggests that doctors recognize risks for firearms injury (including the very presence of any gun in the home) and talk to their patients about risky behaviors and conditions such as depression.

Webster, Daniel W., et al. "Flawed Gun Policy Research Could Endanger Public Safety." *The American Journal of Public Health*, vol. 87, June 1997, pp. 918ff. Attacks the methodology of John Lott and David Mustard's recent study that claims that liberalizing gun-carry laws reduces the crime rate. Among other things, the authors argue that Lott and Mustard mishandled variables and did not take into account the cyclical nature of crime trends.

Weil, Douglas S. "Effects of Limiting Handgun Purchases on Interstate Transfer of Firearms." *JAMA, The Journal of the American Medical*

Association. vol. 275, June 12, 1996, pp. 1759–1761. Study suggests that Virginia's law restricting firearms purchases to one gun per month reduced the number of firearms purchased in Virginia recovered by law enforcement officers from 27 percent to 19 percent.

Wildes, Kevin W. M. "Medicalization and Social Ills." *America,* vol. 180, April 3, 1999, p. 16. Argues that treating firearms misuse as a disease (akin to alcoholism) will fail. Such an approach treats people as passive victims of a condition beyond their control, requiring medical intervention. People are then unlikely to take responsibility for their actions or develop a robust ability to cope with life's challenges.

Wintermute, Garen J. [Testimony Before Senate Judiciary Committee, Subcommittee on Crime, March 31, 1995], in Tamara L. Roleff, ed. *Gun Control: Opposing Viewpoints,* San Diego, Calif.: Lucent, 1997, p. 117–123. Criticizes Gary Kleck's estimate of more than 1 million defensive gun uses annually as too high and gives his own estimate of 82,000. Argues that Kleck's survey sample was too small and that the questions used were imprecise and open to varying interpretation. Wintermute suggests that more modest defensive benefits must be weighed against the risks of domestic violence, of gun accidents, and of criminals stealing guns from homes.

———. "The Relationship between Firearm Design and Firearm Violence, Handguns in the 1990s." *Journal of the American Medical Association,* vol. 275, June 12, 1996, n.p. Identifies disturbing trends in firearm manufacturing in recent years, including more semiautomatic pistols, higher capacity and power handguns, and guns that are easier to conceal and to operate. Many of these factors may result in higher rates of gun fatalities.

Wintermute, Garen J., et al. "The Choice of Weapons in Firearms Suicides." *American Journal of Public Health,* vol. 78, no. 4, July 1988, n.p. Breaks down firearm suicides by type of weapon used and by gender. Handguns are used in 60 percent of the suicides, probably due to their ready availability and easy handling.

Wright, James D. "In the Heat of the Moment." *Reason,* vol. 22, August–September 1990, pp. 44ff. Suggests that by examining the "acquaintance" of shooters and victims to show that most gun deaths are within families is misleading because, for example, two members of rival gangs who simply know each other are counted the same as people who are actually close friends or relatives.

Zimring, Franklin E. "Firearms, Violence and Public Policy." *Scientific American,* vol. 265, November 1991, pp. 48ff. Concludes that increases in the number of firearms in the United States correlate with increases in the crime rate and that existing gun control laws have failed to reverse the trend. A good look at early attempts to frame the gun debate in scientific or medical terms.

Annotated Bibliography

———. "On the Needle-in-the-Haystack and the Deadly Long Gun," in Lee Nisbet, ed. *The Gun Control Debate*, New York: Prometheus, 1990, pp. 165–169. Gun control opponents often argue that with the huge number of guns available in the country, criminals who are willing to break the law will always be able to arm themselves. Zimring argues that they overestimate the ratio of available guns to criminals and that the argument that a handgun ban would lead to substitution of deadlier long guns is unsubstantiated.

INTERNET DOCUMENTS

Blackman, Paul H. "Criminology's Astrology: An Evaluation of Public Health Research on Firearms and Violence." Available online. URL: http://teapot.usask.ca/pub/cdn-firearms/Blackman/medbash1.txt. Posted on January 31, 1995. Takes on the "gun violence epidemic" researchers, arguing that their studies are simplistic, focus only on the "bottom line" of deaths and injuries without understanding context, ignore sound principles of criminology, and are driven by a policy agenda.

Center to Prevent Handgun Violence. "Concealed Truth: Concealed Weapons Laws and Trends in Violent Crime in the United States." Available online. URL: http://www.handguncontrol.org/concealed.htm. Updated on August 9, 1999. Attacks John Lott's research that suggests that allowing more citizens to carry concealed weapons reduces crime. The center's own study concludes that in states with liberalized gun-carry laws, crime either increased or decreased to a smaller extent than the national trends. The article includes charts.

———. "Research on Gun Violence and Gun Violence Prevention." Available online. URL: http://www.handguncontrol.org/research.htm. Downloaded on July 6, 1999. Collects latest studies said to refute arguments of gun advocates and to demonstrate the effectiveness of gun control legislation. Issues include concealed weapons carry, waiting/cooling-off periods, and "one gun a month" laws.

Federal Bureau of Investigation. "Crime in the United States, 1997." Available online. URL: http://www.fbi.gov/pressrm/pressrel98/ucrpress.htm. Posted on November 22, 1998. Summarizes crime figures and trends from 1997 data released in the Uniform Crime Report.

———. "Uniform Crime Reports." Available online. URL: http://www.fbi.gov/ucr.htm. Downloaded on July 7, 1999. Provides access to the most comprehensive and authoritative compilation of crime-related statistics, including those relating to firearms. Statistics are issued annually.

Kistner, William. "Firearm Injuries: The Gun Battle Over Science." Available online. URL: http://www.pbs.org/wgbh/pages/frontline/shows

/guns/procon/injuries.html. Posted in May 1997. Describes the science and politics of research into gun violence, including the NRA's attempt to remove funding for the Centers for Disease Control's research, claiming that it is biased "junk science." This article accompanies a PBS *Frontline* episode called "Ring of Fire."

Kopel, David B. "Polls: Anti-Gun Propaganda." Available online. URL: http://www.nraila.org/research/19990716-MediaPress_001.html. Posted in April 1998. Gives examples to argue that pollsters such as Gallup and Harris often frame their questions on gun issues in a biased way. For example, "assault rifles" are conflated with fully automatic weapons, the NRA "instant background check" is not presented as an alternative to waiting periods, and polls are sometimes "warmed up" with emotional material on gun violence.

Langer, Gary. "Support for Gun Control Stable: But Poll Also Finds Lack of Confidence in Lawmakers." Available online. URL: ABCNews Online. http://more.abcnews.go.com/sections/us/DailyNews/guns_poll990518. html. Posted on May 18, 1999. According to an ABC News/*The Washington Post* poll, public support for gun control in general remains steady at about 80 percent, with about 70 percent favoring a ban on assault weapons. But much lower percentages believe that politicians will actually do something reasonable about the issue. Surprisingly, approval for the National Rifle Association has risen to 48 percent, with 31 percent opposed.

Lott, John R., Jr., and David B. Mustard. "Crime, Deterrance, and Right-To-Carry Concealed Handguns." Available online. URL: http://www.journals.uchicago.edu/JLS/lott.pdf. Downloaded on June 7, 1999. In the most extensive study of the effects of laws allowing the concealed carry of handguns, the authors conclude that the result was an average reduction in murders of 8.5 percent, rapes 5 percent, and aggravated assault 7 percent. This translates to a reduction of murders by 1,570 if such laws were enacted in the whole country.

Physicians for Social Responsibility (Los Angeles). "Resources in Medicine and Firearms." Available online. URL: http://home.glassla.org/PSR/resources.html. Updated on August 29, 1996. Collects resource links (including fact sheets and journal abstracts) on firearms-violence-related topics including costs, impact on youth and minorities, suicide, and interventions to promote gun safety and peaceful behavior.

"Ring of Fire." Available online. URL: http://www.pbs.org/wgbh/pages/frontline/shows/guns/. Downloaded on June 15, 1999. PBS *Frontline* series reports on the small number of California-based companies in the "Ring of Fire" who are responsible for the distribution of most of the cheap handguns (Saturday night specials) in the United States. The web site suggests that marketing practices and lax security at these companies feed the illegal gun market.

Schekall, Regina. "Organized Crime: A Crime Statistics Page." Available online. URL: http://www.crime.org/homepage.html. Downloaded on July 7, 1999. Provides a useful "front end" to crime statistics databases and explains what is available on the web and the appropriate use of different sources of data.

U.S. Department of Justice. Office of Justice Programs. "Bureau of Justice Statistics." Available online. URL: http://www.ojp.usdoj.gov/bjs/. Downloaded on July 7, 1999. This statistical database provides access to a large volume of statistics relating to crime and the justice system collected by federal agencies.

GUNS, CHILDREN, AND SCHOOLS

This section deals with what has become a major concern in the gun debate: children and gun violence (and accidental shootings) at home and in the schools. It includes both reports about this phenomenon and some materials written for young people to educate them about guns and gun violence.

BOOKS

Apel, Lorelei. *Dealing With Weapons at School and at Home.* New York: Rosen Publication Group's PowerKids Press, 1997. Simple guide to help young people avoid danger from guns and other weapons they may encounter in their daily life.

Cox, Vic. *Guns, Violence, and Teens.* Springfield, N.J.: Enslow, 1997. Written for teenagers and takes a teen viewpoint in looking at guns in schools, gang violence, and the positions in the public debate over gun control. Cox includes statistics and suggestions for nonviolent approaches to conflict resolution.

Schulson, Rachel, and Mary Jones (Illustrator). *Guns—What You Should Know.* Morton Grove, Ill.: A. Whitman, 1997. For children 4–8. Without taking sides, this book clearly and simply describes how guns work and how dangerous they can be. The authors include a list of simple rules for a child to follow if he or she finds a gun.

Schwarz, Ted. *Kids and Guns: The History, the Present, the Dangers, and the Remedies.* New York: Franklin Watts, 1999. For young readers. Gives an overview of the history and issues involved in gun control, including recent events, facts, and statistics.

Sheley, Joseph F. *In the Line of Fire: Youths, Guns, and Violence in Urban America.* New York: A. de Gruyter, 1995. Describes an extensive study that focused on the growing problem of gun violence among youth. Sheley points to fear rather than criminal intent as the main motivating factor for young people to get guns and suggests addressing the conditions for such fear rather than focusing on the guns themselves.

Sheley, Joseph F., and James D. Wright. *High School Youths, Weapons, and Violence: A National Survey.* Washington, D.C.: National Institute of Justice, 1998. Reports and analyzes national survey results on youth violence.

Sheley, Joseph F., Zina T. McGee, and James D. Wright. *Weapon-Related Victimization in Selected Inner-City High School Samples.* Washington, D.C.: National Institute of Justice, 1995. An analysis of the types of weapons and circumstances involved in high school violence.

ARTICLES AND PAPERS

Allen, Tom. "Keep Guns out of School." *Education Digest*, vol. 64, December 1998, pp. 27ff. Suggests approaches to keeping guns out of schools. Allen argues that metal detectors are no substitute for creating a social environment that rewards cooperation and discourages resorting to violence.

Ayor, Massad. "Arm Teachers to Stop School Shootings." *The Wall Street Journal*, May 21, 1999, p. A12. Suggests that having some trained and qualified teachers with weapons in school could prevent mass killings like the Littleton High School shootings.

"Children and Guns." *Pediatrics for Parents*, vol. 16, May 1995, p. 1. Reports a study by Sara M. Naureckas, M.D., of Chicago's Children's Memorial Hospital that found that, contrary to popular belief, even very young children have the strength to fire most available handguns.

Cole, Thomas B. "Authorities Address U.S. Drug-Related 'Arms Race.'" *JAMA, The Journal of the American Medical Association*, vol. 275, March 6, 1996, pp. 672ff. Reports on a 1996 "Conference on Guns and Violence in America." Participants concluded that the distribution of guns among youth, initially fueled by drugs, is increasing the risk of mortality in the population as guns spread to youths who are not involved in the drug trade. Cole quotes opinions based on studies by a variety of criminologists and other researchers, with no consensus on banning all guns but with some agreement on measures to regulate more tightly the gun trade, such as through registration and banning of private sales.

Cummings, Peter, et al. "State Gun Safe Storage Laws and Child Mortality Due to Firearms." *JAMA, The Journal of the American Medical Association*, vol. 278, October 1, 1997, pp. 1084ff. Finds that unintentional deaths from firearms dropped an average of 23 percent in 12 states that had passed laws making parents liable for injuries caused by guns that were not securely stored.

Davis, James W. "More Guns and Younger Assailants: A Combined Police and Trauma Center Study." *JAMA, The Journal of the American Medical Association*, vol. 279, March 4, 1998, p. 640. Studies admissions to a regional trauma center. Davis finds that more young assailants are using guns than before and that the average age of victims is getting younger.

Fortgang, Erika. "How They Got the Guns." *Rolling Stone*, June 10, 1999, pp. 51ff. Explores the question of where young mass shooters, such as the high school students in Littleton, obtain their guns. The main sources are gun shows (where no background check is required) and unlicensed dealers, though guns are also stolen from parents or others.

Gest, Ted. "Firearms Folk." *U.S. News & World Report*, vol. 122, January 13, 1997, pp. 19ff. Reports that veteran folk trio Peter, Paul, and Mary have rewritten their song "Where Have All the Flowers Gone?" to point out the toll gun violence is taking on children.

Gibbs, Nancy. "TIME Special Report (Guns in America; Troubled Kids)." *Time*, vol. 153, May 31, 1999, p. 32. Reflects on the feeling of helplessness as people in the media, who love to provide answers, can find no answers to the violence erupting in the schools.

Heim, David. "American Mayhem: School Shootings." *The Christian Century*, vol. 115, June 3, 1998, pp. 563ff. Explores the disturbing increase in the number and severity of school shootings (prior to the Littleton incident). Heim suggests that although poverty, family breakdown, and the availability of guns all play a role, the responsibility of the media cannot be ignored. Media creators cannot at the same time tout the power of imagination and refuse to take some responsibility for its effects.

"High-School Violence Reportedly Declining: National Survey Probes Beyond Sensational Incidents." *Los Angeles Times* in *San Francisco Chronicle*, August 4, 1999, p. A4. Reports on a study from the U.S. Centers for Disease Control and Prevention that found that the number of high school students who said they carried a weapon to school fell by 28 percent from 1993 to 1997. However, significant violence and the perception of lack of safety persists in many areas.

Jourdan, Jeanne. "A Community's Answer to Teen Violence." *Children Today*, vol. 23, Winter–Spring 1994, pp. 20ff. Describes a program started by volunteers in South Bend, Indiana, who were concerned about teen violence. The "This is My Neighborhood—No Shooting Allowed" program teaches children alternatives to violence as a way of solving disputes and tries to change attitudes toward violence.

Kachur, S. Patrick. "School-Associated Violent Deaths in the United States, 1992 to 1994." *JAMA, The Journal of the American Medical Association*, vol.

275 (1996), pp. 1729–1733. Surveys data on violent deaths in schools, breaking it down by age, size of community, and other factors. Kachur suggests that such deaths are more common than previously estimated and that a "comprehensive approach" is needed.

Kopel, David B. "Gun Play: What Kids Don't Know About Guns Can Kill Them." *Reason*, vol. 25, July 1993, pp. 18ff. Argues that new gun laws are actually endangering children by making it harder to give them proper training in safe handling of firearms. Youngsters are left to learn about guns from TV or their peers. Kopel also argues that distortion of facts and figures is making rational gun policy difficult.

Levin, Bob. "Casualties of the Right to Bear Arms: Today's Outcasts Can Grab a Handy Semiautomatic and, Taking Cool Moves from the Latest Flick, Go Kill Their Classmates." *Maclean's*, May 3, 1999, p. 27. Author provides a Canadian, pro gun control viewpoint on the Littleton High School shootings. Levin ridicules the U.S. gun culture in recounting his personal experience with aspects of it.

Merina, Anita. "Fighting School Violence Means Taking on Guns." *NEA Today*, vol. 12, March 1994, pp. 4ff. Reports that the incidence of gun-related violence in schools is rising and discusses measures being taken to combat it, such as using metal detectors and taking legal action against offenders.

Noonan, Peggy. "Sins of the Fathers." *Good Housekeeping*, vol. 227, July 1998, p. 178. Suggests that although the right to keep and bear arms is important, gun owners must personally exercise more "gun control" by handling and storing their guns safely, teaching youngsters that guns are not toys, and combating the glorification of violence in the media.

Page, Randy M., and Jon Hammermeister. "Weapon-Carrying and Youth Violence." *Adolescence*, vol. 32, Fall 1997, pp. 505ff. Reviews surveys and studies on the prevalence and patterns of weapons carrying among youth. The authors suggest that weapons carrying is associated more with aggressive or criminal behavior than the desire for self-defense. The authors also describe specifics involving firearms and the need for schools to develop policies and practices to keep guns out of schools, as well as specifics for promoting gun control legislation.

Pipho, Chris. "Living With Zero Tolerance." *Phi Delta Kappan*, vol. 79, June 1998, pp. 725ff. Discusses the problems of crafting weapons bans for schools to comply with federal mandates. Some states ban a broader range of weapons including knives, which are not covered under the federal law. This has led to embarrassing incidents such as a student being suspended for having a tiny paring knife for cutting a lunchtime apple. Some states have also broadened their policy to include drugs, alcohol, and other items. Pipho gives examples of state provisions.

"Rates of Homicide, Suicide, and Firearm-Related Death Among Children—26 Industrialized Countries." *Morbidity and Mortality Weekly Report*, vol. 46, February 7, 1997, pp. 101ff. Concludes that the United States has by far the highest rates of child homicide, suicide, and firearms-related deaths among the industrialized nations.

Rivo, Marc. "Counseling Parents About Firearm Safety." *American Family Physician*, vol. 53, February 1, 1996, p. 693. Reports a survey of physicians that indicates that although a majority of the doctors believe they should counsel patients about firearms safety, few actually do so.

Schoolfield, Susan H. "Can Children and Guns Coexist in the Home?" *USA Today (Magazine)*, vol. 122, January 1994, pp. 40ff. Gives statistics on the prevalence of guns in homes and the rate of gun-related murder, suicide, and accidents. Schoolfield describes emerging organizations promoting gun safety, new safety devices, and recommendations for gun owners. She also recommends that parents be held responsible for guns accessed by children, comparing it to sanctions against drunk driving.

Senturia, Yvonne D., et al. "Gun Storage Patterns in U.S. Homes With Children: A Pediatric Practice-Based Survey." *Archives of Pediatrics & Adolescent Medicine*, vol. 150, March 1996, pp. 265ff. Finds that the majority of gun owners do not lock up their guns and that persons who use guns at work or for self-protection are most likely to have them loaded at home. The authors suggest that childrens' doctors talk to parents about the need to store firearms safely.

Shapiro, Bruce. "The Guns of Littleton." *The Nation*, vol. 268, May 17, 1999, p. 4. Insists that whatever the complex social and psychological causes that alienated Littleton shooters Dylan Klebold and Eric Harris, what adds a new dimension to the threat is today's ready availability of powerful firearms. Gun makers have flooded the market, with many sales targeted to young people.

"Teens Under Siege: How Kids Can Go Wrong—And What Parents Can Do." *Maclean's*, May 3, 1999, p. 22. Reports on Canadian reaction to the Littleton, Colorado, high school shootings. Although Canada has fewer guns and stricter gun laws (including registration), gun control is only part of what needs to be addressed in dealing with the social forces that are breeding alienation among youth.

Tyson, Anne Scott. "How to Keep Firearms Out of Children's Hands." *The Christian Science Monitor*, vol. 89, April 6, 1998, p. 3. Gives suggestions for storing firearms safely and keeping them out of the hands of children.

Walsh, Edward. "Big Drop in Kids Expelled for Guns at School." *San Francisco Chronicle*, August 11, 1999, p. A3. Reports a survey by the federal Department of Education that found that the number of students expelled from schools for gun possession during the 1997–1998 school year has declined sharply from previous years. Both demographics and heightened security efforts may be responsible for the decline.

Wilkinson, Todd. "At Home With Guns." *The Christian Science Monitor,* May 26, 1999, p. 11. Describes the relationship between youngsters and guns in communities where hunting is popular. Such families often practice gun safety and tend to support some gun control, especially on assault weapons and Saturday night specials. But the declining number of hunters and the shock of school shootings may be eroding rural gun culture.

Wintermute, Garen J. "When Children Shoot Children: 88 Unintended Deaths in California." *JAMA, The Journal of the American Medical Association,* vol. 257, no. 22, June 12, 1987, pp. 3107–3109. Studies gun accidents involving children. Wintermute concludes that the keeping of guns in the home in the mistaken belief that they are good protection is a major factor in such accidents. Another is deficiencies in firearm design, such as lack of proper safety devices.

Witkin, Gordon. "Stopping Youth Violence By Stopping Gun Theft." *U.S. News & World Report,* vol. 123, no. 23, December 15, 1997, p. 26(1). Argues that schools can do only so much to keep guns out. The root of the problem is stolen guns—about a half million a year, 80 percent from private homes. Better locking and "personalization" devices may eventually keep guns from being stolen.

Wolcott, Jennifer. "Parent-to-Parent: Is the Gun Safely Stored?" *The Christian Science Monitor,* May 26, 1999, p. 15. Discusses approaches to parents talking to their neighbors about the safe storage of firearms. The recent school shootings can provide a springboard for such discussion while concern is high.

INTERNET DOCUMENTS

American Academy of Pediatrics and Center to Prevent Handgun Violence. "Steps to Prevent Firearm Injury in the Home (STOP2)." Available online. URL: http://www.handguncontrol.org/protecting/D3/d3stop2.htm. Downloaded on June 5, 1999. Describes newest version of the STOP program and package of materials to help pediatricians and other health professionals counsel families about ways to reduce the risk of firearms-related injuries.

Center to Prevent Handgun Violence. "Children and Firearms." Available online. URL: http://www.aacap.org/factsfam/firearms.htm. Downloaded on July 7, 1999. Describes the risks of guns in the home and urges that guns be removed. Failing that, the web site offers safe storage suggestions.

———. "Clarence and Guns." Available online. URL: http://www.handguncontrol.org/game.htm. Downloaded on June 5, 1999. A simple web-based interactive game where youngsters learn to make good decisions about how to deal with guns.

———. "Kids Shooting Kids." Available online. URL: http://www.cphv.org/news/may97.htm#kids. Downloaded on July 7, 1999. Describes a new report about recent incidents where children intentionally or accidentally shot other children.

Centers for Disease Control. "1997 Youth Risk Behavior Surveillance System (YRBSS)." Available online. URL: http://www.cdc.gov/nccdphp/dash/yrbs/natsum97/susc.htm. Posted on May 24, 1999. Summarizes data from a survey measuring the extent of students' risky (violent) behavior and perception of risk in the school environment.

Handgun Control and Center To Prevent Handgun Violence. "Is My Family Safe: STOP2 Quiz." Available online. URL: http://www.handguncontrol.org/protecting/D3/stop.htm. Posted on February 14, 1999. Interactive true/false quiz that helps determine whether a family is safe from firearms injuries.

Kopel, David B. "Children and Guns: Sensible Solutions." Independence Institute. Available online. URL: http://rkba.org/research/kopel/kidsgun.html. Downloaded on April 25, 1993. Argues that safety education, youth development, and proper law enforcement can reduce gun accidents and violence involving children, while "gimmicky" safety devices, laws, and lawsuits are unlikely to be effective.

———. "President's Politicking Won't Achieve Goal." Independence Institute. Available online. URL: http://i2i.org/SuptDocs/OpEdArcv/1999/GunControlNoAnswer.htm. Posted on May 6, 1999. Argues that although President Clinton is using the Littleton High School shooting tragedy to push a new package of gun control measures, none of them could have prevented the year-long premeditated murder plan of two high school killers.

National Center for Injury Prevention and Control. "Facts About Violence Among Youth and Violence in Schools." Available online. URL: http://www.cdc.gov/ncipc/dvp/schoolvi.htm. Downloaded on July 7, 1999. Describes facts and circumstances relating to homicide and other serious violence involving youth, particularly in schools.

———. "Youth Violence in the United States Fact Sheet." Available online. URL: http://www.cdc.gov/ncipc/dvp/yvpt/newfacts.htm. Downloaded on July 7, 1999. Describes the magnitude of the youth violence problem, identifies primary risk factors, summarizes studies and findings. The web page includes references.

INTERNATIONAL PERSPECTIVES

Gun control is generally not a public issue outside of North America, but there are exceptions, including Great Britain and other English-speaking countries such as Australia and New Zealand. This section is a representative sampling of writings about the gun control issue in these countries, as well as comparisons with the United States.

BOOKS

Crook, John. *Gun Massacres in Australia: The Case for Gun Control.* Chelsea, Victoria, Australia: Gun Control Australia, n.d. An overview of 21 gun killings that took place in Australia during the years 1987 to mid-1994, and an examination of the attempts to control gun misuse as a result of the killings.

Halbrook, Stephen P. *Target Switzerland: Swiss Armed Neutrality in World War II.* Rockville Centre, N.Y.: Sarpedon, 1998. Argues that Switzerland's armed neutrality during World War II was made possible by its decentralized federal system and its unique system of "citizen soldier" militia. Although the book does not focus on gun rights, the relationship of the Swiss system to the U.S. Second Amendment and collective self-defense makes this book relevant to the gun debate.

Kopel, David B. *Gun Control in Great Britain: Saving Lives or Constricting Liberty?* Chicago: Office of International Criminal Justice, University of Illinois at Chicago, 1992. Analysis of British gun control laws and their effectiveness.

Simkin, J., and Aaron Zelman. *Gun Control: Gateway to Tyranny: The Nazi Weapons Law, 18 March 1938.* Hartford, Wisc.: Jews for the Preservation of Firearms Ownership, 1992. Describes Nazi gun control legislation and asserts that it became the model for U.S. gun control efforts starting in the 1960s. The authors generally view gun control as a key element in the totalitarian project.

ARTICLES AND PAPERS

"America and Guns." *The Economist*, vol. 346, April 4, 1998, pp. 16ff. Presents a British viewpoint on U.S. gun problems, giving statistics comparing gun deaths in the United States with other countries and expressing incredulity concerning the U.S.'s gun culture.

"America's Vigilante Values." *The Economist*, vol. 323, June 20, 1992, pp. 17ff. British viewpoint that argues that the refusal of Americans to embrace gun control comes not only from claims about the Constitution but also from "vigilante values" that are also seen in the willingness of the U.S. government to kidnap suspects abroad.

Beltrame, Julian, and John Urquhart. "Shootings Mar Canadian Confidence in Tough Gun Laws Curbing Bloodbaths." *The Wall Street Journal*, April 30, 1999, p. B8. Reports that Canadians are discouraged about two recent multiple shootings in their country and are wondering whether the tough new Canadian gun laws can really have an effect on such tragedies.

Bonner, Raymond. "21 Nations Seek to Limit the Traffic in Light Weapons." *The New York Times*, vol. 147, July 13, 1998, p. A3. Describes an international conference in Oslo, Norway, that is attempting to forget agreements that would reduce the distribution of small arms (mostly rifles) that are plentiful in the world's trouble spots.

———. "After Land-Mine Triumph, Groups Combat Small Arms; Weapons Wreak Havoc Around the World." *The New York Times*, vol. 147, January 7, 1998, p. A8. Reports that groups that had spearheaded an international campaign to stop the use of land mines are turning their attention to the proliferation of small arms that are involved in violent clashes and crime in many countries.

"Cambodia's City of Guns." *The Economist*, October 24, 1998, p. 40. Describes the situation of Cambodia's capital Phnom Penh, where decades of civil war have left the population with 50,000 guns. Afraid of crime and disorder, most people have refused the government's request that the guns be turned in. The article suggests that the government must offer real security and reduce corruption before the populace will cooperate.

Centerwall, Brandon S. "Homicide and the Prevalence of Handguns: Canada and the United States, 1976 to 1980." *American Journal of Epidemiology*, vol. 124, December 1, 1991, n.p. Suggests that in actual border areas the homicide rates for the United States and Canada are comparable and generally low. These areas tend to be similar demographically and sociologically. Since the U.S. areas have 3–10 times more handguns than their Canadian counterparts, this suggests that the prevalence of handguns has little effect on the murder rate.

Cordner, Stephen, and Kathy Ettershank. "Gun-Toting Australians Take Aim at New Weapons-Control Law." *The Lancet*, vol. 347, no. 9015, June 8, 1996, p. 1616(1). Reports on the growing militancy of Australian gun owners who are trying to block a ban on semiautomatic weapons.

Ettershank, Kathy, and Stephen Cordner. "Landmark Australian Gun Laws Finally Get Go-Ahead." *The Lancet*, vol. 348, no. 9023, August 3, 1996, p. 327(1). Describes new strict Australian gun laws that are taking effect that ban all semiautomatic weapons, require registration for all other guns, and allow gun ownership only for "valid reasons," such as belonging to a legitimate shooting club.

Fennell, Tom. "Taking Aim on Guns: A Rash of Brutal Murders Sparks Calls for More Controls on Firearms." *Maclean's*, vol. 107, April 25, 1994, pp. 10ff. Describes the upsurge in Canadian interest in gun control following brutal murders in Toronto. But a recent undercover police investigation suggests that the main source for crime guns in Canada is smuggling from the United States, which is hard to stop with domestic laws.

"Firing at Gun Control." *Maclean's*, vol. 110, September 22, 1997, p. 33. Describes the constitutional battle as provincial attorneys general try to overturn Canada's national gun registration law as unconstitutional. Their arguments are based on local jurisdiction over private property and what they claim is the irrelevance of regulation of long guns to crime control.

Fisher, Luke. "In the Crossfire: Firearms Owners Lobby Ottawa to Drop Plans for Tougher Gun Control." *Maclean's*, vol. 107, October 3, 1994, pp. 14ff. Reports that gun owners, aided by the Reform Party in western Canada, are organizing to oppose the Liberal government's plans for further gun controls.

Goldring, Natalie J. "The NRA Goes Global." *Bulletin of the Atomic Scientists*, vol. 55, January 1999, p. 61. Argues that gun control will only become a reality when the international flow of arms is stopped. The NRA is using its formidable resources to try to detail efforts of nongovernmental organizations (NGOs) to create international laws that would regulate weapons manufacture and distribution.

"Gun Control: Canada." *The Economist*, vol. 333, October 29, 1994, p. 50ff. Describes Canada's battle over gun control, which pits the Coalition for Gun Control against the National Firearms Association, Canada's version of the NRA. Canada already has stricter gun laws than the United States, and gun control is favored by a majority of the population.

"Gun Law in Brazil." *The Economist (U.S.)*, vol. 351, June 19, 1999, p. 29. Reports that Brazil's government is pushing for a total ban on gun ownership but is being opposed by a newly formed gun lobby. Brazil has experienced a high rate of crime and mass shootings in recent years. Police corruption and government inefficiency may undermine the effectiveness of such laws.

Hewlett, Bill. "Innocents Lost: The People of Dunblane, Scotland Bid Farewell to the Victims of a Day That Will Never Be Forgotten." *People Weekly*, vol. 45, April 1, 1996, pp. 42ff. Describes the somber and reflective mood following the killing of 17 kindergarten children and their teacher in Dunblane, Scotland. People wonder how the shooter, Thomas Hamilton, had been able to get a gun permit: Though he had broken no laws, he had frequently been accused of improprieties in supervising youth activities.

Annotated Bibliography

"Hey, Anybody Want a Gun?" *The Economist*, vol. 347, May 16, 1998, pp. 47ff. Reports that the United States and 45 other nations have recently begun work on a protocol to control the proliferation of small arms, which often lead to unstable conditions in emerging nations. Opposition by the NRA, however, resulted in outright gun bans being dropped from the agenda.

"Hitting the Right Target." *New Statesman*, vol. 125, August 16, 1996, p. 5. Considers the possibility that the committee investigating the Dunblane shootings may recommend a total ban on handguns in Britain. The article argues that such a ban would hurt gun owners without reducing crime. If the society is serious about the crime problem, it must reexamine its values and social priorities.

Howe, Darcus. "Brixton Is in Shock. Gun Law Is a Different Order of Threat, Impossible To Respond To." *New Statesman*, vol. 126, June 13, 1997, p. 17. Describes the aftermath of gang shootings in a black neighborhood in Brixton, England. With the failure, to prevent the violence, despite strict gun laws, the community appears demoralized and must rally.

Kelly, Ned. "The Kiwis & Their Guns." *American Rifleman*, vol. 141, January 1993, pp. 42ff. Reports that recent gun control developments in New Zealand are making it harder for legitimate hunters and sports shooters to obtain firearms.

Knox, Neal. "Lesson from Australia, U.K." *American Rifleman*, vol. 145, May 1997, p. 17. Argues that the same tactics of guile and deception used by politicians to pass gun laws in Australia and the United Kingdom are likely to be used in the United States; gun rights advocates must be ready to respond.

Kopel, David B. "The Allure of Foreign Gun Laws." *Journal of the Medical Association of Georgia*, vol. 83, March 1994, pp. 153–155. Gun control advocates often suggest that the strict gun control laws in nations such as Great Britain and Japan are responsible for their having much lower murder rates than the United States. Kopel points to the counterexample of Switzerland, where all citizens receive military training and have assault rifles in their homes, as well as easy access to many other weapons. Yet Switzerland has a low murder rate, similar to Japan's. Kopel suggests that because it has a strong family and social structure and no gun control, the country can keep its crime rates low.

Kopel, David B., and Stephen D'Andrilli. "The Swiss and Their Guns." *American Rifleman*, vol. 138, February 1990, pp. 38ff. Describes the role of guns in Switzerland, where citizens receive military training and have automatic weapons and other firearms; yet there is little gun violence.

McGuire, Stryker. "The Dunblane Effect: Horror from the Massacre Prompts a Ban on Handguns." *Newsweek*, vol. 128, October 28, 1996,

p. 46. Suggests that horror at the killing of kindergarten children in Dunblane, Scotland, has made the British impatient with reform and willing to push for a total ban on handguns.

Metaksa, Tanya K. "Global Gun Control Is on the March." *American Rifleman*, vol. 145, August 1997, pp. 42ff. Criticizes the United Nations for adopting a Japanese proposal for international firearms regulations as it is based on faulty data and possibly could result in infringement on Americans' gun rights.

———. "Gun Owners Branded 'A Threat to Mankind.'" *American Rifleman*, vol. 146, April 1998, pp. 38ff. Reports that the United Nations is moving toward institutionalizing an anti-gun position in international law and relations. The NRA has been trying to become an accredited nongovernmental organization so that it can monitor UN efforts from inside.

Nemeth, Mary. "Fighting Back: Farmers, Hunters and Firearms Enthusiasts Are Turning the Gun-Control Debate into Trench Warfare." *Maclean's*, vol. 108, June 5, 1995, pp. 14ff. Reports on proposed tougher gun control laws in Canada and the mobilization of gun rights groups to oppose them. Nemeth quotes a variety of people on both sides and summarizes current and proposed gun laws.

Otchet, Amy. "Small Arms, Many Hands." *UNESCO Courier*, November 1998, pp. 37ff. Describes the efforts of a group of nongovernmental organizations that is waging an international campaign against the proliferation of light weapons (such as automatic rifles) around the world. Otchet also describes the extent of the problem (500 million small arms worldwide) and the politics involved in coming to a consensus for control measures.

"Out of Control: Australia." *The Economist*, vol. 341, November 30, 1996, p. 36. Reports on the mass shooting in Hobart, Australia, where 35 people were killed by Martin Bryant with a semiautomatic rifle. In response, there has been a push for tighter gun control and all Australian states have banned semiautomatic rifles and shotguns.

Riddell, Mary. "Dunblane and the Damned Politicians." *New Statesman*, vol. 125, October 18, 1996, p. 7. Suggests that although the goals of gun control advocates are reasonable, the rush to take advantage of popular emotions following the Dunblane shootings can result in bad public policy that makes promises that can't be delivered.

Safran, Claire. "A Tale of Two Cities—And the Difference Guns Make." *Good Housekeeping*, vol. 217, November 1993, pp. 134ff. Discusses research led by Dr. John Henry Sloan of Seattle's Harborview Medical Center that shows that although Vancouver, British Columbia, and Seattle, Washington, have similar demographics and overall crime rates, the

Canadian city has far fewer gun deaths. The obvious difference is that Canada has much stricter gun laws.

Schneider, Howard. "Check Your Guns at the City Limits." *The Washington Post*, September 14, 1998, p. A15. Reports on new gun control laws in Yemen, a country that has been beset by its share of bandits and lawlessness.

Selick, Karen. "Gun Control Way Off Target." *Reader's Digest (Canadian)*, vol. 148, May 1996, pp. 115ff. Criticizes Canada's 1996 gun control bill as a violation of the right to choice about self-defense.

Sewell, Dennis. "Guns 'N' Red Roses." *New Statesman & Society*, vol. 9, May 24, 1996, p. 11. Reports that although the British public supports gun control, the attempts by opportunistic politicians such as Jack Straw to capitalize on the Dunblane shooting tragedy may be backfiring. Sewell also presents arguments by gun rights advocates.

Simonds, Merilyn. "Code of Arms." *Canadian Geographic*, vol. 116, March–April 1996, pp. 44ff. Describes the gun scene in Canada, which has a reasonable number of guns but doesn't have the emotional attachment to them that many people in the United States have. Simonds reviews the different historical experiences that people in Canada and the United States have had with firearms. She also discusses events that have heated up the gun control debate in Canada. A related article gives a brief chronology of gun control in Canada.

Sloan, John Henry, et al. "Handgun Regulations, Crime, Assaults, and Homicide: A Tale of Two Cities." *New England Journal of Medicine*, vol. 319, November 10, 1988, pp. 1256–1261. Compares gun regulations and crime rates in Seattle and Vancouver, British Columbia. Concludes that because the cities are similar in many respects, Vancouver's much lower crime rate is due to its much stricter gun controls.

Smith, James F. "Mexican Congress Takes Aim at Illegal Guns from U.S." *Los Angeles Times*, vol. 117, September 7, 1998, p. A3. Reports on Mexican crackdown on people from the United States who smuggle guns into the country, including the jailing of U.S. citizens charged with smuggling.

"A Tale of Two Lobbies: Why Do Two Similar Countries Disagree So Profoundly About Guns?" *The Economist*, vol. 341, October 19, 1996, p. 20. Notes that although the United States and Britain have many cultural similarities, the shootings at Dunblane, Scotland, are propelling the United Kingdom to stricter gun laws, while similar incidents in the United States have thus far failed to lead to substantial new gun control measures. One difference is that the United States has a constitutional amendment that sometimes comes into conflict with public opinion, and the United States, unlike Britain, has a powerful gun lobby.

"Uplift That Gun." *The Economist*, vol. 312, September 23, 1989, p. 37. Reports on a movement for gun control in the Philippines, where the legacy of civil unrest, crime, and corruption has flooded the country with guns and a "cowboy ethic."

Wilson, Chris Oliver. "Disarming News: Why Bobbies Have No Guns." *U.S. News & World Report*, vol. 124, February 9, 1998, pp. 46ff. Describes the total ban on handguns that Britain put into effect in response to the 1996 school shootings at Dunblane, Scotland, that left 16 dead. Wilson notes that 95 percent of British police officers are unarmed, and four out of five say they don't wish to carry guns.

Wilson-Smith, Anthony. "Allan Rock's War on Guns: The Justice Minister Unveils a Set of Proposals to Restrict Firearms." *Maclean's*, vol. 107, December 12, 1994, pp. 22ff. Discusses tough new gun laws proposed by Canada's justice minister. The proposals, which include registration of gun owners and firearms and banning of most handguns and assault weapons, have met with vigorous, well-organized opposition by gun advocates.

INTERNET DOCUMENTS

Coalition to Stop Handgun Violence. "International Comparisons." Available online. URL: http://www.gunfree.org/csgv/bsc_int.htm. Posted on August 11, 1997. Compares firearms-related regulation in 49 countries, generally pointing out that the United States does not regulate many aspects of firearms use that are regulated in most other industrialized nations. U.S. firearms death rates are also much higher than in other countries. The web page also provides a chart summarizing this data.

Kates, Don B. "Gun Laws Around the World: Do They Work?" Available online. URL: http://www.nraila.org/research/19990728-InternationalGunControl-001.htm. Downloaded on July 7, 1999. Describes gun laws, gun use, and homicide and suicide rates around the world. Argues that peaceful, well-ordered societies do not need gun laws to be that way and that violent, disordered societies do not benefit from gun laws.

"Skeeter's Home Page." Available online. URL: http://teapot.usask.ca/cdn-firearms/homepage.html. Downloaded on July 7, 1999. Provides resource links on Canadian gun law, safety, pro-gun activism, and other categories.

CHAPTER 8

ORGANIZATIONS AND AGENCIES

The following organizations are national in scope (a few are international). There are hundreds of local organizations of gun enthusiasts who often take an interest in gun control issues, and there are a growing number of local groups that work for gun violence prevention and gun control. The web sites of national organizations often have links to local organizations, as do some of the web sites listed in Chapter 7 in the Reference section.

Academics for the Second Amendment
P.O. Box 131254
St. Paul, MN 55113
Educational and advocacy organization dedicated to giving the Second Amendment its full and proper place in constitutional discourse; sponsors scholarship and conferences.

American Academy of Pediatrics Center to Prevent Handgun Violence Project
Phone: (708) 228-5505 or (800) 433-9016
141 Northwest Point Boulevard
P.O. Box 927
Elk Grove Village, IL 60009
Provides background, data, and guidance to help doctors lobby for laws that can reduce handgun violence.

American Firearms Association
c/o Maconald and Associates
4020 University Drive
Suite 207
Fairfax, VA 22030
Considers itself to be the moderate alternative to the NRA, reconciling gun rights with "reasonable gun control."

Arming Women Against Rape and Endangerment (AWARE)
URL: http://www.aware.org/
E-mail: info@aware.org
Phone: (877) 672-9273
P.O. Box 242
Bedford, MA 01730-0242
Promotes self-defense for women through education and training, including firearms training.

Brass Roots
URL: http://www.brassrootsusa.org
Phone: (800) 555-GUNS
P.O. Box 246
Hazel Park, MI 48030
Michigan-based national gun rights organization.

Bureau of Alcohol, Tobacco, and Firearms
URL: http://www.atf.treas.gov/
Phone: (202) 287-4097
650 Massachusetts Avenue NW
Washington, DC 20226
The agency of the U.S. Treasury Department that has responsibility for investigation and enforcement of all federal firearms laws.

Canadian Institute for Legal Action
Phone: (905) 571-2150
National Office
P.O. Box 44030
600 Grandview St. S.
Oshawa, ON L1H 8P4
Canada
Canadian coalition in defense of gun rights, including gun advocacy and shooting sports organizations.

Cease Fire, Inc.
URL: http://www.ceasefire.org
E-mail: info@ceasefire.org
P.O. Box 33424
Washington, DC 20033-0424
Educational organization dedicated to reducing gun-related deaths of children. Cease Fire, Inc., produces public service announcements and other material urging "handgun-free homes."

Center to Prevent Handgun Violence
URL: http://www.cphv.org
Phone: (202) 289-7319
1225 I St. NW, Ste. 1100
Washington, DC 20005
Emphasizes education about the dangers of handgun possession, particularly involving children; develops programs to educate young people about guns and gun violence; organizes research and legal action projects.

Children's Safety Network National Maternal & Child Health Clearinghouse
Phone: (703) 821-8955, Ext. 254
8201 Greensboro Drive, Ste. 600
McLean, VA 22102
Publishes newsletters and bibliographies focusing on firearms issues affecting child safety.

Citizens Committee for the Right to Keep and Bear Arms
Phone: (425) 454-4911
12500 NE 10th Place
Bellevue, WA 98005
Anti-gun control group emphasizing Second Amendment issues.

Coalition for Gun Control (Australia and New Zealand)
URL: http://www.health.usyd.edu.au/cgc/
E-mail: cgc@pub.health.su.oz.au
Phone: 041 960-3527
P.O. Box 167

Camperdown 2050 NSW
Australia
A coalition of medical and other groups supporting gun control; engages in research, advocacy, and cooperation with like-minded groups.

Coalition to Stop Gun Violence
URL: http://www.gunfree.org
Phone: (202) 530-0340
100 16th Street, NW, Suite 603
Washington, DC 20036
A large coalition of labor, religious, medical, educational, civic, and other groups united to fight gun violence. The coalition seeks a total ban on civilian ownership of handguns and assault weapons, lobbies and provides technical support to advocacy organizations, and has a separate unit, the Educational Fund to End Gun Violence.

Doctors for Integrity in Research and Public Policy
Phone: (510) 277-0333
5201 Norris Canyon Rd.,
Suite 140
San Ramon, CA 94583
Organizes, physicians to counteract what it sees as the shoddy and biased pro–gun control research being done by those who say that there is "an epidemic of gun violence." The organization also publishes critiques of such studies.

Federal Bureau of Investigation (FBI)
URL: http://www.fbi.gov/
Phone: (202) 324-3691

935 Pennsylvania Ave., NW
Washington, DC 20525
Performs background checks and gun traces for local authorities and compiles many statistics involving gun violence and guns used in crime.

Firearms Coalition
URL: http://www.nealknox.com/
7771 Sudley Rd., No. 44
Manassas, VA 20109
A hard-core pro-gun group founded by Neal Knox that reports on legislation in Congress and other gun-related news.

Gun Control Network
URL: http://www.gun-control-network.org/gcnhome.htm
P.O. Box 11495
London N3 2FE
United Kingdom
British organization promoting gun control, founded in the aftermath of the Dunblane, Scotland, shootings. The network seeks to change British laws to ban those types of handguns that remain legal to own.

Gun Owners of America
URL: http://www.gunowners.org/
Phone: (703) 321-8585
8001 Forbes Place
Springfield, VA 22151
Smaller than the NRA but more radical in its advocacy of gun rights, it focuses on activism and lobbying.

Guns Save Lives
URL: http://gunssavelives.com

7481 Huntsman Blvd., Suite 525
Springfield, VA 22153
Militantly opposes gun control but instead supports self-defense and the right to carry concealed weapons.

Handgun Control, Inc.
URL: http://www.handguncontrol.org
Phone: (202) 898-0792
1225 Eye Street NW, Suite 1100
Washington, DC 20005
The nation's largest gun control organization founded in 1974 and now led by Sarah and James Brady following the latter's serious wounding in an assassination attempt against President Reagan. Handgun Control, Inc., goes head-on against the NRA in fighting to preserve existing legislation (such as the assault weapons ban and gun purchase waiting periods) and to promote new laws, such as one requiring that trigger locks be sold with guns.

Handgun Epidemic Lowering Plan (HELP)
E-mail: cmh-helpnet@nwu.edu
Phone: (773) 880-3826
Children's Memorial Hospital
2300 Children's Plaza, #88
Chicago, IL 60614-3394
Medically oriented organization that seeks to educate and to strengthen gun control to reduce gun violence. Their web site provides news summaries, policy statements, and help for survivors of shootings.

International Shooting Sport Federation
URL: http://www.issf-shooting.org/
E-mail: issfmunich@compuserve.com
Phone: 49-89-5443550
Bavariaring 21, D-80336
München,
Germany
International organization and governing body for shooting sports.

Jews for the Preservation of Firearms Ownership
URL: http://www.jpfo.org/
Phone: (414) 673-9745
P.O. Box 270143
Hartford, WI 53027
A radical group that sees firearms ownership as bound together with the historical and moral imperatives of Judaism and necessary if future Holocausts are to be prevented. The group often attacks what it considers to be the liberal Jewish establishment's advocacy of gun control.

Join Together
URL: http://www1.jointogether.org/gv/
E-mail: info@jointogether.org
Phone: (617) 437-1500
441 Stuart Street
Boston, MA 02116
Education and advocacy group focusing on issues of gun violence and substance abuse. It is a project of the Boston University School of Public Health.

Justice for Shooters
URL: http://home.rednet.co.uk/homepages/markg/index.html

E-mail: JFS@online.rednet.co.uk
Phone: (01753) 738314
P.O. Box 705
Bourne End
Buckinghamshire SL8 5FS
United Kingdom
British rights organization.

**Law Enforcement Alliance of
   America (LEAA)**
URL: http://web.wt.net/~tat/
   leaa.htm
Phone: (703) 847-COPS
7700 Leesburg Pike, Suite 421
Falls Church, VA 22043
An organization that seeks to bring
law enforcement officers and citizens together to fight crime. The
organization seeks stricter penalties for criminals and promotes
victim's rights; it opposes gun control as not being effective crime
control.

**Legal Community Against
   Violence**
URL: http://www.lcav.org/
E-mail: joinus@lcav.org
268 Bush St., Suite 555
San Francisco, CA 94104
Organization founded after mass
shootings in a San Francisco office
building in 1993. The group works
to strengthen local gun control laws
as well as to defend gun control at
the state and federal level.

**National Association of Federally
   Licensed Firearms Dealers**
URL: http://www.amfire.com/
E-mail: afi@amfire.com
Phone: (954) 561-3505

2455 E. Sunrise Boulevard,
Suite 916
Fort Lauderdale, FL 33304
A trade group for firearms dealers.
The association, as of 1999, was engaged in trying to counteract liability suits being filed against gun
makers by cities.

**National Center for Injury
   Prevention/Control Centers
   for Disease Control
   and Prevention**
URL: http://www.cdc.gov/ncipc/
   ncipchm.htm
Phone: (770) 488-1506
Mailstop K65 4770 Buford
   Highway NE
Atlanta, GA 30341-3724
Division of the Centers for Disease
Control that deals with injury
prevention, including gun-related
injuries. This center has undertaken
a considerable amount of research
that appears in medical literature.

National Concealed Carry, Inc.
URL: http://www.concealcarry.org
A militant conservative group working to secure the right to carry a
concealed weapon in all 50 states.

National Firearms Association
URL: http://www.nfa.ca/
Phone: (403) 640-1110
Box 4384, Station C
Calgary AB T2T 5N2
Canada
Canada's largest gun rights group,
the rough equivalent of the U.S.'s
National Rifle Association. The

group currently is fighting Canada's new gun law, called "C-68."

National Rifle Association
URL: http://www.nra.org/
Phone: (800) NRA-3888
1600 Rhode Island Avenue NW
Washington, DC 20036
The U.S.'s largest and most effective gun rights group—what people usually mean when they refer to "the gun lobby." Its political arm is the Institute for Legislative Action. The NRA has about 3 million members.

National Shooting Sports Foundation
URL: http://www.nssf.org
E-mail: info@nssf.org
Phone: (203) 426-1320
11 Mile Hill Road
Newtown, CT 06470-2359
A large trade organization representing gun manufacturers, distributors, and dealers. The organization promotes hunting, recreational shooting, and gun safety and, as of 1999, was emphasizing greater participation of women in shooting sports.

Pacific Center for Violence Prevention
URL: http://www.pcvp.org/
E-mail: pcvp@pcvp.org
Phone: (415) 285-2563
San Francisco General Hospital
1001 Potrero Avenue
San Francisco, CA 94110
Addresses prevention of violence; has a section on firearm violence. Its web site presents statistics, fact sheets, and other resources. It is a project of the Trauma Foundation.

Physicians for Social Responsibility
URL: http://www.psr.org
E-mail: psrnatl@psr.org
Phone: (202) 898-0150
1101 14th Street Northwest
Suite 700
Washington, DC 20005
Organization of medical professionals involved in social issues. The group has a section on Violence Prevention that emphasizes gun control issues.

Second Amendment Foundation
URL: http://www.saf.org/
E-mail: info@saf.org
Phone: (800) 426-4302
James Madison Building
12500 NE Tenth Place
Bellevue, WA 98005
Educational and advocacy organization focusing on the Second Amendment, considered as an individual right to keep and bear arms.

Sporting Shooters Association of Australia
URL: http://www.ssaa.org.au/
Phone: 08 8272 7622
P.O. BOX 2066 Kent Town
South Australia 5071
Australian shooting and gun-rights organization.

Sporting Shooters Association of New Zealand
P.O. Box 41 013
St. Lukes, Auckland
New Zealand

New Zealand gun enthusiasts and gun rights advocacy group.

Student Pledge Against Gun Violence
URL: http://www.pledge.org/
E-mail: mlgrow@microassist.com
Phone: (507) 645-5378
112 Nevada St.
Northfield, MN 55057
Seeks pledges (commitments) from young people not to bring guns to school and to work to persuade fellow students to avoid guns.

Violence Policy Center
URL: http://www.vpc.org
E-mail: comment@vpc.org
1140 19th Street, NW, Suite 600
Washington, DC 20036
A "gun control think tank," research, education, and advocacy group.

Violence Prevention Research Program
URL: http://web.ucdmc.ucdavis.edu/vprp/
Phone: (916) 734-3539
Western Fairs Building
University of California, Davis

2315 Stockton Blvd.
Sacramento, CA 95817
Researches violence prevention with an emphasis on gun-related violence and the effectiveness of gun laws and policies (such as gun purchase waiting periods).

Women Against Gun Control
URL: http://www.wagc.com/
E-mail: inf.@wagc.com
Phone: (801) 328-9660
P.O. Box 521000
Salt Lake City, UT 84152-1000
Advocates gun ownership as a feminist issue.

World Forum on the Future of Sport Shooting Activities
URL: http://www.wfsa.net
Phone: +39 06 5903510
WFSA c/o ANPAM
Viale dell'Astronomia 30
1-00144 Roma
Italy
An international educational and advocacy group promoting sport shooting. As of 1999, it was focusing on combating international gun control efforts in the United Nations.

PART III

APPENDICES

APPENDIX A

RESEARCH STUDIES, POLLS, AND OTHER REPORTS RELATING TO GUN CONTROL

This appendix presents a collection of recent data relevant to gun control issues, including polls, surveys, government statistics, and studies. For this book, the statistics and reports gathered and compiled were the most up-to-date statistics that could be found as of July 1999; more-recent statistics may well be available at the time of reading. Most material within each of these pages dates from the mid- to late 1990s. URLs have been supplied to each source notation to browse web sites (such as the Department of Justice) for updated materials. Additional research suggestions can be found in Chapter 6.

This appendix has been divided into the following topics:

1. Crime, Weapons Offenses, and Gun Deaths
2. Gun Owners and Ownership
3. Risks and Benefits of Gun Ownership
4. Gun Laws and Their Effectiveness
5. Children and Guns
6. Public Support for Gun Control

CRIME, WEAPONS OFFENSES, AND GUN DEATHS

Most rates for serious violent crime (homicide, robbery, aggravated assault, and rape) peaked in the early 1980s and again in the mid-1990s. As of the year 1998, they were down sharply, although the rate of crime reported to the police and of arrests made by police also shows a more modest decline.

LONG-TERM TRENDS FOR RATES OF SERIOUS VIOLENT CRIME

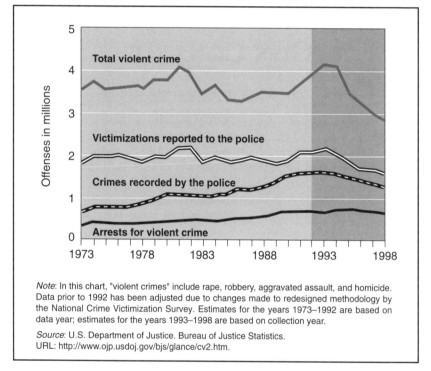

Note: In this chart, "violent crimes" include rape, robbery, aggravated assault, and homicide. Data prior to 1992 has been adjusted due to changes made to redesigned methodology by the National Crime Victimization Survey. Estimates for the years 1973–1992 are based on data year; estimates for the years 1993–1998 are based on collection year.

Source: U.S. Department of Justice. Bureau of Justice Statistics.
URL: http://www.ojp.usdoj.gov/bjs/glance/cv2.htm.

LONG-TERM TRENDS FOR ARRESTS FOR WEAPONS OFFENSES

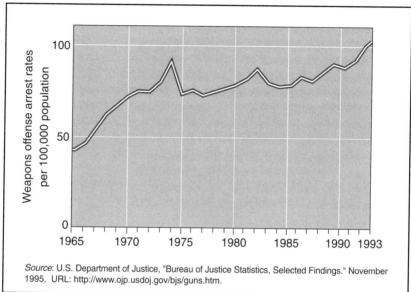

Source: U.S. Department of Justice, "Bureau of Justice Statistics, Selected Findings." November 1995. URL: http://www.ojp.usdoj.gov/bjs/guns.htm.

Arrests for weapons offenses more than doubled between 1965 and 1993. The FBI also reports that in 1993:

• 92 percent of persons arrested for weapons offenses were males.

• 77 percent were age 18 or over.

• Proportionately, five times as many blacks were arrested for weapons offenses as whites.

• 77 percent of weapons arrests occurred in cities, 16 percent suburban, and only 8 percent rural.

Although rates for murder and other crimes are declining, on average, gun criminals are younger in age. The U.S. Bureau of Justice indicates that firearm killings by 25-year-olds and older decreased by about half to about 5,000 between 1980 and 1997, but gun killings by young people 18 to 24 years old increased from about 5,000 in 1980 to more than 7,500 in 1997. (*Source:* CNN Online. URL: http://cnn.com/US/9901/02/murder.rate/index.html.)

GEOGRAPHICAL DISTRIBUTION OF WEAPONS OFFENSES

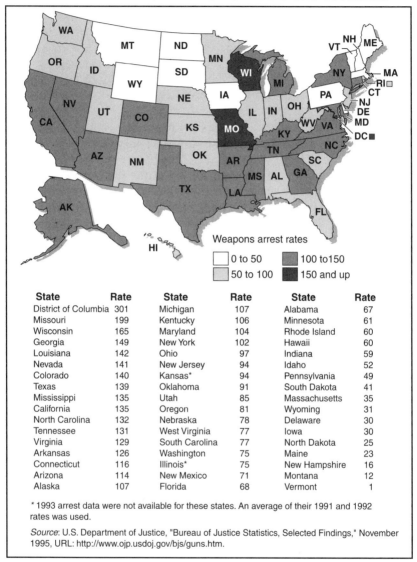

Weapons arrest rates

☐ 0 to 50   ▨ 100 to150
▨ 50 to 100   ▨ 150 and up

State	Rate	State	Rate	State	Rate
District of Columbia	301	Michigan	107	Alabama	67
Missouri	199	Kentucky	106	Minnesota	61
Wisconsin	165	Maryland	104	Rhode Island	60
Georgia	149	New York	102	Hawaii	60
Louisiana	142	Ohio	97	Indiana	59
Nevada	141	New Jersey	94	Idaho	52
Colorado	140	Kansas*	94	Pennsylvania	49
Texas	139	Oklahoma	91	South Dakota	41
Mississippi	135	Utah	85	Massachusetts	35
California	135	Oregon	81	Wyoming	31
North Carolina	132	Nebraska	78	Delaware	30
Tennessee	131	West Virginia	77	Iowa	30
Virginia	129	South Carolina	77	North Dakota	25
Arkansas	126	Washington	75	Maine	23
Connecticut	116	Illinois*	75	New Hampshire	16
Arizona	114	New Mexico	71	Montana	12
Alaska	107	Florida	68	Vermont	1

* 1993 arrest data were not available for these states. An average of their 1991 and 1992 rates was used.

Source: U.S. Department of Justice, "Bureau of Justice Statistics, Selected Findings," November 1995, URL: http://www.ojp.usdoj.gov/bjs/guns.htm.

The above map codes states according to their rate of weapons offenses per population of 100,000 in 1993. The District of Columbia had the highest rate (301); Vermont had the lowest (1).

TYPES OF WEAPONS USED IN MURDERS

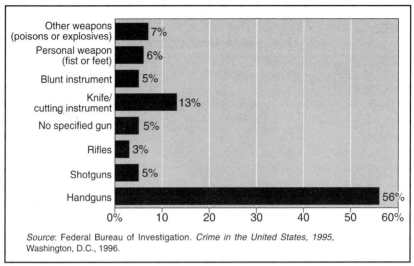

Source: Federal Bureau of Investigation. *Crime in the United States, 1995,* Washington, D.C., 1996.

FBI reports show that firearms of all kinds account for about two-thirds of murder weapons, with handguns being the overwhelming choice.

FIREARMS DEATH RATE

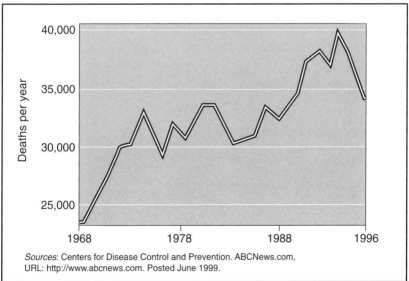

Sources: Centers for Disease Control and Prevention. ABCNews.com, URL: http://www.abcnews.com. Posted June 1999.

Despite the increase in public concern about gun violence and gun safety in the home, the total U.S. deaths from firearms (both intentional and accidental) has been declining since about 1994.

225

HOW CRIMINALS GET GUNS

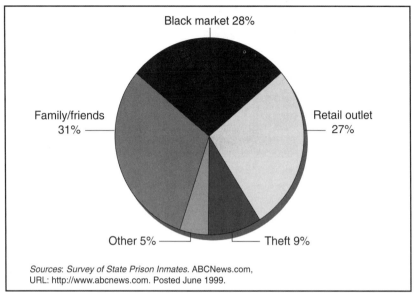

Sources: *Survey of State Prison Inmates.* ABCNews.com,
URL: http://www.abcnews.com. Posted June 1999.

According to a survey of state prison inmates, retail outlets, the black market, and friends and relatives each account for a bit less than a third of guns obtained by criminals. Although it is often argued that guns in the home are likely to be stolen and used by criminals, theft appears to be only a minor source of criminal guns.

A more recent study by *The New York Times* reports that nearly 40 percent of guns used in crimes were purchased from federally licensed firearms dealers (who presumably followed applicable screening procedures). Such data is likely to be used as ammunition by litigants suing firearms manufacturers for negligent marketing. However, critics point out that such data does not account for stolen guns. (*Source:* Associated Press and Nando Media Online, URL: http://www.nando.net/newsroom/ntn/nation/112898/nation8_19850_noframes.html.)

HOW GUNS KILL

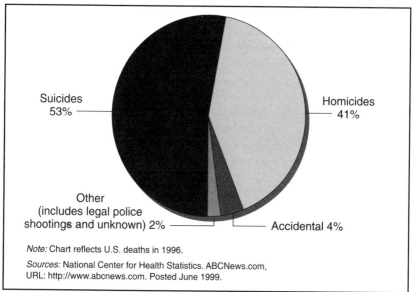

Suicides
53%

Homicides
41%

Other
(includes legal police
shootings and unknown) 2%

Accidental 4%

Note: Chart reflects U.S. deaths in 1996.

Sources: National Center for Health Statistics. ABCNews.com, URL: http://www.abcnews.com. Posted June 1999.

Although much of the gun debate focuses on crime, as the above chart shows, suicide is actually the most common motive for gun deaths.

HOW AGE RELATES TO THE CHANCE OF BECOMING A VICTIM OF GUN VIOLENCE

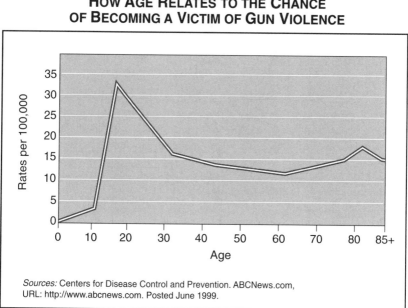

Sources: Centers for Disease Control and Prevention. ABCNews.com, URL: http://www.abcnews.com. Posted June 1999.

Teenagers and young adults (15 to 24 years old) have the highest chance of becoming victims of gunshot wounds.

227

Gun Control

TYPES OF FIREARM DEATHS AND AGE OF VICTIM

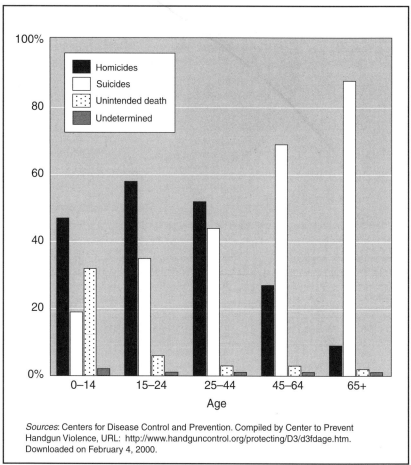

Sources: Centers for Disease Control and Prevention. Compiled by Center to Prevent Handgun Violence, URL: http://www.handguncontrol.org/protecting/D3/d3fdage.htm. Downloaded on February 4, 2000.

According to the Centers for Disease Control, "When a child is very young—0–14—the highest percentage of firearm deaths are homicides and unintended shootings. . . . For 15–24-year-olds, the majority of firearm deaths are homicides, with suicides increasing. . . . For 25–44-year-olds, the majority of firearm deaths are still homicides, but the percentage of suicides is not far behind. . . . For older adults, 45–64, suicide becomes the primary reason people are dying by firearms, and this greatly outweighs the percentage of firearm murders. . . . And for people 65 and older, we see that almost 90 percent of firearm deaths are suicides."

Appendix A

PERCENTAGES OF SUICIDES COMPLETED BY VARIOUS MEANS, AGES 0–19, 1992

Method	Percentage completed
Firearm	66%
Strangulation (hanging, etc.)	20%
Poison	10%
Other methods	3%

Source: Center to Prevent Handgun Violence, "Suicide Completion: Comparison of Firearms and Other Methods. Ages 0–19, United States. 1992." Posted on URL: http://www.handguncontrol.org/protecting/D3/d3suicde.htm.

According to the Center to Prevent Handgun Violence, a person who attempts suicide with a firearm is much more likely to succeed than with other methods. When a suicide attempt is "a cry for help," it is likely to be too late if a firearm is used.

HOW GUNS COMPARE WITH DISEASE AND ACCIDENT AS A CAUSE OF DEATH

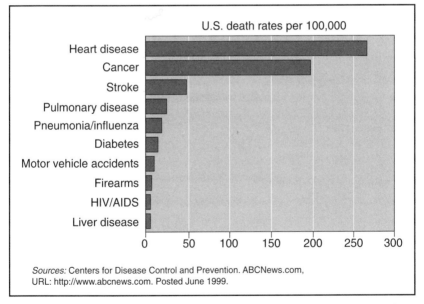

Sources: Centers for Disease Control and Prevention. ABCNews.com, URL: http://www.abcnews.com. Posted June 1999.

Disease (especially heart disease and cancer) kills many more people than do firearms. But among unnatural causes of death, only death by automobile accident occurs more often than death by firearms.

GUN OWNERS AND OWNERSHIP

ADULTS WHO HAVE A GUN IN THEIR HOME

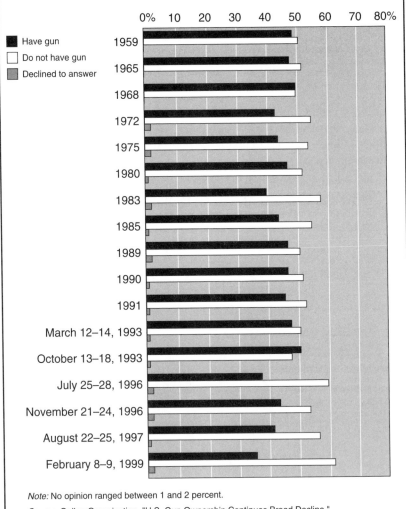

Note: No opinion ranged between 1 and 2 percent.

Source: Gallup Organization, "U.S. Gun Ownership Continues Broad Decline," URL: http://www.gallup.com/poll/ released/pr990406.asp. Poll released April 6, 1999.

Appendix A

The graph on the previous page is based on a Gallup poll released April 6, 1999. The survey concluded that the percentage of Americans who own a gun continues a steady decline. Gun ownership "skews toward rural residents, those living in the South, men, and whites." Gallup also noted: "Perhaps not surprisingly, guns are much more likely to be found in rural homes than they are in urban or suburban dwellings. Fifty-two percent of rural Americans admit to keeping a gun at home, compared to 25 percent of urban residents and 36 percent of suburban residents."

GENDER BREAKDOWN IN GUN OWNERSHIP

	Male (508)	Female (546)
Yes	47%	27%
No	51	71
No opinion	2	2
	100%	100%

Note: For results based on the survey conducted February 8–9, 1999 (N=1,054), the margin of error is ±3 percentage points.

Source: Gallup Organization, URL: http://www.gallup.com/poll/releases/pr990406.asp.

Gallup asked survey participants, "Do you have a gun in your home?" and then tabulated the results by gender. Most people are probably not surprised to learn that males are almost twice as likely to own guns as females.

HOW WHITES AND NONWHITES COMPARE IN GUN OWNERSHIP

	Whites (893)	Nonwhites (154)
Yes	40%	19%
No	59	79
No opinion	1	2
	100%	100%

Note: For results based on the survey conducted February 8–9, 1999 (N=1,054), the margin of error is ±3 percentage points.

Source: Gallup Organization, URL: http://www.gallup.com/poll/releases/pr990406.asp.

Gallup also broke down its results by race. Whites are about twice as likely to be gun owners as nonwhites.

HOW GUN OWNERSHIP CHANGES WITH AGE

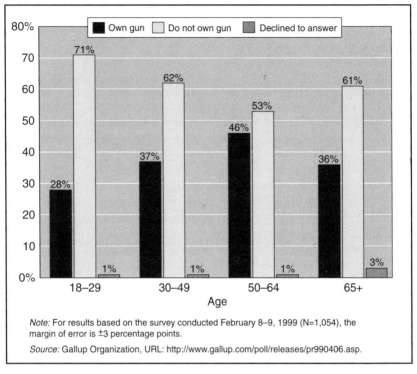

Note: For results based on the survey conducted February 8–9, 1999 (N=1,054), the margin of error is ±3 percentage points.

Source: Gallup Organization, URL: http://www.gallup.com/poll/releases/pr990406.asp.

Despite their predominance in crime statistics, young adults are actually less likely than other age groups to own a gun. The percentage of gun owners peaks in the 50–64 age range.

Appendix A

PARTS OF THE UNITED STATES WITH THE HIGHEST RATE OF SELF-REPORTED GUN OWNERSHIP

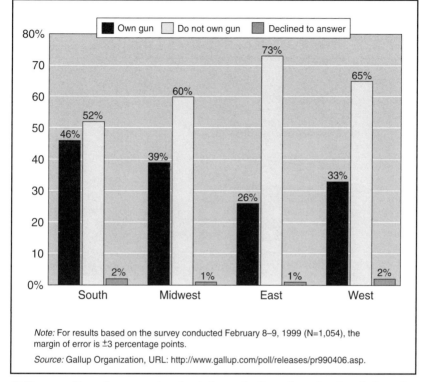

Note: For results based on the survey conducted February 8–9, 1999 (N=1,054), the margin of error is ±3 percentage points.

Source: Gallup Organization, URL: http://www.gallup.com/poll/releases/pr990406.asp.

Gallup confirmed conventional wisdom, finding that the South has the highest rate of gun ownership and the East the lowest. But it is perhaps a little surprising that the Midwest beats out the "wild" West.

RISKS AND BENEFITS OF GUN OWNERSHIP

WHY PEOPLE KEEP GUNS IN THE HOME

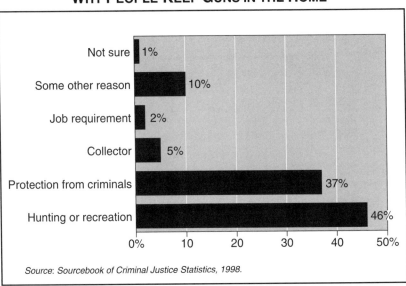

Source: *Sourcebook of Criminal Justice Statistics, 1998.*

According to surveys, hunting/recreation and protection from criminals are the most popular reasons to have a gun in the home.

DOES HAVING A GUN IN THE HOME INCREASE THE RISK OF DEATH BY SUICIDE OR HOMICIDE?

According to medical researchers Peter Cummings and Thomas D. Koepsell, who collected results from six published studies, having a gun in the home is associated with a 1.4 to 4.8 times higher risk of suicide. They also reported on two studies that found a 2.2 to 2.7 times higher risk of homicide. (*Source:* "Does Owning a Firearm Increase or Decrease the Risk of Death?" Peter Cummings, MD, MPH; Thomas D. Koepsell, MD, MPH; *JAMA, The Journal of the American Medical Association*, August 5, 1998, vol. 280 pp. 280: 471–473. Posted on URL: http://www.ama-assn.org/sci-pubs/journals/archive/jama/vol_280/no _5/cv80003x.htm.)

Appendix A

SOME POTENTIAL PROBLEMS WITH CORRELATING GUN OWNERSHIP AND SUICIDE OR HOMICIDE

Gary Kleck, a critic of gun control, notes that "probably less than 5 percent of U.S. homicides are committed in the victim's home by killers using guns kept in that home. Further, the slight risk of such an event occurring is almost completely confined to unusually high-risk subsets of the population, since contrary to widespread belief, gun violence is largely confined to persons with a prior history of criminal behavior.

"Even within these high-risk groups, it is not known whether the net causal effect of gun ownership is to increase the risks of homicide victimization, given that the gun–homicide association found in the previous research on high-risk populations was at least partly spurious. High-risk groups have a higher-than-average probability of both violence-increasing offensive uses of guns and of violence-reducing defensive uses, but it cannot yet be firmly stated whether the net effect is to increase homicides.

"Defensive uses of guns are both effective in preventing injury and more common than aggressive uses, in the home or outside it. The average American household is unlikely to experience a serious gun victimization or to use a gun defensively, but the latter is far more likely than the former. In light of the flaws and weak associations of case-control research, currently available data do not provide a sound empirical basis for recommending to the average American that he or she not keep a gun in the home." (*Source:* Kleck, "Remarks," *JAMA, The Journal of the American Medical Association*, August 5, 1998, vol. 280, pp. 473–475)

HOW EFFECTIVE A GUN IN THE HOME IS FOR SELF-DEFENSE

The effectiveness of a gun as a source of protection is a matter of great controversy between gun control and gun rights advocates. Gun control advocates point to studies that show that gun ownership increases the risk of death by suicide or murder by three to five times. However, although 20 percent of persons who attempt to defend against a criminal with a firearm are injured, 50 percent of those who use another type of weapon (or no weapon) are injured.

Another side of the equation is the number of times a gun is used successfully in self-defense. The National Crime Victimization Survey estimates 108,000 defensive uses of a gun per year, but criminologist Gary Kleck has given estimates from about 1.8 to 2.5 million. Criticism of such estimates is often based on the size and nature of the sample and whether it is based on police reports or surveys. (*Source:* Gary Kleck and Marc Gertz. "Armed Resistance to Crime: The Prevalence and Nature of Self-Defense With a Gun." *Journal of Criminal Law and Criminology* 86(1): pp. 150–187. This also includes a survey of other estimates including some based on data from the National Crime Victimization Survey.)

THE SAFEST WAY TO KEEP A GUN IF YOU HAVE ONE AT HOME

In the report "Safe Storage of Handguns: What Do the Police Recommend?" by medical researchers Donna M. Denno, David C. Grossman, John Britt, and Abraham B. Bergman, the researchers discussed results from a survey they took of police departments in which they assumed the role of concerned gun owners calling for advice.

They reported that "Usable responses were generated for 93 (91%) of the departments sampled. Only 3 departments (3.2%) refused to give advice over the telephone. The most commonly suggested storage methods were trigger locks (55 departments [59%]), portable lockboxes for handguns (48 [52%]), and the separation of guns from ammunition (30 [32%]). Seven percent of departments suggested removing the gun from the household. Over half of those suggesting trigger locks and lockboxes considered these devices safe (35 [64%] for trigger locks and 27 [56%] for lockboxes) and yet rapidly accessible to an adult (36 [65%] for trigger locks and 36 [75%] for lockboxes). Responding police officers most commonly reported using the following storage methods at home: no storage method (31 [38%]), portable lockboxes (23 [28%]), out-of-reach location (11 [13%]), separation of gun and ammunition (10 [12%]), and trigger locks (5 [6%])." (*Source: Archive Pediatric Adolescent Medicine*, 1996; 150: 927–931. Posted on URL: http://www.ama-assn.org/sci-pubs/journals/archive/ajdc/vol_150/no_9/oa5492a.htm.)

Appendix A

GUN LAWS AND THEIR EFFECTIVENESS

IS A "COOLING-OFF PERIOD" FOR HANDGUN PURCHASES LIKELY TO REDUCE THE NUMBER OF HOMICIDES?

Bureau of Alcohol, Tobacco, and Firearms (BATF) statisticians note that "Overall, 6.6% (3,882/58,152) of the firearms BATF traced within 3 years of purchase had been recovered as part of homicide investigations, while a significantly higher percentage of guns traced within 1 week and even 2–4 weeks after purchase were associated with homicide investigations. Specifically, 20% (32/159) of guns traced within 7 days, and 10% (165/1,503) traced 8–31 days from when they were purchased were suspected by police to have been used in a murder."

HOW THE BRADY ACT AFFECTED THE BLACK MARKET IN GUNS

According to a study by the Center to Prevent Handgun Violence, "the percentage of recovered crime guns that were traced to dealers in the four Brady states was greater for guns purchased before the Act took effect when compared to guns purchased after the Act took effect." Therefore, ". . . implementation of the Brady Act disrupted established flow of guns across state lines, resulting in Brady states becoming less important as source states for gun traffickers." (*Source:* Center for the Prevention of Handgun Violence, "Traffic Stop: How the Brady Act Disrupts Interstate Gun Trafficking.")

DOES LIMITING PURCHASES TO ONE GUN A MONTH AFFECT THE ILLEGAL GUN TRADE?

According to a report published in *JAMA, The Journal of the American Medical Association*, "for firearms recovered anywhere in the United States, 3,201 (27%) of 11,876 acquired prior to the implementation of the law and 519 (19%) of 2,730 purchased after the law was enacted were traced to Virginia." (*Source:* Douglas S. Weil and Rebecca C. Knox, "Effects of Limiting Handgun Purchases on Interstate Transfer of Firearms," *JAMA, The Journal of the American Medical Association*, 1996, pp. 275: 1759–1761.)

Gun Control

KINDS OF GUNS THE POLICE ENCOUNTER MOST IN CRIMINAL INVESTIGATIONS

According to Department of Justice statistics, the types of guns police ask the Federal ATF to trace are as follows:

Type of gun	Percent of all 1994 traces
Handguns	79.1
Pistols	*53.0*
—Pistol revolvers	24.7
—Pistol derringers	1.4
Rifles	11.1
Shotguns	9.7
Other, including machine guns	0.1
Total	**100.0%**

They concluded that "Most trace requests concern handguns. Over half of the guns that police agencies asked ATF to trace were pistols and another quarter were revolvers." (*Source:* Bureau of Justice Statistics, "Selected Findings Guns Used in Crime: Firearms, Crime, and Criminal Justice NCJ-148201." Posted on URL: http://www.ojp.usdoj.gov/bjs/pub/ascii/guic.txt.)

HAS THE BRADY ACT KEPT GUNS AWAY FROM CRIMINALS?

A Justice Department survey estimates that 69,000 handgun sales to ineligible purchasers were blocked in 1997, amounting to a rejection rate of about 2.7 percent of about 2.6 million applications. (*Source:* CNN Online, "Background Checks Stopped 69,000 Handgun Sales in 1997," URL: http://cnn.com/US/9806/21/brady.law/index.html.)

In 1999 statements, President Clinton has said that by then the law had stopped about 400,000 sales. Critics, however, point out the difficulty in isolating the effect of Brady from existing state laws as well as the possibility that many people with criminal records who could not pass a Brady check obtained a gun anyway, perhaps using an eligible person as a "straw purchaser." (The "one gun a month" restrictions have been promoted in part as a way to reduce the use of straw purchasers.)

A 1997 study by the Center to Prevent Handgun Violence focused on states such as Ohio that had no background check until the Brady Act went into effect in 1994. It concludes that Brady has substantially reduced the number of crime guns being traced back to such states. For example, "Ohio's share of out-of-state crime guns recovered in Michigan fell by 66%, in Illinois by 87.5%, in New York by 78.5%, and in Pennsylvania by 36%." (*Source:* Center to Prevent Handgun Violence.)

Appendix A

HAS THE BRADY ACT REDUCED THE RATE OF VIOLENT GUN CRIME?

The Center to Prevent Handgun Violence notes that "According to the FBI's Uniform Crime Report, the use of guns in crime rose significantly from 1985 to 1993. However, since implementation of the Brady Law in February 1994, there has been a significant drop in the percentage of violent crimes committed with a firearm. A recent Bureau of Justice Statistics study estimated that in all 50 states, 173,000 transactions were not completed since the implementation of the Brady Law because background checks revealed that the buyers were not allowed to take possession of a handgun. . . . Since the Brady Law was implemented in early 1994 through the end of 1996, the overall proportion of aggravated assaults involving a firearm fell by 12.4% (25.1% to 22.0%). Additionally, the proportion of robberies committed with a firearm fell by 4.0% (42.4% to 40.7%) and murders committed with a firearm fell by 2.6% (69.6% to 67.8%). . . .

"Analysis of the FBI data provides more compelling evidence that the Brady Law is working. The significant drop in the percentage of violent crimes committed with a firearm shows that, since all 50 states began doing the background checks in 1994, the Brady Law is working to make America safer from violent crime." (*Source:* FBI, "Crimes with Guns Down Faster than Violent Crimes Overall: 1996 FBI Data Show Brady Law's Continuing Effectiveness in Reducing Gun Crimes," *Crime in the United States,* 1996, and Center to Prevent Handgun Violence.)

TIME BETWEEN PURCHASE AND INITIATION OF TRACE

	0–7 days	8–31 days	32–365 days	366–730 days	731–1,095 days
Homicide	32 (20.1%)	165 (9.9%)	1,425 (6.7%)	1,239 (6.4%)	1,021 (6.5%)
Other crime	127	1,503	19,953	17,919	14,768

Source: Bureau of Alcohol, Tobacco, and Firearms Trace Database, "Guns Traced as Part of Homicide Investigations Provide Evidence for the Need for a Cooling Off Period for Handgun Purchases," and Center to Prevent Handgun Violence.

This study concludes that "a disproportionate share of murders (relative to other crimes) occur within days of the purchase of a gun and might, therefore be prevented by a waiting period."

Gun Control

STRICTNESS OF STATE GUN LAWS

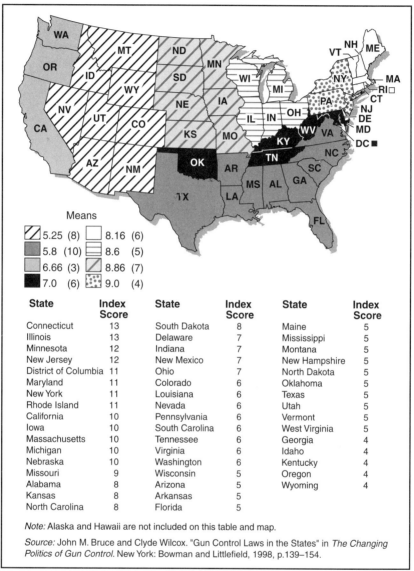

Means

5.25 (8)		8.16 (6)	
5.8 (10)		8.6 (5)	
6.66 (3)		8.86 (7)	
7.0 (6)		9.0 (4)	

State	Index Score	State	Index Score	State	Index Score
Connecticut	13	South Dakota	8	Maine	5
Illinois	13	Delaware	7	Mississippi	5
Minnesota	12	Indiana	7	Montana	5
New Jersey	12	New Mexico	7	New Hampshire	5
District of Columbia	11	Ohio	7	North Dakota	5
Maryland	11	Colorado	6	Oklahoma	5
New York	11	Louisiana	6	Texas	5
Rhode Island	11	Nevada	6	Utah	5
California	10	Pennsylvania	6	Vermont	5
Iowa	10	South Carolina	6	West Virginia	5
Massachusetts	10	Tennessee	6	Georgia	4
Michigan	10	Virginia	6	Idaho	4
Nebraska	10	Washington	6	Kentucky	4
Missouri	9	Wisconsin	5	Oregon	4
Alabama	8	Arizona	5	Wyoming	4
Kansas	8	Arkansas	5		
North Carolina	8	Florida	5		

Note: Alaska and Hawaii are not included on this table and map.

Source: John M. Bruce and Clyde Wilcox. "Gun Control Laws in the States" in *The Changing Politics of Gun Control*. New York: Bowman and Littlefield, 1998, p.139–154.

240

Appendix A

The map and table on the previous page are based on an index that rates the number of selected gun law provisions enforced in each state, with the mean then taken for each region. The Northeast has the most restrictive state gun laws, while the South, Midwest, and West have relatively weak laws. Note, however, that the strictness of gun laws varies considerably within a region. California, for example, has laws almost as strict as New Jersey and New York, while Washington and Oregon are more comparable to Utah or Texas.

WHAT GUN RIGHTS ADVOCATES SAY ABOUT THE USE OF GUN TRACE STATISTICS

According to Paul H. Blackman of the National Rifle Association of America: "This report is based on tracing data, although such data are 'not designed to collect statistics.' Most crime guns are not traced; most traced guns are not involved in violent crimes and, as even this report acknowledges, traced guns may not be representative of recovered guns. Guns that are traced are not randomly chosen and are not representative of guns used in crime." Blackman also suggests that alternative explanations for reduction in guns traced were not considered. (*Source:* Douglas S. Weil and Rebecca C. Knox, "Effects of Limiting Handgun Purchases on Interstate Transfer of Firearms," *JAMA/The Journal of the American Medical Association*, 1996, pp. 275: 1759–1761.)

CHILDREN AND GUNS

WHAT PEOPLE BLAME FOR SCHOOL VIOLENCE

According to a set of Gallup polls, gun availability is rated "very important" as a possible cause of school violence, but family breakdown and drugs were chosen by slightly more respondents. Factors blamed for school violence, in descending order of support, with the percentage of those saying "very important" in causing school violence:

1. Breakdown of the American family, *76%*
2. Increased use of drugs and alcohol among school-aged youth, *74%*
3. Easy availability of weapons including guns and knives, *72%*
4. Growth of youth gangs, *71%*
5. Schools not having the authority for discipline that they once had, *69%*
6. Inability of school staff to resolve conflicts between students, *64%*
7. Increased portrayal of violence in media (especially in movies and on TV), *62%*
8. Trying to deal with troubled or emotionally disturbed students in the regular classroom instead of in special classes or schools, *61%*
9. Shortages of school personnel, *55%*
10. Cutbacks in many school support programs, *54%*
11. A school curriculum that is out of touch with the needs of today's students, *50%*
12. Increased cultural, racial, and ethnic diversity among the public school student population, *41%*
13. Increased poverty among parents, *39%*

In another poll, respondents were asked to volunteer their suggestions for preventing future school shooting incidents. The top three responses were:

• More parental involvement and parent responsibility, *32%*

• More security at schools, *16%*

• Better gun control, *12%*

(*Source:* Newport, Frank. "Public Continues to Believe a Variety of Factors Caused Littleton." Gallup News Service. Available online. URL: http://www.gallup.com/poll/releases/pr990513.asp. Posted on May 13, 1999.)

Appendix A

TEENAGERS WHO WORRY ABOUT VIOLENCE AND WEAPONS IN SCHOOL

A Gallup survey shows surprisingly high proportions of students who have such worries and who have seen violence and weapons among their classmates:

- "One teen in six (17%) says that 'students bringing weapons to school' is a 'very big' or 'big' problem in their school.

- Seven in 10 (70%) say they would report someone who brought a weapon to school.

- 'Gangs' and 'violence' are the third most often cited problem teenagers say faces people their age.

- Three in 10 teens (in a 1996 Gallup Youth Survey) said that when they are in school, they fear for their physical safety.

- One teen in five has a best friend who was attacked within the period of a year by someone wielding a lethal weapon.

- Seven in 10 report seeing people fighting each other at their schools.

- Three in 10 say they are aware of peers who have carried or regularly carry guns and knives when they are in school.

- Six in 10 say that laws governing the sale of firearms should be stricter; 54% would favor a total ban on assault rifles; 70% say Americans should NOT have the right to own large quantities of weapons.

- Nearly half of teens say there are guns in their homes.

- About half of teens say it is very or somewhat important to know how to shoot a gun.

- Six percent say it is very or somewhat important to belong to a gang or posse.

- One teen in five (based on a Gallup Youth Survey scale) falls into the category of 'alienated.' About one-tenth of teenagers say they are unhappy with the way they are.

- Six teens in 10 believe that media containing violence contributes to violent behavior in life.

- Only about one in five says their parents are very strict about what they are permitted to watch on TV."

(*Source:* Gallup Organization, "One-Third of Teenagers Feel Unsafe at School; One in Six Says that Weapons Are a Big Problem in Their School," URL: http://www.gallup.com/poll/releases/pr990422b.asp. This poll was released April 22, 1999.)

Gun Control

SUPPORT FOR GUN CONTROL IN THE WAKE OF LITTLETON

How important is the availability of guns in explaining the Littleton tragedy?

Great deal	60%
Moderate amount	19
Not much	9
Not at all	9
No opinion	3

How effective would stricter gun control for teenagers be?

Very effective	62%
Somewhat effective	18
Not too effective	6
Not effective at all	12
No opinion	2

How effective would it be to "[hold] parents legally responsible for crimes their children commit with their parents' guns?"

Very effective	47%
Somewhat effective	28
Not too effective	12
Not effective at all	12
No opinion	1

Source: Gallup Organization, "Public Continues to Believe a Variety of Factors Caused Littleton." Posted on URL: http://www.gallup.com/poll/releases/pr990423.asp. Posted on May 13, 1999.

HOW CHILDREN'S DOCTORS ARE INVOLVED WITH TREATING AND PREVENTING FIREARMS VIOLENCE

According to a survey published in a pediatrics journal: "Almost 1 in 5 pediatricians treated a gun injury in the past 12 months. In 1988, 86.5% of pediatricians supported restricting the sale and possession of handguns; in 1994, support for such legislation increased to 92.5% (P<.01). Also in 1994, 76% supported banning the sale or possession of handguns. Most respondents (82%) believe anticipatory guidance on firearm safety can reduce injury and death; 95% support asking parents to unload and lock firearms, and 66% support encouraging parents to remove handguns from the home." (*Source:* Archive of Pediatrics and Adolescent Medicine, 1997, pp. 151: 352–359. Posted on URL: http://www.ama-assn.org/sci-pubs/journals/archive/ajdc/vol_151/no _4/oa6295a.htm.)

Appendix A

HOW DOCTORS COUNSEL PATIENTS ABOUT FIREARM SAFETY

According to another survey in a pediatrics journal: "Of the respondents, 80% stated that they should counsel on firearm safety; only 38% do so. Of those clinicians who currently counsel, only 20% counsel more than 10% of their patient families. Firearm safety counseling behavior is positively associated with a clinician being 49 years or younger (odds ratio [OR] = 2.19, P = .02); a perception that counseling is beneficial (OR = 2.62, P = .02); and household handgun ownership (OR = 2.47, P = .02). Clinician households that report gun ownership counsel differently than those clinicians who report not possessing a household gun." (*Source:* Shari Barkin, Naihua Duan, Arlene Fink, Robert H. Brook, Lillian Gelberg, "The Smoking Gun: Do Clinicians Follow Guidelines on Firearm Safety Counseling?" Archive of Pediatrics and Adolescent Medicine, 1998, pp. 152: 749–756, URL: http://www.ama-assn.org/sci-pubs/journals/archive/ajdc/vol_152/no _8/poa8035.htm.)

HOW THE PERCENTAGE OF STUDENTS ENGAGED IN WEAPONS-RELATED RISKY BEHAVIORS CHANGED DURING THE 1990S

Behavior (At least one incidence in past 30 days)	Year			
	1991	1993	1995	1997
Carried weapon	26.1	22.1	20.0	18.3
Carried gun	NA	7.9	7.6	5.9
Carried weapon on school property	NA	11.8	9.8	8.5

Source: Centers for Disease Control and Prevention, "Youth Risk Behavior Trends," *Youth Risk Behavior Survey.* Posted on URL: http://www.cdc.gov/nccdphp/dash/yrbs/trend.htm.

Teenage arrest rates for weapons offenses started to soar in the mid-1980s, but teenage involvement with weapons has actually declined since then. Despite the horrific shootings in the news in the 1990s, the incidence of guns and weapons being carried in schools actually continued to decline. A National Institute of Justice survey found that, of 10th and 11th grade boys, 29 percent of them owned a firearm of some type, but only 6 percent carry guns outside the home. The main purpose of guns owned by the boys was for hunting and recreation, not for crime or for defense from crime.

Gun Control

PUBLIC SUPPORT FOR GUN CONTROL

SUPPORT FOR GUN CONTROL SINCE 1990

In general, do you feel that the laws covering the sale of firearms should be made more strict, less strict, or kept as they are now?

	More strict	Less strict	Kept as now	No opinion
April 26–27, 1999	66%	7%	25%	2%
Feb. 8–9, 1999	60	9	29	2
April 23–24, 1995**	62	12	24	2
Dec. 17–19, 1993	67	7	25	1
March 1993	70	4	24	2
1991	68	5	25	2
1990	78	2	17	3

Which of the following statements comes closest to your view: There should be no restrictions on owning guns; there should be minor restrictions—such as a 5-day waiting period to buy a gun—and gun registrations; there should be major restrictions that would also ban ownership of some guns altogether—such as handguns and certain semiautomatic rifles—or all guns should be illegal for everyone except police and authorized persons?

	April 26–27, 1999	Feb. 8–9, 1999	May 8–10, 1998**	Dec.17–19, 1993
No restrictions	4%	5%	8%	6%
Minor restrictions	30	37	28	35
Major restrictions	38	36	37	38
Some restrictions (unspecified)	4	0	2	0
All guns illegal, except for authorized persons	22	18	24	20
No opinion	2	4	1	1
	100%	100%	100%	100%

** Asked of half sample

Note: For results based on the sample of national adults (N=1,073) surveyed April 26–27, 1999, the margin of sampling error is ±3 percentage points. Note that the first column reflects opinion following the Littleton High School shootings.

Source: Gallup Organization, "Gun Control Support Increases Modestly in Wake of Littleton Tragedy." Posted on URL: http://www.gallup.com/poll/releases/pr990503.asp.

Appendix A

SUPPORT FOR BASIC GUN CONTROL MEASURES

	Support		Oppose	
	Total	% Strong*	Total	% Strong*
Stricter gun control	67	82	31	68
Background checks at gun shows	89	87	11	64
Ban on assault weapons	79	85	19	63
Mandatory trigger locks	75	81	22	64
Ban on mail order and Internet gun sales	70	86	28	68

*Percentage of total who say they feel that way "strongly."

Source: ABC News/Washington Post Poll, "Opinions on Gun Issues." Posted on URL: http://more. abcnews.go.com/sections/us/DailyNews/guns_poll990518. html.

According to an ABC News/*The Washington Post* poll conducted on May 16, 1999, the following percentages support and oppose each measure. Note the second column in each case is the percentage of supporters or opponents who say they feel "strongly" about the issue. The survey also notes: "Just 39 percent of Americans trust the Democrats more to handle gun control, while 31 percent prefer the Republicans—hardly a great advantage, given the Democrats' closer proximity to public preferences. Instead, an unusually large number, 22 percent, volunteer that they don't trust either party to deal with the issue."

APPENDIX B

FEDERAL AND STATE CONSTITUTIONAL PROVISIONS

Much of the legal debate over gun control measures involves their constitutionality. The federal constitution and many state constitutions contain guarantees of the right to keep and bear arms. When a state gun control law is challenged, it is the state constitution that comes into play because the Second Amendment of the federal constitution has not been applied to the states.

The language of many of the state provisions (such as those of Alaska and Hawaii) matches or resembles that of the Second Amendment, referring to the right to bear arms in the context of the militia. Other state provisions (such as Illinois and Kentucky) refer to the right to bear arms for the defense of oneself and the state, for hunting (Nebraska and Nevada, for example), or for other purposes. A number of state provisions (such as that of Louisiana) explicitly give the state the power to regulate the carrying of concealed weapons. Note that the following states do not have constitutional provisions relating to the right to keep and bear arms: California, Iowa, Maryland, Minnesota, New Jersey, and New York.

Federal: "A well-regulated militia, being necessary to the security of a free State, the right of the people to keep and bear arms, shall not be infringed." (Second Amendment)

Alabama: "That every citizen has a right to bear arms in defense of himself and the state." (Article I, Section 26)

Alaska: "A well-regulated militia being necessary to the security of a free state, the right of the people to keep and bear arms shall not be infringed." (Article I, Section 19)

Arizona: "The right of the individual citizen to bear arms in defense of himself or the State shall not be impaired, but nothing in this Section shall be construed as authorizing individuals or corporations to organize, maintain, or employ an armed body of men." (Article II, Section 26)

Arkansas: "The citizens of this State shall have the right to keep and bear arms for their common defense." (Article II, Section 5)

Appendix B

Colorado: "The right of no person to keep and bear arms in defense of his home, person and property, or in aid of the civil power when thereto legally summoned, shall be called in question; but nothing herein contained shall be construed to justify the practice of carrying concealed weapons." (Article II, Section 13)

Connecticut: "Every citizen has a right to bear arms in defense of himself and the state." (Article 1, Section 15)

Delaware: "A person has the right to keep and bear arms for the defense of self, family, home and State, and for hunting and recreational use." (Article I, Section 20)

Florida: "The right of the people to keep and bear arms in defense of themselves and of the lawful authority of the state shall not be infringed, except that the manner of bearing arms may be regulated by law." (Article I, Section 8)

Georgia: "The right of the people to keep and bear arms shall not be infringed, but the General Assembly shall have the power to prescribe the manner in which arms may be borne." (Article I, Section I, par. VIII)

Hawaii: "A well regulated militia being necessary to the security of a free state, the right of the people to keep and bear arms shall not be infringed." (Article I, Section 15)

Idaho: "The people have the right to keep and bear arms, which right shall not be abridged; but this provision shall not prevent the passage of laws to govern the carrying of weapons concealed on the person, nor prevent passage of legislation providing minimum sentences for crimes committed while in possession of a firearm, nor prevent passage of legislation providing penalties for the possession of firearms by a convicted felon, nor prevent the passage of legislation punishing the use of a firearm. No law shall impose licensure, registration or special taxation on the ownership or possession of firearms or ammunition. Nor shall any law permit the confiscation of firearms, except those actually used in the commission of a felony." (Article I, Section 11)

Illinois: "Subject only to the police power, the right of the individual citizen to keep and bear arms shall not be infringed." (Article 1, Section 22)

Indiana: "The people shall have a right to bear arms, for the defense of themselves and the State." (Article I, Section 32)

Kansas: "The people have the right to bear arms for their defense and security; but standing armies, in time of peace, are dangerous to liberty, and shall not be tolerated, and the military shall be in strict subordination to the civil power." (Bill of Rights, Section 4)

Kentucky: "All men are, by nature, free and equal, and have certain inherent and inalienable rights, among which may be reckoned: . . . Seventh: The right to bear arms in defense of themselves and of the state, subject to the power of the general assembly to enact laws to prevent persons from carrying concealed weapons." (Bill of Rights, Section I, par. 7)

Louisiana: "The right of each citizen to keep and bear arms shall not be abridged, but this provision shall not prevent the passage of laws to prohibit the carrying of weapons concealed on the person." (Article I, Section 11)

Maine: "Every citizen has a right to keep and bear arms and this right shall never be questioned." (Article I, Section 16)

Massachusetts: "The people have a right to keep and bear arms for the common defence [sic]. And as, in time of peace, armies are dangerous to liberty, they ought not to be maintained without the consent of the legislature; and the military power shall always be held in an exact subordination to the civil authority, and be governed by it." (Declaration of Rights, Part I, Article XVII)

Michigan: "Every person has a right to keep and bear arms for the defense of himself and the state." (Article I, Section 6)

Mississippi: "The right of every citizen to keep and bear arms in defense of his home, person, or property, or in aid of the civil power when thereto legally summoned, shall not be called in question, but the legislature may regulate or forbid carrying concealed weapons." (Article 3, Section 12)

Missouri: "That the right of every citizen to keep and bear arms in defense of his home, person and property, or when lawfully summoned in aid of the civil power, shall not be questioned; but this shall not justify the wearing of concealed weapons." (Article I, Section 23)

Montana: "The right of any person to keep or bear arms in defense of his own home, person, and property, or in aid of the civil power when thereto legally summoned, shall not be called in question, but nothing herein contained shall be held to permit the carrying of concealed weapons." (Article II, Section 12)

Nebraska: "All persons are by nature free and independent, and have certain inherent and inalienable rights; among these are . . . the right to keep and bear arms for security or defense of self, family, home, and others, and for lawful common defense, hunting, recreational use, and all other lawful purposes, and such rights shall not be denied or infringed by the state or any subdivision thereof." (Article I, Section 1)

Nevada: "Every citizen has the right to keep and bear arms for security and defense, for lawful hunting and recreational use and for other lawful purposes." (Article I, Section II, Par. 1)

New Hampshire: "All persons have the right to keep and bear arms in defense of themselves, their families, their property, and the state." (Part 1, Article IIa)

Appendix B

New Mexico: "No law shall abridge the right of the citizen to keep and bear arms for security and defense, for lawful hunting and recreational use and for other lawful purposes, but nothing herein shall be held to permit the carrying of concealed weapons. No municipality or county shall regulate, in any way, an incident of the right to keep and bear arms." (Article II, Section 6)

North Carolina: "A well regulated militia being necessary to the security of a free State, the right of the people to keep and bear arms shall not be infringed; and, as standing armies in time of peace are dangerous to liberty, they shall not be maintained, and the military shall be kept under strict subordination to, and governed by, the civil power. Nothing herein shall justify the practice of carrying concealed weapons, or prevent the General Assembly from enacting penal statutes against that practice." (Article I, Section 30)

North Dakota: "All individuals are by nature equally free and independent and have certain inalienable rights, among which are . . . to keep and bear arms for the defense of their person, family, property, and the state, and for lawful hunting, recreational, and other lawful purposes, which shall not be infringed." (Article I, Section 1)

Ohio: "The people have the right to bear arms for their defense and security; but standing armies, in time of peace, are dangerous to liberty, and shall not be kept up; and the military shall be in strict subordination to the civil power. (Article I, Section 4)

Oklahoma: "The right of a citizen to keep and bear arms in defense of his home, person, or property, or in aid of the civil power, when thereunto legally summoned, shall never be prohibited; but nothing herein contained shall prevent the Legislature from regulating the carrying of weapons." (Article II, Section 26)

Oregon: "The people shall have the right to bear arms for the defence [sic] of themselves, and the State, but the Military shall be kept in strict subordination to the civil power." (Article I, Section 27)

Pennsylvania: "The right of the citizens to bear arms in defence [sic] of themselves and the State shall not be questioned." (Article I, Section 21)

Rhode Island: "The right of the people to keep and bear arms shall not be infringed." (Article I, Section 22)

South Carolina: "A well regulated militia being necessary to the security of a free State, the right of the people to keep and bear arms shall not be infringed. As, in times of peace, armies are dangerous to liberty, they shall not be maintained without the consent of the General Assembly. The military power of the State shall always be held in subordination to the civil authority and be governed by it. No soldier shall

251

in time of peace be quartered in any house without the consent of the owner nor in time of war but in the manner prescribed by law." (Article I, Section 20)

South Dakota: "The right of the citizens to bear arms in defense of themselves and the state shall not be denied." (Article VI, Section 24)

Tennessee: "That the citizens of this State have a right to keep and to bear arms for their common defense; but the Legislature shall have power, by law, to regulate the wearing of arms with a view to prevent crime." (Article I, Section 26)

Texas: "Every citizen shall have the right to keep and bear arms in lawful defense of himself or the State; but the Legislature shall have power, by law, to regulate the wearing of arms, with a view to prevent crime." (Article I, Section 23)

Utah: "The individual right of the people to keep and bear arms for security and defense of self, family, others, property, or the State, as well as for the other lawful purposes shall not be infringed; but nothing herein shall prevent the legislature from defining the lawful use of arms." (Article I, Section 6)

Vermont: "That the people have a right to bear arms for the defence [sic] of themselves and the State—and as standing armies in time of peace are dangerous to liberty, they ought not to be kept up; and that the military should be kept under strict subordination to and governed by the civil power." (Chapter I, Article XVI)

Virginia: "That a well regulated militia, composed of the body of the people, trained to arms, is the proper, natural, and safe defense of a free state, therefore, the right of the people to keep and bear arms shall not be infringed; that standing armies, in time of peace, should be avoided as dangerous to liberty; and that in all cases the military should be under strict subordination to, and governed by, the civil power." (Article I, Section 13)

Washington: "The right of the individual citizen to bear arms in defense of himself, or the state, shall not be impaired, but nothing in this Section shall be construed as authorizing individuals or corporations to organize, maintain, or employ an armed body of men." (Article I, Section 24)

West Virginia: "A person has the right to keep and bear arms for the defense of self, family, home and state, and for lawful hunting and recreational use." (Article 3, Section 22)

Wisconsin: "The people have the right to keep and bear arms for security, defense, hunting, recreation, or any other lawful purpose." (Article I, Section 25)

Wyoming: "The right of citizens to bear arms in defense of themselves and of the state shall not be denied." (Article I, Section 24)

APPENDIX C

PROVISIONS OF STATE FIREARMS LAWS

The following two charts summarize key provisions of state firearms laws as of mid-1999.

The first chart deals with provisions of regulations of gun purchases and includes bans on certain types of firearms, the status of the NICS (National Instant Check System for gun purchasers), waiting periods for handguns and long guns, requirements for a license or permit to purchase handguns or long guns, and the existence of a registration system for handguns or long guns.

The second chart deals with laws concerning the carrying of concealed firearms, including whether carrying is presumptively permitted ("shall issue"), presumptively prohibited ("may issue"), or prohibited outright.

There are several things to keep in mind while looking at these summary charts:

- Many states pass new firearms laws (or modify existing ones) each year.
- Many municipalities or counties have additional gun restrictions, such as bans on the purchase of handguns or the concealed carrying of firearms.
- There are also many federal laws and regulations that affect gun purchase, ownership, or use.
- Stricter federal laws may preempt more lax state laws, but the existence of federal regulation does not generally preclude enacting stricter state regulations.
- Some state firearms laws may preempt localities from legislating on the same topic, but this varies by state and is often the subject of litigation.

Because of these considerations, it is best to view the charts as a "snapshot" of the status of state gun control laws in 1999 rather than as a definitive

253

reference. Individuals who are directly affected by gun laws (such as gun owners, dealers, or manufacturers) should recheck the cited web site and check with the appropriate state agency for up-to-date information.

Key to the following charts:

1. In certain cities or counties.
2. **National Instant Check System (NICS) exemption codes:**

   RTC: Carry permit holders who are exempt from NICS.
   GRTC: Holders of RTC permits issued before November 30, 1998, are exempt from NICS. Holders of more recent permits are not exempt.
   L: Holders of state license to possess or purchase or firearms ID cards and who are exempt from NICS.
   O: Other, See Note 3.

3. **NICS exemptions notes: Indiana:** Personal protection and hunting and target permits; **Mississippi:** Permit issued to security guards does **not** qualify; **Texas:** Texas Peace Officer license, TCLEOSE Card, is grandfathered only.
4. Chicago only. No handgun not already registered may be possessed.
5. **Arkansas** prohibits carrying a firearm "with a purpose to employ it as a weapon against a person." **Tennessee** prohibits carrying "with the intent to go armed." **Vermont** prohibits carrying a firearm "with the intent or purpose of injuring another."
6. Loaded.
7. New York City only.
8. A permit is required to acquire another handgun before 30 days have elapsed following the acquisition of a handgun.
9. **Maryland** subjects purchases of "assault weapons" to a seven-day waiting period.
10. May be extended by police to 30 days in some circumstances. An individual not holding a driver's license must wait 90 days.
11. Carrying a handgun openly in a motor vehicle requires a license.
12. Every person arriving in **Hawaii** is required to register any firearm(s) brought into the state within three days of arrival of the person or firearm(s), whichever occurs later. Handguns purchased from licensed dealers must be registered within five days.
13. Concealed-carry laws vary significantly between the states. Ratings reflect the real effect a state's particular laws have on the ability of citizens to carry firearms for self-defense.

14. Purchases from licensed dealers only.
15. The state waiting period does not apply to a person holding a valid permit or license to carry a firearm. In **Connecticut,** a hunting license also exempts the holder for long-gun purchases. In **Indiana,** only persons with unlimited carry permits are exempt.
16. **Connecticut:** A permit to purchase or a carry permit is required to obtain a handgun, and a carry permit is required to transport a handgun outside your home. **District of Columbia:** No handgun may be possessed unless it was registered prior to September 23, 1976, and reregistered by February 5, 1977. A permit to purchase is required for a rifle or shotgun. **Hawaii:** Purchase permits, required for all firearms, may not be issued until 14 days after application. A handgun purchase permit is valid for 10 days for one handgun; a long-gun permit is valid for one year, for multiple long guns. **Illinois:** A Firearm Owner's Identification Card (FOI) is required to possess or purchase a firearm, must be issued to qualified applicants within 30 days, and is valid for 5 years. **Iowa:** A purchase permit is required for handguns and is valid for one year, beginning three days after issuance. **Massachusetts:** Firearm owners must possess a Firearms Owner's ID Card (FID) or a license to carry. Handgun purchasers must have a (a) license to carry, (b) purchase permit and an FID, or (c) purchase permit and proof of exempt status. A handgun permit is valid for 10 days. A long-gun purchaser must have a carry license, FID, or proof of exempt status. **Michigan:** A handgun purchaser must obtain a license to purchase from local law enforcement, and within 10 days present the license and handgun to obtain a certificate of inspection. **Minnesota:** A handgun transfer or carrying permit or a seven-day waiting period and handgun transfer report is required to purchase handguns or "assault weapons" from a dealer. A permit or transfer report must be issued to qualified applicants within seven days. A permit is valid for one year; a transfer report for 30 days. **Missouri:** A purchase permit is required for a handgun, must be issued to qualified applicants within seven days, and is valid for 30 days. **New Jersey:** Firearm owners must possess an FID, which must be issued to qualified applicants within 30 days. To purchase a handgun, an FID and a purchase permit, which must be issued within 30 days to qualified applicants and is valid for 90 days, are required. An FID is required to purchase long guns. **New York:** The purchase, the possession, and/or the carrying of a handgun requires a single license, which includes any restrictions placed on the bearer. New York City also requires a license for long guns. **North Carolina:** To purchase a handgun, a license or permit is required, which must be

issued to qualified applicants within 30 days. **Ohio:** Some cities require a permit-to-purchase or firearm owner ID card.

17. Preemption through judicial ruling. Local regulation may be instituted in **Massachusetts** if ratified by the legislature.
18. Except Gary and East Chicago and local laws enacted before January 1994.
19. **Vermont** law respects your right to carry without a permit.
20. **California, Connecticut, New Jersey, New York City** and other local jurisdictions in **New York,** and some local jurisdictions in **Ohio** prohibit "assault weapons." **Hawaii** prohibits "assault pistols." **Illinois:** Chicago, Evanston, Oak Park, Morton Grove, Winnetka, Wilmette, and Highland Park prohibit handguns; some cities prohibit other kinds of firearms. **Maryland** prohibits several small, low-caliber, inexpensive handguns and "assault pistols." **Massachusetts:** It is unlawful to sell, transfer, or possess "any assault weapon or large capacity feeding device" [more than 10 rounds] that was not legally possessed on September 13, 1994. **Ohio:** Some cities prohibit handguns of certain magazine capacities. **Virginia** prohibits "street sweeper" shotguns. The **District of Columbia** prohibits new acquisition of handguns and any semiautomatic firearm capable of using a detachable ammunition magazine of more than 12 rounds capacity. (With respect to some of these laws and ordinances, individuals may retain prohibited firearms owned previously, with certain restrictions.)
21. Local jurisdictions may opt out of prohibition.
22. Preemption only applies to handguns.

Appendix C

STATE REGULATIONS ON FIREARMS PURCHASES

State	Gun ban	Exemptions to NICS[2]	State waiting period number of days		License or permit to purchase		Registration	
			Hand-guns	Long guns	Hand-guns	Long guns	Hand-guns	Long guns
Ala.	. . .	. . .	2	. . .	. . .	. . .	. . .	. . .
Alaska	. . .	RTC	. . .	. . .	. . .	. . .	. . .	. . .
Ariz.	. . .	RTC	. . .	. . .	. . .	. . .	. . .	. . .
Amer. Samoa	. . .	GRTC	. . .	. . .	. . .	. . .	. . .	. . .
Calif.	X[20]	. . .	10	10	. . .	. . .	. . .	. . .
Colo.	. . .	. . .	. . .	. . .	. . .	. . .	. . .	. . .
Conn.	X[20]	GRTC	14[14,15]	14[14,15]	X[16]	. . .	. . .	. . .
Del.	. . .	GRTC	. . .	. . .	. . .	. . .	. . .	. . .
Fla.	. . .	GRTC	3[14,15]	. . .	. . .	. . .	. . .	. . .
Ga.	. . .	RTC	. . .	. . .	. . .	. . .	. . .	. . .
Hawaii	X[20]	L	. . .	. . .	X[16]	X[16]	X[12]	X[12]
Idaho	. . .	RTC	. . .	. . .	. . .	. . .	. . .	. . .
Ill.	[20]	. . .	3	1	X[16]	X[16]	4	4
Ind.	. . .	RTC, O[3]	. . .	. . .	. . .	. . .	. . .	. . .
Iowa	. . .	L, RTC	. . .	. . .	X[16]	. . .	. . .	. . .
Kans.	. . .	. . .	1	. . .	1	. . .	1	. . .
Ky.	. . .	GRTC	. . .	. . .	. . .	. . .	. . .	. . .
La.	. . .	GRTC	. . .	. . .	. . .	. . .	. . .	. . .
Maine	. . .	. . .	. . .	. . .	. . .	. . .	. . .	. . .
Md.	X[20]	GRTC	7	7[9]	8	. . .	. . .	. . .
Mass.	X[20]	GRTC	7	. . .	X[16]	X[16]	. . .	. . .
Mich.	. . .	L	. . .	. . .	X[16]	. . .	X	. . .
Minn.	. . .	GRTC	7[16]	16	X[16]	X[16]	. . .	. . .
Miss.	. . .	RTC[3]	. . .	. . .	. . .	. . .	. . .	. . .
Mo.	. . .	GRTC	7	. . .	X[16]	. . .	. . .	. . .
Mont.	. . .	RTC	. . .	. . .	. . .	. . .	. . .	. . .
Neb.	. . .	L	. . .	. . .	X	. . .	. . .	. . .

Source: National Rifle Association. "Compendium of State Firearms Laws." Available on-line. Posted on URL: http://www.nraila.org/.

State	Gun ban	Exemptions to NICS[2]	State waiting period number of days		License or permit to purchase		Registration	
			Hand-guns	Long guns	Hand-guns	Long guns	Hand-guns	Long guns
Nev.	. . .	RTC	1	. . .	. . .	. . .	1	. . .
N.H.	. . .	. . .	. . .	. . .	. . .	. . .	. . .	. . .
N.J.	X[20]	. . .	. . .	. . .	X[16]	X[16]	. . .	X
N.Mex.	. . .	. . .	. . .	. . .	. . .	. . .	. . .	. . .
N.Y.	20	L	. . .	. . .	X[16]	16	X	7
N.C.	. . .	L, RTC	. . .	. . .	X[16]	. . .	. . .	. . .
N.Dak.	. . .	GRTC	. . .	. . .	. . .	. . .	. . .	. . .
Ohio	20	. . .	1	. . .	16	. . .	1	. . .
Okla.	. . .	GRTC	. . .	. . .	. . .	. . .	. . .	. . .
Oreg.	. . .	GRTC	. . .	. . .	. . .	. . .	. . .	. . .
Pa.	. . .	GRTC	2	. . .	. . .	. . .	. . .	. . .
R.I.	. . .	. . .	7	7	. . .	. . .	. . .	. . .
S.C.	. . .	RTC	8	. . .	8	. . .	. . .	. . .
S.Dak.	. . .	GRTC	2	. . .	. . .	. . .	. . .	. . .
Tenn.	. . .	. . .	. . .	. . .	. . .	. . .	. . .	. . .
Tex.	. . .	RTC[3]	. . .	. . .	. . .	. . .	. . .	. . .
Utah	. . .	RTC	. . .	. . .	. . .	. . .	. . .	. . .
Vt.	. . .	. . .	. . .	. . .	. . .	. . .	. . .	. . .
Va.	X[20]	. . .	1,8	. . .	1,8	. . .	. . .	. . .
Wash.	. . .	GRTC	5[10]	. . .	. . .	. . .	. . .	. . .
W.Va.	. . .	. . .	. . .	. . .	. . .	. . .	. . .	. . .
Wis.	. . .	. . .	2	. . .	. . .	. . .	. . .	. . .
Wyo.	. . .	RTC	. . .	. . .	. . .	. . .	. . .	. . .
D.C.	X[20]	GRTC	. . .	. . .	X[16]	X[16]	X[16]	X

Source: National Rifle Association. "Compendium of State Firearms Laws." Available online. Posted on URL: http://www.nraila.org/.

Appendix C

Concealed carry codes:

R: Right-to-Carry: "shall issue" or less restrictive discretionary permit system (Ala., Conn.)
(See also note #21.)
L: Right-to-Carry Limited by local authority's discretion over permit issuance.
D: Right-to-Carry Denied, no permit system exists; concealed carry is prohibited.

STATE LAWS RELATING TO CARRYING OF FIREARMS

State	Record of sale reported to state or local govt.	State provision for right-to-carry concealed[15]	Carrying openly prohibited	Owner ID cards or licensing	Firearm rights constitutional provison	State firearms preemption laws	Range protection law
Ala.	X	R	X[11]	. . .	X	X[22]	. . .
Alaska	. . .	R	. . .	. . .	X	. . .	X
Ariz.	. . .	R	. . .	. . .	X	X	. . .
Amer. Samoa	. . .	R	X[5]	. . .	X	X	X
Calif.	X	L	X[6]	. . .	. . .	X	X
Colo.	. . .	L	. . .	. . .	X	. . .	X
Conn.	X	R	X	. . .	X	X[17]	X
Del.	. . .	L	. . .	. . .	X	X	. . .
Fla.	. . .	R	X	. . .	X	X	. . .
Ga.	. . .	R	X	. . .	X	X	X
Hawaii	X	L	X	. . .	X	. . .	. . .
Idaho	. . .	R	. . .	. . .	X	X	X
Ill.	X	D	X	X	X	. . .	X
Ind.	X	R	X	. . .	X	X[18]	X
Iowa	X	L	X	. . .	. . .	X	X
Kans.	. . .	D	1	. . .	X	. . .	. . .
Ky.	. . .	R	. . .	. . .	X	X	X
La.	. . .	R	. . .	. . .	X	X	X
Maine	. . .	R	. . .	. . .	X	X	X
Md.	X	L	X	. . .	. . .	X	X
Mass.	X	L	X	X	X	X[17]	X
Mich.	X	L	X[11]	. . .	X	X	X
Minn.	X	L	X	. . .	. . .	X	. . .

Source: National Rifle Association. "Compendium of State Firearms Laws." Available on-line. Posted on URL: http://www.nraila.org/.

State	Record of sale reported to state or local govt.	State provision for right-to-carry concealed[15]	Carrying openly prohibited	Owner ID cards or licensing	Firearm rights constitutional provison	State firearms preemption laws	Range protection law
Miss.	. . .	R	. . .	. . .	X	X	. . .
Mo.	X	D	. . .	. . .	X	X	X
Mont.	. . .	R	. . .	. . .	X	X	X
Neb.	. . .	D	. . .	. . .	X	. . .	. . .
Nev.	. . .	R	. . .	. . .	X	X	X
N.H.	X	R	. . .	. . .	X	. . .	X
N.J.	X	L	X	X	. . .	X[17]	X
N.Mex.	. . .	D	. . .	. . .	X	X	. . .
N.Y.	X	L	X	X	. . .	X[17]	X
N.C.	X	R	. . .	. . .	X	X	X
N.Dak.	X	R	X[6]	. . .	X	X	X
Ohio	[1]	D	[1]	[16]	X	. . .	X
Okla.	. . .	R	X[6]	. . .	X	X	X
Oreg.	X	R	. . .	. . .	X	X	X
Pa.	X	R	X[11]	. . .	X	X	X
R.I.	X	L	X	. . .	X	X	X
S.C.	X	R	X	. . .	X	X	. . .
S.Dak.	X	R	. . .	. . .	X	X	X
Tenn.	X	R	X[5]	. . .	X	X	X
Tex.	. . .	R	X	. . .	X	X	. . .
Utah	. . .	R	X[6]	. . .	X	X	X
Vt.	. . .	R[19]	X[5]	. . .	X	X	X
Va.	[1]	R	. . .	. . .	X	X	X
Wash.	X	R	X[21]	. . .	X	X	. . .
W.Va.	. . .	R	. . .	. . .	X	X	X
Wis.	X	D	. . .	. . .	X	X	X
Wyo.	. . .	R	. . .	. . .	X	X	X
D.C.	X	D	X	X	NA	. . .	. . .

Source: National Rifle Association. "Compendium of State Firearms Laws." Available on-line. Posted on URL: http://www.nraila.org/.

APPENDIX D

THE BRADY HANDGUN VIOLENCE PREVENTION ACT

H.R. 1025
One Hundred Third Congress
of the
United States of America
AT THE FIRST SESSION
Begun and held at the City of Washington on Tuesday, the fifth day of
January, one thousand nine hundred ninety-three

AN ACT

To provide for a waiting period before the purchase of a handgun, and for
the establishment of a national instant criminal background check system to
be contacted by firearms dealers before the transfer of any firearm.

Be it enacted by the Senate and House of Representatives of the United
States of America in Congress assembled,

TITLE I—BRADY HANDGUN CONTROL

SEC. 101. SHORT TITLE.

This title may be cited as the "Brady Handgun Violence Prevention Act."

SEC. 102. FEDERAL FIREARMS LICENSEE REQUIRED TO CONDUCT CRIMINAL BACKGROUND CHECK BEFORE TRANSFER OF FIREARM TO NON-LICENSEE.

(a) INTERIM PROVISION.—

(1) IN GENERAL.—Section 922 of title 18, United States Code, is
amended by adding at the end the following:

"(s)(1) Beginning on the date that is 90 days after the date of enactment
of this subsection and ending on the day before the date that is 60 months

261

after such date of enactment, it shall be unlawful for any licensed importer, licensed manufacturer, or licensed dealer to sell, deliver, or transfer a handgun to an individual who is not licensed under section 923, unless—

"(A) after the most recent proposal of such transfer by the transferee—

"(i) the transferor has—

"(I) received from the transferee a statement of the transferee containing the information described in paragraph (3);

"(II) verified the identity of the transferee by examining the identification document presented;

"(III) within 1 day after the transferee furnishes the statement, provided notice of the contents of the statement to the chief law enforcement officer of the place of residence of the transferee; and

"(IV) within 1 day after the transferee furnishes the statement, transmitted a copy of the statement to the chief law enforcement officer of the place of residence of the transferee; and

"(ii)(I) 5 business days (meaning days on which State offices are open) have elapsed from the date the transferor furnished notice of the contents of the statement to the chief law enforcement officer, during which period the transferor has not received information from the chief law enforcement officer that receipt or possession of the handgun by the transferee would be in violation of Federal, State, or local law; or

"(II) the transferor has received notice from the chief law enforcement officer that the officer has no information indicating that receipt or possession of the handgun by the transferee would violate Federal, State, or local law;

"(B) the transferee has presented to the transferor a written statement, issued by the chief law enforcement officer of the place of residence of the transferee during the 10-day period ending on the date of the most recent proposal of such transfer by the transferee, stating that the transferee requires access to a handgun because of a threat to the life of the transferee or of any member of the household of the transferee;

"(C)(i) the transferee has presented to the transferor a permit that—

"(I) allows the transferee to possess or acquire a handgun; and

"(II) was issued not more than 5 years earlier by the State in which the transfer is to take place; and

"(ii) the law of the State provides that such a permit is to be issued only after an authorized government official has verified that the information available to such official does not indicate that possession of a handgun by the transferee would be in violation of the law;

"(D) the law of the State requires that, before any licensed importer, licensed manufacturer, or licensed dealer completes the transfer of a handgun to an individual who is not licensed under section 923, an authorized government official verify that the information available to such official does not indicate that possession of a handgun by the transferee would be in violation of law;

"(E) the Secretary has approved the transfer under section 5812 of the Internal Revenue Code of 1986; or

"(F) on application of the transferor, the Secretary has certified that compliance with subparagraph (A)(i)(III) is impracticable because—

"(i) the ratio of the number of law enforcement officers of the State in which the transfer is to occur to the number of square miles of land area of the State does not exceed 0.0025;

"(ii) the business premises of the transferor at which the transfer is to occur are extremely remote in relation to the chief law enforcement officer;

and

"(iii) there is an absence of telecommunications facilities in the geographical area in which the business premises are located.

"(2) A chief law enforcement officer to whom a transferor has provided notice pursuant to paragraph (1)(A)(i)(III) shall make a reasonable effort to ascertain within 5 business days whether receipt or possession would be in violation of the law, including research in whatever State and local recordkeeping systems are available and in a national system designated by the Attorney General.

"(3) The statement referred to in paragraph (1)(A)(i)(I) shall contain only—

"(A) the name, address, and date of birth appearing on a valid identification document (as defined in section 1028(d)(1)) of the transferee containing a photograph of the transferee and a description of the identification used;

"(B) a statement that the transferee—

"(i) is not under indictment for, and has not been convicted in any court of, a crime punishable by imprisonment for a term exceeding 1 year;

"(ii) is not a fugitive from justice;

"(iii) is not an unlawful user of or addicted to any controlled substance (as defined in section 102 of the Controlled Substances Act);

"(iv) has not been adjudicated as a mental defective or been committed to a mental institution;

"(v) is not an alien who is illegally or unlawfully in the United States;

"(vi) has not been discharged from the Armed Forces under dishonorable conditions; and

"(vii) is not a person who, having been a citizen of the United States, has renounced such citizenship;

"(C) the date the statement is made; and

"(D) notice that the transferee intends to obtain a handgun from the transferor.

"(4) Any transferor of a handgun who, after such transfer, receives a report from a chief law enforcement officer containing information that receipt or possession of the handgun by the transferee violates Federal, State, or local law shall, within one business day after receipt of such request, communicate any information related to the transfer that the transferor has about the transfer and the transferee to—

"(A) the chief law enforcement officer of the place of business of the transferor; and

"(B) the chief law enforcement officer of the place of residence of the transferee.

"(5) Any transferor who receives information, not otherwise available to the public, in a report under this subsection shall not disclose such information except to the transferee, to law enforcement authorities, or pursuant to the direction of a court of law.

"(6)(A) Any transferor who sells, delivers, or otherwise transfers a handgun to a transferee shall retain the copy of the statement of the transferee with respect to the handgun transaction, and shall retain evidence that the transferor has complied with subclauses (III) and (IV) of paragraph (1)(A)(i) with respect to the statement.

"(B) Unless the chief law enforcement officer to whom a statement is transmitted under paragraph (1)(A)(i)(IV) determines that a transaction would violate Federal, State, or local law—

"(i) the officer shall, within 20 business days after the date the transferee made the statement on the basis of which the notice was provided, destroy the statement, any record containing information derived from the statement, and any record created as a result of the notice required by paragraph (1)(A)(i)(III);

"(ii) the information contained in the statement shall not be conveyed to any person except a person who has a need to know in order to carry out this subsection; and

"(iii) the information contained in the statement shall not be used for any purpose other than to carry out this subsection.

"(C) If a chief law enforcement officer determines that an individual is ineligible to receive a handgun and the individual requests the officer to provide the reason for such determination, the officer shall provide such reasons to the individual in writing within 20 business days after receipt of the request.

"(7) A chief law enforcement officer or other person responsible for providing criminal history background information pursuant to this subsection shall not be liable in an action at law for damages—

"(A) for failure to prevent the sale or transfer of a handgun to a person whose receipt or possession of the handgun is unlawful under this section; or

"(B) for preventing such a sale or transfer to a person who may lawfully receive or possess a handgun.

"(8) For purposes of this subsection, the term 'chief law enforcement officer' means the chief of police, the sheriff, or an equivalent officer or the designee of any such individual.

"(9) The Secretary shall take necessary actions to ensure that the provisions of this subsection are published and disseminated to licensed dealers, law enforcement officials, and the public."

(2) HANDGUN DEFINED.—Section 921(a) of title 18, United States Code, is amended by adding at the end the following:

"(29) The term 'handgun' means—

"(A) a firearm which has a short stock and is designed to be held and fired by the use of a single hand; and

"(B) any combination of parts from which a firearm described in subparagraph (A) can be assembled".

(b) PERMANENT PROVISION.—Section 922 of title 18, United States Code, as amended by subsection (a)(1), is amended by adding at the end the following:

"(t)(1) Beginning on the date that is 30 days after the Attorney General notifies licensees under section 103(d) of the Brady Handgun Violence Prevention Act that the national instant criminal background check system is established, a licensed importer, licensed manufacturer, or licensed dealer shall not transfer a firearm to any other person who is not licensed under this chapter, unless—

"(A) before the completion of the transfer, the licensee contacts the national instant criminal background check system established under section 103 of that Act;

"(B)(i) the system provides the licensee with a unique identification number; or

"(ii) 3 business days (meaning a day on which State offices are open) have elapsed since the licensee contacted the system, and the system has not notified the licensee that the receipt of a firearm by such other person would violate subsection (g) or (n) of this section; and

"(C) the transferor has verified the identity of the transferee by examining a valid identification document (as defined in section 1028(d)(1) of this title) of the transferee containing a photograph of the transferee.

"(2) If receipt of a firearm would not violate section 922 (g) or (n) or State law, the system shall—

"(A) assign a unique identification number to the transfer;

"(B) provide the licensee with the number; and

"(C) destroy all records of the system with respect to the call (other than the identifying number and the date the number was assigned) and all records of the system relating to the person or the transfer.

"(3) Paragraph (1) shall not apply to a firearm transfer between a licensee and another person if—

"(A)(i) such other person has presented to the licensee a permit that—

"(I) allows such other person to possess or acquire a firearm; and

"(II) was issued not more than 5 years earlier by the State in which the transfer is to take place; and

"(ii) the law of the State provides that such a permit is to be issued only after an authorized government official has verified that the information available to such official does not indicate that possession of a firearm by such other person would be in violation of law;

"(B) the Secretary has approved the transfer under section 5812 of the Internal Revenue Code of 1986; or

"(C) on application of the transferor, the Secretary has certified that compliance with paragraph (1)(A) is impracticable because—

"(i) the ratio of the number of law enforcement officers of the State in which the transfer is to occur to the number of square miles of land area of the State does not exceed 0.0025;

"(ii) the business premises of the licensee at which the transfer is to occur are extremely remote in relation to the chief law enforcement officer (as defined in subsection (s)(8)); and

"(iii) there is an absence of telecommunications facilities in the geographical area in which the business premises are located.

"(4) If the national instant criminal background check system notifies the licensee that the information available to the system does not demonstrate that the receipt of a firearm by such other person would violate subsection (g) or (n) or State law, and the licensee transfers a firearm to such other person, the licensee shall include in the record of the transfer the unique identification number provided by the system with respect to the transfer.

"(5) If the licensee knowingly transfers a firearm to such other person and knowingly fails to comply with paragraph (1) of this subsection with respect to the transfer and, at the time such other person most recently proposed the transfer, the national instant criminal background check system was operating and information was available to the system demonstrating that receipt of a firearm by such other person would violate subsection (g) or (n) of this section or State law, the Secretary may, after notice and opportunity for a hearing, suspend for not more than 6 months or revoke any license issued to the licensee under section 923, and may impose on the licensee a civil fine of not more than $5,000.

"(6) Neither a local government nor an employee of the Federal Government or of any State or local government, responsible for providing information to the national instant criminal background check system shall be liable in an action at law for damages—

"(A) for failure to prevent the sale or transfer of a firearm to a person whose receipt or possession of the firearm is unlawful under this section; or

"(B) for preventing such a sale or transfer to a person who may lawfully receive or possess a firearm."

(c) PENALTY.—Section 924(a) of title 18, United States Code, is amended—

(1) in paragraph (1), by striking "paragraph (2) or (3) of"; and

(2) by adding at the end the following:

"(5) Whoever knowingly violates subsection (s) or (t) of section 922 shall be fined not more than $1,000, imprisoned for not more than 1 year, or both."

SEC. 103. NATIONAL INSTANT CRIMINAL BACKGROUND CHECK SYSTEM.

(a) DETERMINATION OF TIMETABLES.—Not later than 6 months after the date of enactment of this Act, the Attorney General shall—

(1) determine the type of computer hardware and software that will be used to operate the national instant criminal background check system and the means by which State criminal records systems and the telephone or electronic device of licensees will communicate with the national system;

(2) investigate the criminal records system of each State and determine for each State a timetable by which the State should be able to provide criminal records on an on-line capacity basis to the national system; and

(3) notify each State of the determinations made pursuant to paragraphs (1) and (2).

(b) ESTABLISHMENT OF SYSTEM.—Not later than 60 months after the date of the enactment of this Act, the Attorney General shall establish a national instant criminal background check system that any licensee may contact, by telephone or by other electronic means in addition to the telephone, for information, to be supplied immediately, on whether receipt of a firearm by a prospective transferee would violate section 922 of title 18, United States Code, or State law.

(c) EXPEDITED ACTION BY THE ATTORNEY GENERAL.—The Attorney General shall expedite—

(1) the upgrading and indexing of State criminal history records in the Federal criminal records system maintained by the Federal Bureau of Investigation;

(2) the development of hardware and software systems to link State criminal history check systems into the national instant criminal background check system established by the Attorney General pursuant to this section; and

(3) the current revitalization initiatives by the Federal Bureau of Investigation for technologically advanced fingerprint and criminal records identification.

(d) NOTIFICATION OF LICENSEES.—On establishment of the system under this section, the Attorney General shall notify each licensee and the chief law enforcement officer of each State of the existence and purpose of the system and the means to be used to contact the system.

(e) ADMINISTRATIVE PROVISIONS.—

(1) AUTHORITY TO OBTAIN OFFICIAL INFORMATION.—Notwithstanding any other law, the Attorney General may secure directly from any department or agency of the United States such information on persons for whom receipt of a firearm would violate subsection (g) or (n) of section 922 of title 18, United States Code or State law, as is necessary to enable the system to operate in accordance with this section. On request of the Attorney General, the head of such department or agency shall furnish such information to the system.

(2) OTHER AUTHORITY.—The Attorney General shall develop such computer software, design and obtain such telecommunications and computer hardware, and employ such personnel, as are necessary to establish and operate the system in accordance with this section.

(f) WRITTEN REASONS PROVIDED ON REQUEST.—If the national instant criminal background check system determines that an individual is ineligible to receive a firearm and the individual requests the system to provide the reasons for the determination, the system shall provide such reasons to the individual, in writing, within 5 business days after the date of the request.

(g) CORRECTION OF ERRONEOUS SYSTEM INFORMATION.—If the system established under this section informs an individual contacting the system that receipt of a firearm by a prospective transferee would violate subsection (g) or (n) of section 922 of title 18, United States Code or

State law, the prospective transferee may request the Attorney General to provide the prospective transferee with the reasons therefor. Upon receipt of such a request, the Attorney General shall immediately comply with the request. The prospective transferee may submit to the Attorney General information to correct, clarify, or supplement records of the system with respect to the prospective transferee. After receipt of such information, the Attorney General shall immediately consider the information, investigate the matter further, and correct all erroneous Federal records relating to the prospective transferee and give notice of the error to any Federal department or agency or any State that was the source of such erroneous records.

(h) REGULATIONS.—After 90 days' notice to the public and an opportunity for hearing by interested parties, the Attorney General shall prescribe regulations to ensure the privacy and security of the information of the system established under this section.

(i) PROHIBITION RELATING TO ESTABLISHMENT OF REGISTRATION SYSTEMS WITH RESPECT TO FIREARMS.—No department, agency, officer, or employee of the United States may—

(1) require that any record or portion thereof generated by the system established under this section be recorded at or transferred to a facility owned, managed, or controlled by the United States or any State or political subdivision thereof; or

(2) use the system established under this section to establish any system for the registration of firearms, firearm owners, or firearm transactions or dispositions, except with respect to persons, prohibited by section 922 (g) or (n) of title 18, United States Code or State law, from receiving a firearm.

(j) DEFINITIONS.—As used in this section:

(1) LICENSEE.—The term "licensee" means a licensed importer (as defined in section 921(a)(9) of title 18, United States Code), a licensed manufacturer (as defined in section 921(a)(10) of that title), or a licensed dealer (as defined in section 921(a)(11) of that title).

(2) OTHER TERMS.—The terms "firearm", "handgun", "licensed importer", "licensed manufacturer", and "licensed dealer" have the meanings stated in section 921(a) of title 18, United States Code, as amended by subsection (a)(2).

(k) AUTHORIZATION OF APPROPRIATIONS.—There are authorized to be appropriated, which may be appropriated from the Violent Crime Reduction Trust Fund established by section 1115 of title 31, United States Code, such sums as are necessary to enable the Attorney General to carry out this section.

SEC. 104. REMEDY FOR ERRONEOUS DENIAL OF FIREARM.

(a) IN GENERAL.—Chapter 44 of title 18, United States Code, is amended by inserting after section 925 the following new section:

"S 925A. Remedy for erroneous denial of firearm

"Any person denied a firearm pursuant to subsection (s) or (t) of section 922—

"(1) due to the provision of erroneous information relating to the person by any State or political subdivision thereof, or by the national instant criminal background check system established under section 103 of the Brady Handgun Violence Prevention Act; or

"(2) who was not prohibited from receipt of a firearm pursuant to subsection (g) or (n) of section 922,

may bring an action against the State or political subdivision responsible for providing the erroneous information, or responsible for denying the transfer, or against the United States, as the case may be, for an order directing that the erroneous information be corrected or that the transfer be approved, as the case may be. In any action under this section, the court, in its discretion, may allow the prevailing party a reasonable attorney's fee as part of the costs."

(b) TECHNICAL AMENDMENT.—The chapter analysis for chapter 44 of title 18, United States Code, is amended by inserting after the item relating to section 925 the following new item:

"925A. Remedy for erroneous denial of firearm."

SEC. 105. RULE OF CONSTRUCTION.

This Act and the amendments made by this Act shall not be construed to alter or impair any right or remedy under section 552a of title 5, United States Code.

SEC. 106. FUNDING FOR IMPROVEMENT OF CRIMINAL RECORDS.

(a) USE OF FORMULA GRANTS.—Section 509(b) of title I of the Omnibus Crime Control and Safe Streets Act of 1968 (42 U.S.C. 3759(b)) is amended—

(1) in paragraph (2) by striking "and" after the semicolon;

(2) in paragraph (3) by striking the period and inserting "; and"; and

(3) by adding at the end the following new paragraph:

"(4) the improvement of State record systems and the sharing with the Attorney General of all of the records described in paragraphs (1), (2), and (3) of this subsection and the records required by the Attorney General under section 103 of the Brady Handgun Violence Prevention Act, for the purpose of implementing that Act."

(b) ADDITIONAL FUNDING.—

(1) GRANTS FOR THE IMPROVEMENT OF CRIMINAL RECORDS.—The Attorney General, through the Bureau of Justice Statistics, shall, subject to appropriations and with preference to States that

as of the date of enactment of this Act have the lowest percent currency of case dispositions in computerized criminal history files, make a grant to each State to be used—

(A) for the creation of a computerized criminal history record system or improvement of an existing system;

(B) to improve accessibility to the national instant criminal background system; and

(C) upon establishment of the national system, to assist the State in the transmittal of criminal records to the national system.

(2) AUTHORIZATION OF APPROPRIATIONS.—There are authorized to be appropriated for grants under paragraph (1), which may be appropriated from the Violent Crime Reduction Trust Fund established by section 1115 of title 31, United States Code, a total of $200,000,000 for fiscal year 1994 and all fiscal years thereafter.

TITLE II—MULTIPLE FIREARM PURCHASES TO STATE AND LOCAL POLICE

SEC. 201. REPORTING REQUIREMENT.

Section 923(g)(3) of title 18, United States Code, is amended—

(1) in the second sentence by inserting after "thereon," the following: "and to the department of State police or State law enforcement agency of the State or local law enforcement agency of the local jurisdiction in which the sale or other disposition took place";

(2) by inserting "(A)" after "(3)"; and

(3) by adding at the end thereof the following:

"(B) Except in the case of forms and contents thereof regarding a purchaser who is prohibited by subsection (g) or (n) of section 922 of this title from receipt of a firearm, the department of State police or State law enforcement agency or local law enforcement agency of the local jurisdiction shall not disclose any such form or the contents thereof to any person or entity, and shall destroy each such form and any record of the contents thereof no more than 20 days from the date such form is received. No later than the date that is 6 months after the effective date of this subparagraph, and at the end of each 6-month period thereafter, the department of State police or State law enforcement agency or local law enforcement agency of the local jurisdiction shall certify to the Attorney General of the United States that no disclosure contrary to this subparagraph has been made and that all forms and any record of the contents thereof have been destroyed as provided in this subparagraph."

TITLE III—FEDERAL FIREARMS LICENSE REFORM

SEC. 301. SHORT TITLE.

This title may be cited as the "Federal Firearms License Reform Act of 1993".

SEC. 302. PREVENTION OF THEFT OF FIREARMS.

(a) COMMON CARRIERS.—Section 922(e) of title 18, United States Code, is amended by adding at the end the following: "No common or contract carrier shall require or cause any label, tag, or other written notice to be placed on the outside of any package, luggage, or other container that such package, luggage, or other container contains a firearm."

(b) RECEIPT REQUIREMENT.—Section 922(f) of title 18, United States Code, is amended—

(1) by inserting "(1)" after "(f)"; and

(2) by adding at the end the following new paragraph:

"(2) It shall be unlawful for any common or contract carrier to deliver in interstate or foreign commerce any firearm without obtaining written acknowledgement of receipt from the recipient of the package or other container in which there is a firearm."

(c) UNLAWFUL ACTS.—Section 922 of title 18, United States Code, as amended by section 102, is amended by adding at the end the following new subsection:

"(u) It shall be unlawful for a person to steal or unlawfully take or carry away from the person or the premises of a person who is licensed to engage in the business of importing, manufacturing, or dealing in firearms, any firearm in the licensee's business inventory that has been shipped or transported in interstate or foreign commerce."

(d) PENALTIES.—Section 924 of title 18, United States Code, is amended by adding at the end the following new subsection:

"(i)(1) A person who knowingly violates section 922(u) shall be fined not more than $10,000, imprisoned not more than 10 years, or both.

"(2) Nothing contained in this subsection shall be construed as indicating an intent on the part of Congress to occupy the field in which provisions of this subsection operate to the exclusion of State laws on the same subject matter, nor shall any provision of this subsection be construed as invalidating any provision of State law unless such provision is inconsistent with any of the purposes of this subsection."

SEC. 303. LICENSE APPLICATION FEES FOR DEALERS IN FIREARMS.

Section 923(a)(3) of title 18. United States Code, is amended—

(1) in subparagraph (A), by adding "or" at the end;

(2) in subparagraph (B) by striking "a pawnbroker dealing in firearms other than" and inserting "not a dealer in";

(3) in subparagraph (B) by striking "$25 per year; or" and inserting "$200 for 3 years, except that the fee for renewal of a valid license shall be $90 for 3 years."; and

(4) by striking subparagraph (C).

Speaker of the House of Representatives.
Vice President of the United States and President of the Senate.

APPENDIX E

━━━━━━━━━━━━

U.S. v. MILLER

UNITED STATES v. MILLER ET AL.

APPEAL FROM THE DISTRICT COURT OF THE UNITED STATES FOR THE WESTERN DISTRICT OF ARKANSAS.

[Note: footnotes and references have been omitted]

No. 696. Argued March 30, 1939.—Decided May 15, 1939.

The National Firearms Act, as applied to one indicted for transporting in interstate commerce a 12-gauge shotgun with a barrel less than 18 inches long, without having registered it and without having in his possession a stamp-affixed written order for it, as required by the Act, held:

1. Not unconstitutional as an invasion of the reserved powers of the States. Citing Sonzinsky v. United States, 300 U. S. 506, and Narcotic Act cases.
2. Not violative of the Second Amendment of the Federal Constitution.

The Court can not take judicial notice that a shotgun having a barrel less than 18 inches long has today any reasonable relation to the preservation or efficiency of a well regulated militia; and therefore can not say that the Second Amendment guarantees to the citizen the right to keep and bear such a weapon. 26 F. Supp. 1002, reversed.

APPEAL under the Criminal Appeals Act from a judgment sustaining a demurrer to an indictment for violation of the National Firearms Act.

Opinion of the Court.

Appendix E

Mr. Gordon Dean argued the cause, and Solicitor General Jackson, Assistant Attorney General McMahon, and Messrs. William W. Barron, Fred E. Strine, George F. Kneip, W. Marvin Smith, and Clinton R. Barry were on a brief, for the United States.

No appearance for appellees.

MR. JUSTICE McREYNOLDS delivered the opinion of the Court.

An indictment in the District Court Western District Arkansas, charged that Jack Miller and Frank Layton
"did unlawfully, knowingly, wilfully, and feloniously transport in interstate commerce from the town of Claremore in the State of Oklahoma to the town of Siloam Springs in the State of Arkansas a certain firearm, to-wit, a double barrel 12-gauge Stevens shotgun having a barrel less than 18 inches in length, bearing identification number 76230, said defendants, at the time of so transporting said firearm in interstate commerce as aforesaid, not having registered said firearm as required by Section 1132d of Title 26, United States Code (Act of June 26, 1934, c. 737, Sec. 4 [sec. 5], 48 Stat. 1237), and not having in their possession a stamp-affixed written order for said firearm as provided by Section 1132c, Title 26, United States Code (June 26, 1934, c. 737, Sec. 4, 48 Stat. 1237) and the regulations issued under authority of the said Act of Congress known as the 'National Firearms Act', approved June 26, 1934, contrary to the form of the statute in such case made and provided, against the peace and dignity of the United States."

A duly interposed demurrer alleged: The National Firearms Act is not a revenue measure but an attempt to usurp police power reserved to the States, and is therefore unconstitutional. Also, it offends the inhibition of the Second Amendment to the Constitution—"A well regulated Militia, being necessary to the security of a free State, the right of people to keep and bear Arms, shall not be infringed."
District Court held that section eleven of the Act violates the Second Amendment. It accordingly sustained the demurrer and quashed the indictment.
The cause is here by direct appeal.
Considering *Sonzinsky v. United States* (1937), 300 U.S. 506, 513, and what was ruled in sundry causes arising under the Harrison Narcotic Act (footnote 2)—*United States v. Jin Fuey Moy* (1916), 241 U.S. 394; *United States v. Doremus* (1919), 249 U.S. 86, 94; *Linder v. United States* (1925), 268 U.S. 5; *Alston v. United States* (1927), 274 U.S. 289; *Nigro v. United States*

275

(1928), 276 U.S. 332—the objection that the Act usurps police power reserved to the States is plainly untenable.

In the absence of any evidence tending to show that possession or use of a "shotgun having a barrel of less than eighteen inches in length" at this time has some reasonable relationship to the preservation or efficiency of a well regulated militia, we cannot say that the Second Amendment guarantees the right to keep and bear such an instrument. Certainly it is not within judicial notice that this weapon is any part of the ordinary military equipment or that its use could contribute to the common defense. *Aymette v. State*, 2 Humphreys (Tenn.) 154, 158.

The Constitution as originally adopted granted to the Congress power— "To provide for calling forth the Militia to execute the Laws of the Union, suppress Insurrections and repel Invasions; To provide for organizing, arming, and disciplining, the Militia, and for governing such Part of them as may be employed in the Service of the United States, reserving to the States respectively, the Appointment of the Officers, and the Authority of training the Militia according to the discipline prescribed by Congress." With obvious purpose to assure the continuation and render possible the effectiveness of such forces the declaration and guarantee of the Second Amendment were made. It must be interpreted and applied with that end in view.

The Militia which the States were expected to maintain and train is set in contrast with Troops which they were forbidden to keep without the consent of Congress. The sentiment of the time strongly disfavored standing armies; the common view was that adequate defense of country and laws could be secured through the Militia—civilians primarily, soldiers on occasion.

The signification attributed to the term Militia appears from the debates in the Convention, the history and legislation of Colonies and States, and the writings of approved commentators. These show plainly enough that the Militia comprised all males physically capable of acting in concert for the common defense. "A body of citizens enrolled for military discipline." And further, that ordinarily when called for service these men were expected to appear bearing arms supplied by themselves and of the kind in common use at the time.

Blackstone's Commentaries, Vol. 2, Ch. 13, p. 409 points out "that king Alfred first settled a national militia in this kingdom," and traces the subsequent development and use of such forces.

Adam Smith's *Wealth of Nations*, Book V, Ch. 1, contains an extended account of the Militia. It is there said: "Men of republican principles have been jealous of a standing army as dangerous to liberty." "In a militia, the character of the labourer, artificer, or tradesman, predominates over that of the soldier: in a standing army, that of the soldier predominates over every other character; and in this distinction seems to consist the essential difference between those two different species of military force."

"The American Colonies in the 17th Century," Osgood, Vol. I, ch. XIII, affirms in reference to the early system of defense in New England—

"In all the colonies, as in England, the militia system was based on the principle of the assize of arms. This implied the general obligation of all adult male inhabitants to possess arms, and, with certain exceptions, to cooperate in the work of defence." "The possession of arms also implied the possession of ammunition, and the authorities paid quite as much attention to the latter as to the former." "A year later [1632] it was ordered that any single man who had not furnished himself with arms might be put out to service, and this became a permanent part of the legislation of the colony [Massachusetts]."

Also "Clauses intended to insure the possession of arms and ammunition by all who were subject to military service appear in all the important enactments concerning military affairs. Fines were the penalty for delinquency, whether of towns or individuals. According to the usage of the times, the infantry of Massachusetts consisted of pikemen and musketeers. The law, as enacted in 1649 and thereafter, provided that each of the former should be armed with a pike, corselet, head-piece, sword, and knapsack. The musketeer should carry a 'good fixed musket,' not under bastard musket bore, not less than three feet, nine inches, nor more than four feet three inches in length, a priming wire, scourer, and mould, a sword, rest, bandoleers, one pound of powder, twenty bullets, and two fathoms of match. The law also required that two-thirds of each company should be musketeers."

The General Court of Massachusetts, January Session 1784, provided for the organization and government of the Militia. It directed that the Train Band should "contain all able bodied men, from sixteen to forty years of age, and the Alarm List, all other men under sixty years of age, . . ." Also, "That every non-commissioned officer and private soldier of the said militia not under the controul of parents, masters or guardians, and being of sufficient ability therefor in the judgment of the Selectmen of the town in which he shall dwell, shall equip himself, and be constantly provided with a good fire arm," &c.

By an Act passed April 4, 1786 the New York Legislature directed: "That every able-bodied Male Person, being a Citizen of this State, or of any of the United States, and residing in this State, (except such Persons as are hereinafter excepted) and who are of the Age of Sixteen, and under the Age of Forty-five Years, shall, by the Captain or commanding Officer of the Beat in which such Citizens shall reside, within four Months after the passing of this Act, be enrolled in the Company of such Beat. . . . That every Citizen

so enrolled and notified, shall, within three Months thereafter, provide him-
self, at his own Expense, with a good Musket or Firelock, a sufficient Bayo-
net and Belt, a Pouch with a Box therein to contain not less than
Twenty-four Cartridges suited to the Bore of his Musket or Firelock, each
Cartridge containing a proper Quantity of Powder and Ball, two spare
Flints, a Blanket and Knapsack; . . ."

The General Assembly of Virginia, October, 1785, (12 Hening's
Statutes) declared, "The defense and safety of the commonwealth depend
upon having its citizens properly armed and taught the knowledge of military duty."

It further provided for organization and control of the Militia and directed that "All free male persons between the ages of eighteen and fifty
years," with certain exceptions, "shall be inrolled or formed into companies." "There shall be a private muster of every company once in two
months."

Also that "Every officer and soldier shall appear at his respective muster-
field on the day appointed, by eleven o'clock in the forenoon, armed,
equipped, and accoutred, as follows: . . . every noncommissioned officer
and private with a good, clean musket carrying an ounce ball, and three feet
eight inches long in the barrel, with a good bayonet and iron ramrod well
fitted thereto, a cartridge box properly made, to contain and secure twenty
cartridges fitted to his musket, a good knapsack and canteen, and moreover,
each non-commissioned officer and Private shall have at every muster one
pound of good powder, and four pounds of lead, including twenty blind cartridges; and each serjeant shall have a pair of moulds fit to cast balls for their
respective companies, to be purchased by the commanding officer out of the
monies arising on delinquencies. Provided, That the militia of the counties
westward of the Blue Ridge, and the counties below adjoining thereto, shall
not be obliged to be armed with muskets, but may have good rifles with
proper accoutrements, in lieu thereof. And every of the said officers, non-
commissioned officers, and privates, shall constantly keep the aforesaid
arms, accoutrements, and ammunition, ready to be produced whenever
called for by his commanding officer. If any private shall make it appear to
the satisfaction of the court hereafter to be appointed for trying delinquencies under this act that he is so poor that he cannot purchase the arms herein
required, such court shall cause them to be purchased out of the money arising from delinquents."

Most if not all of the States have adopted provisions touching the right
to keep and bear arms. Differences in the language employed in these have
naturally led to somewhat variant conclusions concerning the scope of the
right guaranteed. But none of them seem to afford any material support for
the challenged ruling of the court below.

In the margin some of the more important opinions and comments by writers are cited.

We are unable to accept the conclusion of the court below and the challenged judgment must be reversed. The cause will be remanded for further proceedings.

MR. JUSTICE DOUGLAS took no part in the consideration or decision of this cause.

APPENDIX F

QUILICI V. MORTON GROVE

Victor D. QUILICI, Robert Stengl, et al., George L. Reichert, and Robert E. Metier, Plaintiffs-Appellants,

VILLAGE OF MORTON GROVE, et al., Defendants-Appellees.

Nos. 82-1045, 82-1076 and 82-1132.

United States Court of Appeals, Seventh Circuit.

Argued May 28, 1982.

Decided Dec. 6, 1982.

As Amended Dec. 10, 1982.

Rehearing and Rehearing En Banc Denied March 2, 1983.

Victor D. Quilici, Bennsonville, Ill., Don B. Kates, Jr., O'Brien & Hallisey, San Francisco, Cal., Richard V. Houpt, Pedersen & Houpt, Donald J. Moran, Chicago, Ill., for plaintiffs-appellants.

Eugene R. Wedoff, Jenner & Block, Chicago, Ill., for defendants-appellees.

Before BAUER, WOOD, and COFFEY, Circuit Judges.

BAUER, Circuit Judge.

This appeal concerns the constitutionality of the Village of Morton Grove's Ordinance No. 81-11, [footnote 1] which prohibits the possession of handguns within the Village's borders. The district court held that the Ordinance was constitutional. We affirm.

Appendix F

I

Victor D. Quilici initially challenged Ordinance No. 81-11 in state court. Morton Grove removed the action to federal court where it was consolidated with two similar actions, one brought by George L. Reichert and Robert E. Metier (collectively Reichert) and one brought by Robert Stengl, Martin Gutenkauf, Alice Gutenkauf, Walter J. Dutchak and Geoffrey Lagonia (collectively Stengl). Plaintiffs alleged that Ordinance No. 81-11 violated article 1, section 22 of the Illinois Constitution and the second, ninth and fourteenth amendments of the United States Constitution. They sought an order declaring the Ordinance unconstitutional and permanently enjoining its enforcement. The parties filed cross motions for summary judgment. The district court granted Morton Grove's motion for summary judgment and denied plaintiffs' motions for summary judgment.

In its opinion, *Quilici v. Village of Morton Grove*, 532 F.Supp. 1169 (N.D.Ill. 1981), the district court set forth several reasons for upholding the handgun ban's validity under the state and federal constitutions. First, it held that the Ordinance which banned only certain kinds of arms was a valid exercise of Morton Grove's police power and did not conflict with section 22's conditional right to keep and bear arms. Second, relying on *Presser v. Illinois*, 116 U.S. 252, 6 S.Ct. 580, 29 L.Ed. 615 (1886), the court concluded that the second amendment's guarantee of the right to bear arms has not been incorporated into the fourteenth amendment and, therefore, is inapplicable to Morton Grove. Finally, it stated that the ninth amendment does not include the right to possess handguns for self-defense. Appellants contend that the district court incorrectly construed the relevant constitutional provisions, assigning numerous errors based on case law, historical analysis, common law traditions and public policy concerns. [footnote 2]

While we recognize that this case raises controversial issues which engender strong emotions, our task is to apply the law as it has been interpreted by the Supreme Court, regardless of whether that Court's interpretation comports with various personal views of what the law should be. We are also aware that we must resolve the controversy without rendering unnecessary constitutional decisions. *Richard Nixon v. A. Ernest Fitzgerald*,—U.S.—, 102 S.Ct. 2690, 73 L.Ed.2d 349 (1982). With these principles in mind we address appellants' contentions.

II

We consider the state constitutional issue first. The Illinois Constitution provides:

Subject only to the police power, the right of the individual citizen to keep and bear arms shall not be infringed.

Ill. Const. art. I, section 22. The parties agree that the meaning of this section is controlled by the terms "arms" and "police power" but disagree as to the scope of these terms.

Relying on the statutory construction principles that constitutional guarantees should be broadly construed and that constitutional provisions should prevail over conflicting statutory provisions, appellants allege that section 22's guarantee of the right to keep and bear arms prohibits a complete ban of any one kind of arm. They argue that the constitutional history of section 22 establishes that the term "arms" includes those weapons commonly employed for "recreation or the protection of person and property," 6 Record of Proceedings, Sixth Illinois Constitutional Convention 87 (Proceedings), and contend that handguns have consistently been used for these purposes.

Appellants concede that the phrase "subject to the police power" does not prohibit reasonable regulation of arms. Thus, they admit that laws which require the licensing of guns or which restrict the carrying of concealed weapons or the possession of firearms by minors, convicted felons, and incompetents are valid. However, they maintain that no authority supports interpreting section 22 to permit a ban on the possession of handguns merely because alternative weapons are not also banned. They argue that construing section 22 in this manner would lead to the anomalous situation in which one municipality completely bans handguns while a neighboring municipality completely bans all arms but handguns.

In contrast, Morton Grove alleges that "arms" is a general term which does not include any specific kind of weapon. Relying on section 22's language, which they characterize as clear and explicit, Morton Grove reads section 22 to guarantee the right to keep only some, but not all, arms which are used for "recreation or the protection of person and property." It argues that the Ordinance passes constitutional muster because standard rifles and shotguns are also used for "recreation or the protection of person and property" and Ordinance No. 81-11 does not ban these weapons.

While Morton Grove does not challenge appellants' assertion that "arms" includes handguns, we believe that a discussion of the kind of arms section 22 protects is an appropriate place to begin our analysis. Because we disagree with Morton Grove's assertion that section 22's language is clear and explicit, we turn to the constitutional debates for guidance on the proper construction of arms. [footnote 3] *Client Follow-Up Co. v. Hynes*, 75 Ill.2d 208, 216, 28 Ill.Dec. 488, 390 N.E.2d 847, 850 (1979), citing *Wolfson v. Avery*, 6 Ill.2d 78, 126 N.E.2d 701 (1955). [footnote 4]

The debates indicate that the category of arms protected by section 22 is not limited to military weapons; the framers also intended to include those arms that "law-abiding persons commonly employ[ed]" for "recreation or the protection of person and property." 6 Proceedings 87. Handguns are undisputedly the type of arms commonly used for "recreation or the protection of person and property."

Our conclusion that the framers intended to include handguns in the class of protected arms is supported by the fact that in discussing the term the Proceedings refer to *People v. Brown*, 253 Mich. 537, 541–42, 235 N.W. 245, 246–47 (1931) and *State v. Duke*, 42 Tex. 455, 458 (1875). Brown defines weapons as those "relied upon . . . for defense or pleasure," including "ordinary guns" and "revolvers." 253 Mich. at 542, 235 N.W. at 247. Duke states that "[t]he arms which every person is secured the right to keep and bear (in defense of himself or the State, subject to legislative regulation), must be such arms as are commonly kept, . . . and are appropriate for . . . self defense, as well as such as are proper for the defense of the State." 42 Tex. at 458. The delegates' statements and reliance on Brown and Duke convinces us that the term *arms* in section 22 includes handguns.

Having determined that section 22 includes handguns within the class of arms protected, we must now determine the extent to which a municipality may exercise its police power to restrict, or even prohibit, the right to keep and bear these arms. The district court concluded that section 22 recognizes only a narrow individual right which is subject to substantial legislative control. It noted that "[t]o the extent that one looks to the convention debate for assistance in reconciling the conflict between the right to arms and the exercise of the police power, the debate clearly supports its narrow construction of the individual right." *Quilici v. Village of Morton Grove*, 532 F.Supp. at 1174. It further noted that while the Proceedings cite some cases holding that the state's police power should be read restrictively, those cases were decided under "distinctly different constitutional provisions" and, thus, have little application to this case. Id. at 1176.

We agree with the district court that the right to keep and bear arms in Illinois is so limited by the police power that a ban on handguns does not violate that right. In reaching this conclusion we find two factors significant. First, section 22's plain language grants only the right to keep and bear arms, not handguns. Second, although the framers intended handguns to be one of the arms conditionally protected under section 22, they also envisioned that local governments might exercise their police power to restrict, or prohibit, the right to keep and bear handguns. For example, Delegate Foster, speaking for the majority, explained:

It could be argued that, in theory, the legislature now [prior to the adoption of the 1970 Illinois Constitution] has the right to ban all firearms in the state as far as individual citizens owning them is concerned. That is the power which we wanted to restrict—an absolute ban on all firearms.

3 Proceedings 1688. Delegate Foster then noted that section 22 "would prevent a complete ban on all guns, but there could be a ban on certain categories." Id. at 1693. [footnote 5] It is difficult to imagine clearer evidence that section 22 was intended to permit a municipality to ban handguns if it so desired.

Appellants argue that construing section 22 to protect only some unspecified categories of arms, thereby allowing municipalities to exercise their police power to enact dissimilar gun control laws, leads to "untenable" and "absurd" results. Quilici br. at 14. This argument ignores the fact that the Illinois Constitution authorizes local governments to function as home rule units to "exercise any power and perform any function pertaining to its government and affairs". Illinois Const. art. VIII, section 6(a). Home rule government [footnote 6] is based on the theory that local governments are in the best position to assess the needs and desires of the community and, thus, can most wisely enact legislation addressing local concerns. *Carlson v. Briceland*, 61 Ill. App.3d 247, 18 Ill.Dec. 502, 377 N.E.2d 1138 (1978). Illinois home rule units have expansive powers to govern as they deem proper, see generally *Hall & Wallack, Intergovernmental Cooperation and the Transfer of Powers*, 1981 U.Ill.L.Rev. 775, 777–79; *Vitullo & Peters, Intergovernmental Cooperation and the Municipal Insurance Crisis*, 30 DePaul L.Rev. 325, 326–29 (1981); including the authority to impose greater restrictions on particular rights than those imposed by the state. See *City of Evanston v. Create, Inc.*, 85 111.2d 101, 51 Ill.Dec. 688, 421 N.E.2d 196 (1981). The only limits on their autonomy are those imposed by the Illinois Constitution, *City of Carbondale ex rel. Ham v. Eckert*, 76 Ill.App.3d 881, 32 Ill.Dec. 377, 395 N.E.2d 607 (1979), or by the Illinois General Assembly exercising its authority to pre-empt home rule in specific instances. Because we have concluded that the Illinois Constitution permits a ban on certain categories of arms, home rule units such as Morton Grove may properly enact different, even inconsistent, arms restrictions. This is precisely the kind of local control envisioned by the new Illinois Constitution.

Appellants concede that municipalities may, under the Illinois Constitution, exercise their police power to enact regulations which prohibit "possession of items legislatively found to be dangerous . . .", Quilici br. at 9. They draw a distinction, however, between the exercise of the police power in general and the exercise of police power with respect to a constitutionally protected right. Indeed, they vehemently insist that a municipality may not exercise its police power to completely prohibit a constitutional guarantee.

We agree that the state may not exercise its police power to violate a positive constitutional mandate, *People v. Warren*, 11 Ill.2d 420, 143 N.E.2d 28 (1957), but we reiterate that section 22 simply prohibits all absolute ban on all firearms. Since Ordinance No. 81-11 does not prohibit all firearms, it does not prohibit a constitutionally protected right. There is no right under the Illinois Constitution to possess a handgun, nor does the state have an overriding state interest in gun control which requires it to retain exclusive control in order to prevent home rule units from adopting conflicting enactments. See *City of Evanston v. Create, Inc.*, 85 Ill.2d 101, 51 Ill.Dec. 688, 421 N.E.2d 196 (1981). Accordingly, Morton Grove may exercise its police power to prohibit handguns even though this prohibition interferes with an individual's liberty or property. *People v. Warren*, 11 Ill.2d 420, 143 N.E.2d 28 (1957).

The Illinois Constitution establishes a presumption in favor of municipal home rule. *Carlson v. Briceland*, 61 111. App.3d 247, 18 Ill.Dec. 502, 377 N.E.2d 1138 (1978). Once a local government identifies a problem and enacts legislation to mitigate or eliminate it, that enactment is presumed valid and may be overturned only if it is unreasonable, clearly arbitrary, and has no foundation in the police power. *Illinois Gamefowl Breeders Ass'n v. Block*, 75 Ill.2d 443, 27 Ill.Dec. 465, 389 N.E.2d 529 (1979); *People v. Copeland*, 92 Ill.App.3d 475, 47 Ill.Dec. 860, 415 N.E.2d 1173 (1st Dist. 1980). Thus, it is not the province of this court to pass judgment on the merits of Ordinance No. 81-11; our task is simply to determine whether Ordinance No. 81-11's restrictions are rationally related to its stated goals. *People ex rel. Difanis v. Barr*, 83 Ill.2d 191, 46 Ill.Dec. 678, 414 N.E.2d 731 (1980). As the district court noted, there is at least some empirical evidence that gun control legislation may reduce the number of deaths and accidents caused by handguns. *Quilici v. Village of Morton Grove*, 532 F.Supp. at 1179. This evidence is sufficient to sustain the conclusion that Ordinance No. 81-11 is neither wholly arbitrary nor completely unsupported by any set of facts. *People v. Copeland*, 92 Ill.App.3d 475, 47 Ill.Dec. 860, 415 N.E.2d 1173 (1st Dist.1980). Accordingly, we decline to consider plaintiffs' arguments that Ordinance No. 81-11 will not make Morton Grove a safer, more peaceful place.

We agree with the district court that Ordinance No. 81-11: (1) is property directed at protecting the safety and health of Morton Grove citizens; (2) is a valid exercise of Morton Grove's police power; and (3) does not violate any of appellants' rights guaranteed by the Illinois Constitution. [footnote 7]

III

We next consider whether Ordinance No. 81-11 violates the second amendment to the United States Constitution. While appellants all contend that Ordinance No. 81-11 is invalid under the second amendment, they offer slightly different arguments to substantiate this contention. All argue, however, that the second amendment applies to state and local governments and that the second amendment guarantee of the right to keep and bear arms exists, not only to assist in the common defense, but also to protect the individual. While reluctantly conceding that *Presser v. Illinois*, 116 U.S. 252, 6 S.Ct. 580, 29 L.Ed. 615 (1886), held that the second amendment applied only to action by the federal government they nevertheless assert that *Presser* also held that the right to keep and bear arms is an attribute of national citizenship which is not subject to state restriction. Reichert br. at 36. Finally, apparently responding to the district court's comments that "[p]laintiffs . . . have not suggested that the Morton Grove Ordinance in any way interferes with the ability of the United States to maintain public security . . ." *Quilici v. Village of Morton Grove*, 532 F.Supp. at 1169, Quilici and Reichert argue in this court that the Morton Grove Ordinance interferes with the federal government's ability to maintain public security by preventing individuals from defending themselves and the community from "external or internal armed threats." Quilici br. at 12; Reichert br. at 37–38. These are the same arguments made in the district court. Accordingly, we comment only briefly on the points already fully analyzed in that court's decision.

As we have noted, the parties agree that *Presser* is controlling, but disagree as to what *Presser* held. It is difficult to understand how appellants can assert that *Presser* supports the theory that the second amendment right to keep and bear arms is a fundamental right which the state cannot regulate when the *Presser* decision plainly states that "[t]he Second Amendment declares that it shall not be infringed, but this . . . means no more than that it shall not be infringed by Congress. This is one of the amendments that has no other effect than to restrict the powers of the National government . . ." *Presser v. Illinois*, 116 U.S. 252, 265, 6 S.Ct. 580, 584, 29 L.Ed. 615 (1886). As the district court explained in detail, appellants' claim that *Presser* supports the proposition that the second amendment guarantee of the right to keep and bear arms is not subject to state restriction is based on dicta quoted out of context. *Quilici v. Village of Morton Grove*, 532 F.Supp. at 1181–82. This argument borders on the frivolous and does not warrant any further consideration.

Apparently recognizing the inherent weakness of their reliance on *Presser*, appellants urge three additional arguments to buttress their claim that the second amendment applies to the states. They contend that: (1) *Presser* is no longer good law because later Supreme Court cases incorporating other amendments into the fourteenth amendment have effectively overruled *Presser*, Reichert br. at 52; (2) *Presser* is illogical, Quilici br. at 12; and (3) the entire Bill of Rights has been implicitly incorporated into the fourteenth amendment to apply to the states, Reichert br. at 48–52.

None of these arguments has merit. First, appellants offer no authority, other than their own opinions, to support their arguments that *Presser* is no longer good law or would have been decided differently today. Indeed, the fact that the Supreme Court continues to cite *Presser*, *Malloy v. Hogan*, 378 U.S. 1, 4 n. 2, 84 S.Ct. 1489, 1491 n. 2, 12 L.Ed.2d 653 (1964), leads to the opposite conclusion. Second, regardless of whether appellants agree with the *Presser* analysis, it is the law of the land and we are bound by it. Their assertion that *Presser* is illogical is a policy matter for the Supreme Court to address. Finally, their theory of implicit incorporation is wholly unsupported. The Supreme Court has specifically rejected the proposition that the entire Bill of Rights applies to the states through the fourteenth amendment. *Adamson v. California*, 332 U.S. 46, 67 S.Ct. 1672, 91 L.Ed. 1903 (1947), overruled on other grounds, *Malloy v. Hogan*, 378 U.S. 1, 84 S.Ct. 1489, 12 L.Ed.2d 653 (1964); *Palko v. Connecticut*, 302 U.S. 319, 58 S.Ct. 149, 82 L.Ed. 288 (1937); *Twining v. New Jersey*, 211 U.S. 78, 29 S.Ct. 14, 53 L.Ed. 97 (1908).

Since we hold that the second amendment does not apply to the states, we need not consider the scope of its guarantee of the right to bear arms. For the sake of completeness, however, and because appellants devote a large portion of their briefs to this issue, we briefly comment on what we believe to be the scope of the second amendment.

The second amendment provides that "A regulated Militia being necessary to the security of a free State, the right of the people to keep and bear Arms, shall not be infringed." U.S. Const. amend. II. Construing this language according to its plain meaning, it seems clear that the right to bear arms is inextricably connected to the preservation of a militia. This is precisely the manner in which the Supreme Court interpreted the second amendment in *United States v. Miller*, 307 U.S. 174, 59 S.Ct. 816, 83 L.Ed. 1206 (1939), the only Supreme Court case specifically addressing that amendment's scope. There the Court held that the right to keep and bear arms extends only to those arms which are necessary to maintain a well regulated militia.

In an attempt to avoid the *Miller* holding that the right to keep and bear arms exists only as it relates to protecting the public security, appellants argue that "[t]he fact that the right to keep and bear arms is joined with language expressing one of its purposes in no way permits a construction which limits or confines the exercise of that right." Reichert br. at 35. They offer no explanation for how they have arrived at this conclusion. Alternatively, they argue that handguns are military weapons. [footnote 8] Stengl's br. at 11–13. Our reading of *Miller* convinces us that it does not support either of these theories. As the Village correctly notes, appellants are essentially arguing that Miller was wrongly decided and should be overruled. Such arguments have no place before this court. Under the controlling authority of *Miller* we conclude that the right to keep and bear handguns is not guaranteed by the second amendment. [footnote 9]

Because the second amendment is not applicable to Morton Grove and possession of handguns by individuals is not part of the right to keep and bear arms, Ordinance No. 81-11 does not violate the second amendment.

IV

Finally, we consider whether Ordinance No. 81-11 violates the ninth amendment. Appellants argue that, although the right to use commonly-owned arms for self-defense is not explicitly listed in the Bill of Rights, it is a fundamental right protected by the ninth amendment. Citing no authority which directly supports their contention, they rely on the debates in the First Congress and the writings of legal philosophers to establish that the right of an individual to own and possess firearms for self-defense is an absolute and inalienable right which cannot be impinged.

Since appellants do not cite, and our research has not revealed, any Supreme Court case holding that any specific right is protected by the ninth amendment, appellants' argument has no legal significance. Appellants may believe the ninth amendment should be read to recognize an unwritten, fundamental, individual right to own or possess firearms; the fact remains that the Supreme Court has never embraced this theory. [footnote 10]

Reasonable people may differ about the wisdom of Ordinance No. 81-11. History may prove that the Ordinance cannot effectively promote peace and security for Morton Grove's citizens. Such issues, however, are not before the court. We simply hold the Ordinance No. 81-11 is a proper exercise of Morton Grove's police power and does not violate art. 1, section 22 of the Illinois Constitution or the second, ninth, or fourteenth amendments of the United States Constitution. Accordingly, the decision of the district court is

AFFIRMED.
[Footnotes omitted]

INDEX

Page numbers in *italic* indicate illustrations (charts, graphs, maps).
Page numbers followed by *t* indicate tables.

Index

Index

LAKE COUNTY PUBLIC LIBRARY
INDIANA